BUSINESS
2010

BUSINESS 2010

FIVE FORCES THAT WILL RESHAPE BUSINESS— AND HOW TO MAKE THEM WORK FOR YOU

FRED HARMON

KIPLINGER BOOKS
Washington, DC

Published by
The Kiplinger Washington Editors, Inc.
1729 H Street, N.W.
Washington, DC 20006

Library of Congress Cataloging-in-Publication Data

Harmon, Frederick G.
   Business 2010 : five forces that will reshape business--and how to make them work for you / Frederick G. Harmon.-- 1st ed.
      p. cm.
   Includes index.
   ISBN 0-938721-84-4 (cloth : alk. paper)
    1. Business forecasting. I. Title.

HD30.27 .H38 2001
658.4'062--dc21   00-069012

This publication is intended to provide guidance in regard to the subject matter covered. It is sold with the understanding that the author and publisher are not herein engaged in rendering legal, accounting, tax or other professional services. If such services are required, professional assistance should be sought.

First edition. Printed in the United States of America.
9 8 7 6 5 4 3 2 1

Kiplinger publishes books and videos on a wide variety of personal-finance and business-management subjects. Check our Web site (www.kiplinger.com) for a complete list of titles, additional information and excerpts. Or write:
         Cindy Greene
         Kiplinger Books & Tapes
         1729 H Street, N.W.
         Washington, DC 20006
         e-mail: cgreene@kiplinger.com
To order, call 800-280-7165; for information about volume discounts, call 202-887-6431.

Dedication

Once again, this book is for Nancy.

Acknowledgments

LTHOUGH MY NAME APPEARS AS AUTHOR ON THIS book, it is, in a real sense, a collaboration among many individuals in several organizations.

In my Preface, I have already noted my debt to Garry Jacobs, Bob Macfarlane and Harlan Cleveland, who provided major contributions to my thoughts on the development of organizations. I also thank members of the World Academy of Art and Science, who invited me to attend a meeting that included presentations that proved most relevant to the themes explored in this book.

I add my great appreciation to the Kiplinger organization for the opportunity to prepare and present the ideas in this book. While I have read Kiplinger publications for many years, I have not previously had the chance to work with the company's outstanding staff.

The basic theme of this book, Business 2010, was the idea of Kiplinger Books publisher David Harrison. When David asked literary agent Rob Kaplan to find a suitable author for the project, Rob, an old friend, as well as my agent, brought this challenging opportunity to me.

Knight Kiplinger, editor in chief of *The Kiplinger Letter* and Kiplingerforecasts.com, showed a special interest in the book from the beginning, reading and commenting on both my detailed outline and the completed draft. In each case, he provided many helpful and insightful comments.

My closest collaborator at the Kiplinger organization was Patricia Mertz Esswein, managing editor of Kiplinger Books. Pat relentlessly pushed me to come up with a better example or a clearer explanation for each of my themes. Despite exceptionally tight deadlines, she maintained such a cheerful and optimistic manner that I found it difficult to object to the additional work on what I had naively supposed was a nearly finished manuscript. The final text benefited enormously from her dedicated effort.

I am also grateful to the editors and writers of the Kiplinger publications. Articles on the Web-based Kiplingerforecasts.com proved to be an invaluable source of information about many of the key business trends discussed in this book.

Thanks also to Priscilla Taylor, who copyedited and smoothed the manuscript, and to Heather Waugh, who designed the book.

Katherine Yarrusso-Mosley of First Coast Business Center in Jacksonville, Fla. once again ably served her invaluable role of helping me with research while providing support for my business consulting assignments. Sue Holmes calmly and effectively kept my Virginia office running smoothly while I worked on the book. Janani Ram of Pondicherry, India, brought high energy and intelligence to demanding research assignments for the book.

To all of the above people and organizations, my deepest thanks.

Table of Contents

Introduction

ARE WE LIVING TODAY IN A TIME MORE EXCITING, more dangerous, more dismaying, more encouraging than any previous era in world history? Well, yes and no.

One of the most misguided human conceits is the assumption that current circumstances are profoundly exceptional, whatever the superlative might be—"the most treacherous," "the fastest changing," "the richest in opportunity"—of all eras. There is a natural human tendency, especially among those who are not avid students of history, to ascribe unique traits to one's own era.

Of course, each new era presents a particular set of challenges and opportunities that have not been seen before in exactly their present form. But before we crown our era as "the most," "the best" or "the worst" of all, let's remember that the world has experienced similarly deep and far-reaching upheaval in the past—but not often, and not very recently.

Consider the incredible changes that will be wrought in the years ahead by such forces as the Internet, biotechnology, and the globalization of world business. Such world-changing upheavals don't come along very often, and are rarely synchronized. Have they equals in world history? Perhaps only the invention of movable type for printing, the steam engine, electricity for motors and lighting, the telephone, the automobile, powered flight, radio and television, antibiotics, high-yield hybrid grains would qualify.

Notice that in this list of world-changing technologies, the time intervals between them has kept shrinking, from several centuries to a few decades to a few years.

This shrinking interval of innovation by itself sums up what is unique about our present era: the sheer speed of change. Yes, people of earlier times had to adjust to changes every bit as daunting as those we face today, but never to so many simultaneously, with every change mutating into a new challenge before there is time to adjust to the one before. For this reason, these are both the best of times and the worst of times for people in business. Every day we seem to be sailing into uncharted waters, heading toward an unknown future that is at once rich in opportunity and strewn with pitfalls.

Fred Harmon's *Business 2010* is a wonderful blend of the visionary and the practical, the theoretical and the applied.

My colleagues at Kiplinger and I explored these themes in a long-range-forecast book first published two years ago, titled *World Boom Ahead.* That book discusses how a confluence of global trends—in technology, government, population and entrepreneurship—will result in world economic growth higher, on average, than that ever before experienced in history.

While *World Boom Ahead* dealt briefly with trends in management, I knew that the future of business—its structures, organizational styles and special challenges—deserved an entire book, one that would be useful not only to the readers of our *Kiplinger Letter* but also to virtually everyone who faces tough strategic decisions.

Fred Harmon's *Business 2010* is just such a book. It is a wonderful blend of the visionary and the practical, the theoretical and the applied. It offers sound forecasts of the forces that will affect business in the years ahead, but, more than that, it lays out the implications of these changes, with concrete suggestions on how to position your business and yourself to benefit.

Mr. Harmon draws on his rich experiences as a business journalist and corporate consultant to illustrate his themes with real-life case studies drawn from the best practices (and occasional blunders) of prominent firms.

We at the Kiplinger organization are aware—on several different levels—of the extraordinary depth and speed of change in today's world. On one level, as forecasting journalists, we are in the business of alerting our readers—mostly people in senior management—to the changes ahead that will affect their enterprises, for good and ill. And as business managers ourselves, running an information service employing a few hundred people, we are whipped by the same winds of change that we write about.

My Kiplinger colleagues and I had the pleasure, as fellow journalists and observers of business, of helping Fred Harmon shape this book, offering suggestions and background research and reading his early drafts. But I know only too well, as an author myself, that the heavy lifting—the struggle to get the words right—is ultimately the author's responsibility. So I tip my hat to Mr. Harmon for accomplishing so sweeping and valuable a tome as *Business 2010*.

Let me return, for a moment, to the idea of change. Institutions, like individuals, are generally resistant to change. They don't modify their ways of living and working simply for refreshment or novelty. On the contrary, they are usually forced to change by the imperatives of the marketplace; it's a case of changing or facing extinction.

But the most successful companies, like the highest-achieving individuals, are more receptive to change than others. Rather than sitting back and waiting to be buffeted by the gales of change, successful businesses try to peer into the darkness and make out the hazy shape of the future, so that they can turn change to their advantage.

All of us at the Kiplinger organization wish you and your colleagues success as you try to adapt to the amazing changes that lie ahead.

Knight Kiplinger

KNIGHT A. KIPLINGER
Editor in Chief, *The Kiplinger Letter and kiplingerforecasts.com*
Washington, D.C.
January, 2001

Preface: Toward Business 2010

ODAY, AMERICAN BUSINESSPEOPLE DEFINE CHANGE primarily in terms of technology or markets, but an equally important element is our changed perspective. In a few decades we moved from relying on limited material assets to depending on virtually limitless, intangible resources.

The foundation of our economic system has shifted from physical production to mental services. In the 1990s, we went from worrying about how we had too many people for too few jobs to wondering how we could find the workers we need. Perhaps most important, we extended our horizon from national borders to global cyberspace.

These are not small changes. Taken together they create a climate of rare challenge and opportunity.

We are certain to miss the true significance of such developments when we constantly look around the corner for the next disaster, or when we interpret the latest stock market gyration as an accurate predictor of long-term trends. It is far more practical—and energizing—to look periodically at the deeper, long-term forces of change in our society than to continually focus on short-term effects.

That's the central message of *Business 2010:* Expand your understanding of five specific forces of change that are reshaping your business, and reposition your company—internally and externally—with those forces.

Part One of this book focuses on the five forces behind the accelerating growth reshaping our world—technology, freedom, education, demographics and globalization—placing these forces in a historical context as well indicating their likely future direction.

Part Two deals with five key components within every company that must be realigned with the forces of change. Whether start-up or established giant, every company must have a *market* for its *products or services*. It requires *people* to make, sell, develop and account for what it sells. *Capital* in the form of cash or other physical assets is the fourth component. Finally, tying the others all together is *organization*—the network of structures and systems the company uses to manage the other components.

The five forces described in Part One have overturned conventional wisdom, and all require fresh thinking. Each chapter in Part Two focuses on one component and shows you how to evaluate the likely evolution of that component in light of the changes described in Part One.

Part Three brings together key issues and priorities that any company must address in accordance with the analysis in Parts One and Two. This part emphasizes how to increase profits and productivity by emphasizing values like speed, value-added service and development of people—all benchmarks of success in the new business equation.

The Question of Development

Although this book frequently deals with growth, the more important theme is development—the process of building competitive advantage by strengthening the components of your business in alignment with the forces of change.

My ideas about business development are adapted from a theory of societal development, produced by my frequent consulting and writing associates, Garry Jacobs and Robert Macfarlane. Their rigorous work on this project focuses on concepts, but their aim is very practical—to increase the speed and effectiveness of any development project, whether for individuals, companies or even countries.

They first presented their ideas in papers published by Mother's Service Society, a research and service organization in Pondicherry, India. Later their core ideas appeared as a key element in the 1994 United Nations report "Uncommon Opportunities: An Agenda for Peace and Equitable Development." Jacobs and Macfarlane have since expanded their work in a series of papers written with political scientist and author Harlan Cleveland, president emeritus of the World Academy of Art and Science.

Many of the dramatic changes we now see around us can be explained by our current evolution to a more mental stage of development.

In their papers (available at www.mirainternational.com), the three authors focus on development as a process by which societies move from lesser to greater levels of accomplishment. They argue that all societies develop through three overlapping stages, which they call physical, vital and mental:

In the first stage, physical aspects of life dominate human existence. Society focuses on physical survival, protection and preservation of the status quo.

In the second stage, increasing productivity of physical resources generates surplus produce, energy and wealth. Commerce replaces agriculture as the predominant source of wealth.

In the third stage, societies advance by mental development. This stage is characterized by the generation of new inventions, higher levels of organization, and an elevation in the status and rights of individuals.

The progression from one stage to the next stimulates an exponential increase in the productivity and accomplishment of society. They contend that our current evolution to a more mental stage of development explains many of the dramatic changes we now see around us.

Up to now, they contend, development has been largely

unconscious, proceeding "by a slow, cumbersome trial and error process from experience to knowledge." Conscious development (the aim of their theory) moves in the other direction, from knowledge to experience. "The more conscious the process, the more rapid the progress." That, of course, is why education is such a powerful lever for development.

I gratefully acknowledge their contribution as well as their generous support for my effort to translate their societal theory into an explanation of business development.

Keeping Up With Change

A CEO of a successful and rapidly growing midwestern company recently confided to me that he was "scared" by the ferocious pace of change, by his uncertainty about whether he or his company could keep up. I certainly empathized with his feeling. A dozen times, while preparing this book, I felt overwhelmed by the volume and complexity of information available all around me. My task was to find patterns, yet each day's newspapers and TV broadcasts brought a deluge of fresh information and analysis. Like my friend, I wondered how I could ever keep up. Over time, however, I learned to ask two questions that always helped me separate the ephemeral from the significant. These questions may prove useful to any reader when confronting change.

First, how does this new development connect with the past? I am convinced that developments that connect with strong historical forces—the expansion of human freedom, for example—are likely to prove the most significant for society and business over time.

Second, what is different this time? Too heavy a reliance on continuity with the past encourages complacency, a world-weary conviction that there is nothing new under the sun. For example, the Internet clearly links with the telegraph, the mid-nineteenth century breakthrough technology that first provided instant communication across great distances. However, the

Internet is also truly new. By giving millions of individuals access to this powerful communication tool at a fraction of the cost of a telegram, the Internet has opened great new possibilities for human development.

I have attempted to reflect this dual perspective throughout this book. I find that answers to both questions continually refresh my feeling of confidence and optimism.

FREDERICK G. HARMON
Annandale, Virginia
January, 2001

BUSINESS
2010

Understanding the Forces of Change

W E'VE TRIED CHANGE THREE TIMES AROUND here," an exasperated manager complained to a consultant friend of mine. "It's never worked." Many executives share this manager's frustration. Keeping your company aligned with technological change, rapid market shifts, rising expectations of customers and employees, and unyielding competitive pressures is a daunting task.

Success begins with a deeper understanding of the forces around you. A partial understanding breeds partial solutions, leading to partial success at best. Just as inevitably, a more comprehensive vision produces a wider perspective, which, in turn, opens the way to integrated, rather than piecemeal, responses to change.

This first three chapters of this book aim to provide that wider perspective. They identify the five predominant forces reshaping business and society today and explain how those forces, acting separately and together, create new opportunities for business growth and development. Chapter Four, the last chapter in Part One, explores how societies and businesses evolve in response to the challenges created by the forces of change.

A Moment of Opportunity

KEY CHAPTER THEMES

■ *Five forces of change*

■ *Technology: Making labor mental*

■ *Freedom: New definitions of competition and choice*

■ *Education: The irreplaceable engine for growth*

"We can't pretend to forecast just what will happen or when. But we already know something more important: why it will happen."
—HARLAN CLEVELAND, PRESIDENT EMERITUS, WORLD ACADEMY OF ART AND SCIENCE

"One cannot manage change. One can only be ahead of it." —PETER F. DRUCKER, AUTHOR, PROFESSOR, CLAREMONT GRADUATE SCHOOL, CALIFORNIA

STRATEGIES TO ANTICIPATE CHANGE REQUIRE FAR MORE than predictions, projections, or forecasts. If you doubt that, take a look at your company's five-year-old, long-term projections of sales, costs and profits. As a management tool to focus attention on what were then the critical issues, the numbers probably had value; as a window on the future they were probably next to useless. As Samuel Goldwyn, the shrewd but sometimes tongue-twisted Hollywood producer, once put it, "Never make forecasts, especially about the future."

Anticipating the future begins not with projections but with an understanding of five fundamental forces that are reshaping business: technology, freedom, education, demographics and globalization. Each of these forces began gathering speed decades or even centuries ago. Each has reached new levels of acceleration in recent years. Individually and collectively they are changing the way that societies, individuals and companies live and work.

Within these five forces, lie find the root causes for the shorter-term trends businesspeople encounter every day. For example, demographics are a major factor behind the current shortage of people, skilled and unskilled, in virtually every industry. Think demographics next time you see a sign in the window of a fast-food restaurant or a local small business announcing, "Now accepting applications." Whom do they think they are kidding? "Now pleading for applications" would be closer to the truth.

Or take the expanding sense of freedom. From time to time, do the expectations and attitudes of young workers in your company frustrate you? If so, you have front-line experience of how an expanded definition of freedom is redefining traditional relationships at work. This expanded sense of freedom also contributes mightily to the pressure that business leaders today feel to decentralize authority and "empower" people.

When you understand these five forces, you will be better able to anticipate the direction of related trends in your market, industry and company. You will also be more alert to unfolding opportunities for your business. That's because the interaction among these forces has placed American business at the center of a new launching point for human choices and opportunities.

If American business realizes the potential of this moment, America's rapid growth in the 1990s will be remembered neither as a fortuitous occurrence nor an extended run of good luck. Instead, the '90s will be recalled as the forerunner of an even more rapid and broader pace of development.

It took the convergence of these five powerful engines of progress to create this moment of opportunity:

Technology hourly extends human capacity and converts physical energy into ever-higher forms of mental energy.

The spread of freedom daily multiplies the potential for human choice within closed societies and organizations.

Education expands mental horizons and intellectual skills at an ever-increasing pace.

Demographics overturn all of our traditional definitions of both customers and employees.

Globalization opens vast new markets while raising hope and opportunities among people whose ancestors had little of either.

This chapter discusses the first three of these forces—technology, freedom and education. Chapter Two reviews the big demographic changes that are coming in American society and analyzes how they will affect markets and the workplace in the years ahead. Chapter Three looks at the outlook for globalization—the powerful force that is creating so many new opportunities for growth and threats of competition today. Chapter Four explains how successful businesses respond and adapt to the increased momentum of these forces of change.

For readers who are already familiar with the demographic trends that are discussed in Chapter Two, projecting even faster economic growth may seem counterintuitive. That's because so much of our growth in the past has resulted from a *quantitative* expansion of population, a trend that will slow in the U.S. in the next 20 to 30 years. This book proposes that accelerating *qualitative* advances now accompany this continuing quantitative expansion, and that the shift becomes more important every year.

Qualitative advances refer to developments like the expansion of lifelong education at home and at work, the rapid evolution of technology to replace a permanent shortage of workers and improve the physical health and longevity of Americans, and the development of new services for the comfort and convenience of people at work and at home.

These advances—and dozens of others discussed later—translate into spectacular opportunities for business. Exploiting those opportunities requires a basic shift in perspective, that is, an understanding that the paths to tomorrow's opportunities lead in vastly different directions from the well-worn trails of yesterday.

For a century or longer, the word *more* has driven business: More cars. More houses. More refrigerators. More TV channels. More hospitals. More retail outlets. And, of course, more people. The new watchword is *better*: Better-quality cars. Better education. Better health care. Better recreation. Better value-added services offered as an addition to standard products.

Adding to the potential of this qualitative expansion at home is the parallel expansion of quantitative growth in the developing world. A growing, global middle class every year exhibits a larger appetite and, increasingly, an expanding purchasing power for U.S.-style comforts.

The resources that have fueled the economic growth of the late 20th century are potentially infinite. We have only begun to see what technology, freedom and education can accomplish individually and, even more important, in combination with greater demographic diversity and globalization.

Driving Force #1: Technology— Extending Human Potential and Making Labor Mental

Technology's power derives from its capacity to enhance human capacities. Our ancestors developed the hand ax to extend the power and reach of their arms. The communications revolution extended the range of our eyes and ears to send and receive information. The computer simulates aspects of our mental powers. By combining communication technologies and the computer, we created the relentless pace of the Information Age.

Information Age technology has radically altered the way American companies do business, creating what some executives call a New Economy. Between 1995 and 1998 the information technology sector (IT), which accounts for only 8% of U.S. gross domestic product (GDP), contributed, on average, 35% of the country's economic growth. At century's end, software companies alone employed 800,000 people. These companies were growing at a rate of 13% a year, compared with 2.5% for the economy as a whole.[1]

More widely defined, IT represents something new in every business. The new technology provides instantaneous information. Business used to count inventory at the end of the year, month or even day. Now, information about inventory is available immediately, reducing inventory stockpiling, unnecessary workers and capital equipment. Some of the productivity gains of the 1990s are clearly linked to these improvements.

American business has been quick to see the potential of this change. As early as 1990, U.S. business was spending more on equipment to automate the handling of information than on the combined outlays for all of physical production, including factory equipment, transportation systems and construction projects. By century's end, shares in a single information company, Microsoft, were worth more than all the shares in every company in the U.S. auto industry, that undisputed symbol of the industrial age.

What is not new about the New Economy is what Harvard professor Joseph Schumpter long ago called "creative destruction." In this continuous process, leading-edge technologies push out the old, as companies replace obsolescent, capital-intensive production equipment with more modern information systems. Creative destruction has been around for centuries. Today it is accelerating, driven by innovations in information technology.

One can celebrate the achievements of technology and still be alert to its limitations. At the creative end, creative destruction is a heady brew for 30-year-old Silicon Valley dot-com millionaires. At the destruction end, the same brew has a bitter taste for 50-year-old redundant Akron factory workers.

Then there is that famous "right to be left alone." Advances in technology make it easy to collect data at home and at work. Databases combining public and consumer information now encompass some 95% of American households. Surveys repeatedly show that when Americans become aware of this electronic snooping, they don't like what they see.

The Biological Frontier

Even greater technological change is just over the horizon. Physics, the dominant science of the 20th century, changed our world through innovations such as the atomic bomb and the transistor. The 21st century promises to be the Century of Biology. At one level, the biotech revolution merely extends developments in the life sciences that have brought vaccines against smallpox and polio, antidepressant drugs, the "green revolution" in agriculture, as well as increases in life spans around the world.

Genetics will be the key enabling technology of the early 21st century, rivaling information technology in importance.

But when Watson and Crick decoded the structure of DNA, they opened new possibilities on the scientific frontier. Genetics will be a key enabling technology of the early 21st century, rivaling information technology, energy technology and materials technology in importance. It is already clear that genetic research opens the potential for us to redirect the evolution of our own and other species. To take just one example, it is no longer certain that there need be any limit to life expectancy. Recent research suggests that aging and cell degeneration are genetically controlled processes that could potentially be turned off.

Explosive Issues

The biotech revolution raises potentially explosive issues. Biotech research is uncovering the genetic foundations of diseases like Alzheimer's, breast cancer and schizophrenia. Now, the "germ-line" research of the future has the potential to eliminate those diseases not only in treated individuals but also in all of their subsequent descendants.

The emerging issue is how to draw the line between legitimate therapy and artificial enhancement of the human race. For example, there is growing evidence that a tendency for violence is both genetically inherited and more characteristic of males than females. Suppose we establish that this is true (which is certainly possible) and we are able to isolate the violence gene (which is even more likely within our capacity)? Why not intervene genetically to correct an obvious danger to society? "Those who think that this sounds like science fiction have simply not been paying attention to…the life sciences recently," says George Mason University Professor Francis Fukuyama.

Business often dismisses people who question technology's cost-benefit relationships as neo-Luddites, those 19th-century

English craftsmen who rioted against the textile machinery that was displacing them. However, the success of activists in the past 20 years in reframing the environmental cost-benefit argument and then winning public support for their position provides a clear model for debates that are only now beginning.

Lists of new technological marvels and miracle cures are now commonplace in every newspaper, magazine and TV show. It is only a small exaggeration to say that Americans have become addicted to technological progress. This widespread support is closely linked to the two trends discussed in the paragraphs that follow. Freedom—of opportunity and from excessive regulation—creates a climate in which innovation thrives. Expanding education in schools and on television produces technologically friendly customers and workers with a growing appetite for the latest innovation.

Driving Force #2: Freedom's Dance

Tom Brokaw, anchor of NBC Nightly News, stood near the Berlin Wall at 1:00 A.M. on November 10, 1989. Hours earlier, the East German government had announced that its citizens could travel to the West. By midnight, East Germans began pouring through border checkpoints.

As Brokaw watched, the "first to reach the wall was a young man in a brown jacket. The crowd parted and cheered as he raised his arms in triumph and danced along the concrete slab that hours before had imprisoned him." For Brokaw, as for many others, "my enduring memory will always be of that young man's dance…he transformed The Wall from a sinister symbol of oppression to a platform for celebration and liberation."

That night could serve as a celebration not just of one victory but of a century of hard-won victories for popular rule. In 1900, only six of 43 then-recognized nation-states had something that could be described as a political democracy. In the U.S., eligible voters included only some men and no women. By the close of the century, democratic rule had extended to 117 of 193 countries, some 54% of world population.[2]

Asian Values

Freedom breeds a hunger for and expectation of greater individual choice. That's why the so-called Asian model, popular in the 1970s and 1980s, could only be a temporary way station to greater freedom. The Asian model held that economic and political freedoms were divisible. In theory, Asian willingness to defer to authority could produce sustained growth without the political upheavals that sometimes shake Western democracies. The Asian model turned sour when key decisions were left to bureaucrats who claimed to have all the answers. Unchecked rule by bureaucrats led to corruption, collusion with favored companies, and questionable loans to friends and family of government leaders.

While the lessons of this setback are important, the fundamental economic strengths of Asia were apparent in its rapid recovery. Necessary reforms that opened up society took hold in the aftermath of the "Asian flu." Assuming that necessary reforms continue, the region should have an expanding production base as well as offering a huge market for most of this century.

Why did Asian values so quickly change from being a strength to being a weakness? Korean economist Ungsuh Kenneth Park identifies the most probable explanation: "Strong governments, meek people and wide cooperation" are valuable in the early takeoff period of economic growth. However, once basic needs are met, "people everywhere demand greater participation in the decisions that shape their lives."[3]

All true development "can be seen as the process of expanding the real freedom that people enjoy," says Amartya Sen, winner of the 1998 Nobel Prize in economics. Future decades will see a widening of definitions of freedom beyond creating political democracy and unchaining markets. Effective development requires the removal of all major sources of "unfreedom," Sen insists. Under this definition, expanding development will inevitably create stronger national agendas to reduce poverty and health risks as well as eliminating political tyranny, and to expand education and economic opportunities as well as liberalizing markets.

Competition and Choice

In the marketplace, people express their greater freedom by demanding more choices. As a result, producers must provide more opportunities for customers to choose what the product looks like, how they purchase it and what customized features they want.

Henry Ford pioneered the vast expansion of the freedom to travel when he offered his customers an $850 automobile, but competition decades ago repealed his famous limitation that customers could have any color car they wanted "as long as it is black." Before long, Ford customers will be able to order their car with exactly the individual features they want and have it delivered from the factory in a matter of days.

Rapidly expanding choice breeds chaotic market competition. Giant corporations cede control in every business field. Entrepreneurial companies rise from nowhere to challenge the giants and become giants themselves. In fewer than 20 years this is the story of MCI, Microsoft, Dell, Federal Express, Wal-Mart and Amazon.com. Today a few entrepreneurs with a Web site can compete for market share, funding and excitement with established giants.

In the 1950s, billion-dollar mergers would have shaken Wall Street and Washington alike. Today, no one worries seriously that merged giants in traditional industries can monopolize markets. The Justice Department expressed far more concern about the potential monopoly of a single company, Microsoft, on the Information Age frontier. As economic power decentralizes, federal antitrust officials will look more closely at a company's domination in particular geographic regions, not just in the country as a whole. An aggressive push by the federal government in this area will mean still further decentralization of the economy and still more competition.

The jobs lost because of mergers would have created greater controversy in earlier eras. In 1999, there were few headlines about the more than 55,000 merger-related job cuts. Smart small-business owners hired some of this talent, acquiring a knowledge pool developed by big companies. Other downsized executives took their skills into the entrepreneurial economy, decentralizing economic power even further.

Erosion of Top-Down Power

Within companies, the expanding, explosive power of freedom translates into decentralized authority and empowered workers. In a fast-moving technological age, the economic freedom represented by "a fair day's wage for a fair day's work" is a given, rather than a competitive advantage. Today's rapid turnover of talented people arises in part from the "unfreedoms" in too many large American corporations. The entrepreneurial economy, in contrast, promises both greater economic freedom and the social freedom of greater personal autonomy.

The same people who demand more choice at the supermarket, who want access to more television channels and who want more control over the curriculum at their local schools hunger for more choices in their work. To keep competition and choice synchronized with the rhythms of Freedom's Dance is a major business opportunity of the new century.

Driving Force #3: Education— The Irreplaceable Engine for Growth

Education is an irreplaceable engine for business growth. "In the knowledge society, the knowledge base is the foundation of the economy," says Peter Drucker.

Education's primary contribution to business is its capacity to transform business's greatest resource—people—into human capital. The quality of that human capital determines how well any business can produce, innovate and compete.

In its second great contribution, education helps business by raising people's aspirations for self-improvement. This increased awareness expands market opportunities. Expanding print literacy sells more books. Expanding computer literacy sells software. Wider health education sells pharmaceuticals.

Third, education accelerates the diffusion of scientific and technical knowledge. The technical know-how used in any industry, from agriculture to computer science, regularly reaches the front-line worker through formal schooling, adult education, correspondence courses or in-company training.

Education's Support for Freedom

Education has traditionally supported the expansion of American freedom and economic opportunity. Education gave the early leaders of the American republic the knowledge of Enlightenment ideas on which they based both our Revolution and our Constitution. Many of these people, including Thomas Jefferson, were the first of their families to attend college. Setting forth the new American perspective, John Adams said henceforth it was education, not birth or privilege, that would make the gentleman.

By the mid-19th century the great educator Horace Mann had won for every American child the right to basic education at state expense. Although it took decades to turn this right into a reality, access to free public schools served as a great cauldron of Americanization. Millions of children walked into school as foreigners and graduated as Americans with a common language, values and the basic skills of a literate society.

The G.I. Bill gave millions of American veterans the opportunity for advanced technical, professional and academic education. For 50 years after World War II, this bold stroke provided the country with educated leadership at every economic level. In addition, by subsidizing a massive expansion of our elitist higher educational system, the G.I. Bill increased access to higher education for millions more.

Our hot political debates about education are justified by the importance of the challenges confronting us, but the clamor of the debates tends to drown out appreciation of the continuing and genuine achievements of our education system. In both quantitative and qualitative terms the numbers are impressive. Consider:

- **In the 1949–50 academic year,** just over 31 million Americans were enrolled at all levels of education. Fifty years later, the number had more than doubled, to 67.6 million.
- **Just 30 years ago,** more than half of Americans who were 25 years of age or older had not graduated from high school. Today, 83% of Americans over 25 years old are graduates of high school.
- **More than 90% of school-age Americans** under age 18 are students.

■ **Many older Americans** are back in the schoolroom. In 1996, nearly 3 million people who were aged 35 or older were enrolled in school.

■ **A college education is no longer an elite entitlement.** In 1994–95 more than 1 million prospective college students took the Scholastic Aptitude Test. That compares with 11,000 in 1941, the first year the test was administered.

■ **Meanwhile, the SAT scores of minority groups** have been rising since 1975–76. Among African Americans, verbal scores in 1994-95 were 24 points higher than they were 20 years earlier. Math scores rose 34 points during the same period.[4]

Absorbing this level of change has put the education system under enormous pressure. Dissatisfaction with quality is at an all-time high. Yet America's fundamental faith in the power and potential of its education system remains strong.

Diffusion of Scientific Information

Technology stalls without effective educational channels to spread scientific and technical information. Recognizing this truth, the French established the Ecole Polytechnique in 1794. Originally designed to train engineering and artillery officers, the school eventually concentrated on math, basic science and technical capability.

The success of the Polytechnique sparked imitators in Prague, Vienna, Zurich and Moscow. German universities invented the teaching laboratory in 1830, a breakthrough in making their university technical education the world model by the end of the 19th century.

This growing reliance on formal education to spread technical and scientific knowledge had "momentous consequences," says historian David S. Landes. As the frontiers of technology shifted to fields like chemicals and electricity, formal instruction grew in importance. Nations that continued to rely too heavily on experiential learning slipped to the rear ranks of economic progress. For example, Landes compares the power of formal schooling on the continent of Europe with the British approach of learning by doing—the experiential strategy that had driven the Industrial Revolution by combining and recombining known techniques. As technology grew more complex, "Continental reliance on schooling paid off, generating and imparting new technologies...while Britain, caught in the net of habit, fell behind."[5]

Educational Requirements for Business

Today, American business needs an effective school system at every level to stay competitive. The raw knowledge available to the average business keeps growing exponentially. According to at least one expert estimate (probably more of a guestimate), the Internet causes available information to double every 80 days. Staying on top of these mounting data dumps requires business owners and managers to have an educated perspective and an ability to organize knowledge across companies. A statistic, no matter eye-catching, represents only a point in time. Even a short-term trend can be misleading when isolated from a deeper, more comprehensive understanding of how the forces of change are reshaping a company's total environment. Before a company can make the best use of new information, that information must be organized and readily available throughout the whole industry. Today, too often, the best pieces of information are isolated in individual company silos called *market research, financial data* and *product development*.

Dissatisfaction with the current system among business leaders and, increasingly, among the American population as a whole has reached such a fevered pitch that reforms and innovations will roll out in the early years of this century. Distance learning is already widely available. In March 1999, Jones International University became the first Internet-only university to be accredited to grant college degrees by the North Central Association of Colleges and Schools, the group responsible for evaluating institutions of higher learning in the midwestern U.S. At century's end, a million people were studying online, a number that is expected to double by 2003. Closed-circuit television has the potential to raise the level of instruction in classrooms throughout the nation by bringing superstar teachers to students in remote locations.

UNext.com provides one innovative model of how education could evolve in the next decade. The founders of the company, Andrew Rosenfield, a lawyer and legal consultant, and Gary Becker, a Nobel Prize-winning economist at the University of Chicago, want to sell online courses to companies eager to improve the skills of their employees. To get the support of brand-name business schools, they offered a deal worth at least $20 million to founding institutions. In short order, *The New York Times* reports, they had signed up Carnegie Mellon, Chicago, Columbia and Stanford universities as well as the London School of Economics. That support enabled UNext to recruit faculty for its courses and acquire curriculum expertise from the institutions.

Business recognizes that, to get the skills it needs, it must educate its own workforce.

UNext is targeting adult learners in client companies like Merrill Lynch and AOL–Time-Warner. One added appeal: students can also accumulate credit toward a diploma from UNext's own business school. Only four months after offering its first online courses, UNext was negotiating to offer courses in Brazil, China, India and elsewhere.[6]

Business Universities

Business recognizes that, to get the skills it needs, it must educate its own workforce. Corporations are now investing as much as $70 billion annually on their own "universities" to train and educate workers at all levels. Employee schools are growing at 100 times the rate of academic institutions, according to a study by the consulting firm KPMG. The need is urgent. KPMG estimates that 75% of today's workforce needs retraining.[7]

At century's end there were about 1,600 company universities, four times as many as there were 15 years ago, according to Corporate University Xchange (CUX), a research and consulting firm. If this pace continues, there will be more corporate universities than traditional ones by 2010. High-tech companies like Motorola and Dell are leading the current expansion. In the next decade, leaders among more traditional industries will certainly expand their education efforts to meet the shortage of skilled workers and to train employees to their own specifications while on the job.[8]

Education for Technologists: A Competitive Advantage

As with any expense, business must ask: Where is the greatest competitive advantage from educational investment? Peter Drucker, who for years has identified pivotal links between education and productivity, offers this surprising answer. Today, training and development budgets focus on bringing senior and middle-level managers and professionals up to speed with changing requirements. In addition, funds are invested in teaching young employees the skills of the business. However, according to Drucker, true competitive advantage may come quickest by educating those he calls "technologists"—the large number of people whose "knowledge work" is relatively subordinate to their manual tasks. This category includes the lab technicians, the machinists running a complicated prototype machine, and all kinds of repair and installation people such as auto mechanics and electricians.

Drucker reasons that theoretical (or *high*) knowledge no longer has national borders. Once knowledge is available, any country can train a substantial number of high-knowledge workers. India, for example, has been training some 75,000, highly skilled computer programmers every year. Similarly, there is no longer much competitive advantage to investing in the development of techniques to improve productivity of manual labor. Everyone knows what to do and how to train for it.

"Only in educating technologists," Drucker says, "can the developed countries still have a meaningful competitive edge, and for some time to come."[9] The U.S. has a current and substantial advantage here in its network of community colleges. For at least 50 years these colleges have been combining technical and academic education in partnership with local businesses. Today, more than 90% of the 1,132 members of the

American Association of Community Colleges have training contracts with local businesses. According to an AACC study, 95% of business organizations that use community colleges would recommend them for workforce education and training programs.

Our educational system is poised for a creative change. Existing technology opens the way for more individualized learning, and more of it at home. We will continue to rely on schoolrooms for socialization and interactive learning in groups. Minorities and immigrants will continue to use education as the vehicle for progress and access to the expanding opportunities of American economic life.

Summary and Conclusions

Powerful forces with deep historic roots are reshaping the business arena. Some changes are already in place. Others just over the horizon are now clearly visible.

Technology, to paraphrase Sir Isaac Newton, progresses on the "shoulders of giants." Every year, information technology will consolidate and expand previous gains. Some of today's high-tech stars will be a memory by 2010, devoured by the revolution they created. Yet faster, more customized communication tools will keep overturning 20th-century business practices. The ability to respond to customers faster, cheaper and more comprehensively will be the watchwords in traditional and leading-edge companies alike.

Today's primitive program crashes and access delays will fade. In the early days of the auto age, drivers acted as mechanics, restarting machines that failed on the road. Before long, drivers could assume that the new horseless carriage would work. Information technology follows the same pattern. More user-friendly machines and programs are on the way.

Fear of Frankenstein

Counterpressures are inevitable. The ancient fear of Frankenstein—science gone amok—will mobilize stronger forces against technology. Critics will focus on the erosion of privacy and unregulated tampering with genes in plants, animals and people. Concern over inequality between technology "haves" and "have-nots" will grow domestically and internationally. Those people who are left out will provide a cause and recruits for reformers.

While pressures will mount, the undeniable benefits of technology will prevail. The failure of the much-heralded Y2K catastrophe to materialize energized technology's proponents, reinforcing the belief that even major downside risks can be managed—at a price. For the next decade at least, business can assume accelerating progress in technology.

More Emphasis on Health, Education and Equality

Freedom's Dance will swing to a faster, wider, more inclusive rhythm. The benefits of free markets and free institutions will continue to gain converts. Other freedoms will move to the forefront. With 2 billion people still living in grinding poverty, democratic governments will place more emphasis on wider definitions of freedom that promote better health, education and equality of opportunity.

Freedom evolving with technology will create unexpected results in economics and politics. Traditional economic theory focuses on scarcity, diminishing returns and finite resources. As technology redefines value as a mental rather than physical resource, allocation enters an exciting new arena. Today's technology theoretically makes it possible to provide everyone on the planet with basic food, health care and education. As this ability becomes more apparent, definitions of freedom will expand to include greater equality of opportunity and access.

Between Education and Catastrophe

"Civilization is in a race between education and catastrophe." That observation is as true today as when the visionary writer H. G. Wells said it at the end of the 19th century. Expanding freedom, coupled with the unfolding wonders of technology, gives humans greater potential for progress—or mischief—than ever before. Education is our best tool to ensure sensible choices.

Practical reasons underpin business's mounting concern about U.S. education. Tomorrow's workers need an educational base that provides an understanding of science, math and technology; a facility to gather, digest and use information; and an awareness of threats and opportunities beyond local and national borders.

In addition to a skilled population of workers, business needs a broadly educated one. Support for economic and political policies that underpin business success depends on an informed, rational electorate. Stability in a democracy depends on reasonably rational judgments by a majority of the population. Making such judgments in the world today depends on some understanding of the principles of science and economics, and of the elements of sustainable growth.

If the education system stalls, freedom and technology will sputter and slow. Business progress will limp, forcing companies to depend too heavily on the knowledge, skills and enthusiasm of educated immigrants. The native born's resentment of immigrants will grow, creating instability and a downward cycle of increased regulation and repressive legislation.

Fortunately, we are entering an era of educational experimentation, supported by media and business attention. As a result, there will be more progress in educational content and methodology in the next 10 years than in the past century. By supporting this effort through funding educational innovation and excellence at the local level and through providing its own educational infrastructure, business helps ensure a favorable outcome for itself.

Later chapters look further at how technology, freedom and education are reshaping business. For example, as a result of these forces, organizational design is undergoing more profound change than any time since business borrowed the military structure of command and control more than a century ago. These forces have catapulted speed of response to an entirely new dimension. What we call the globalization of business began with the commercial empires of the colonial era. Yet the pace and possibilities created by the acceleration of technology, freedom and education are opening the way for a whole new world of business opportunity.

The next chapter, however, highlights a fourth group of important opportunities—shifts in the demographic patterns on which business depends for customers and workers.

21st-Century Demographics

KEY CHAPTER THEMES

- *Population declines in most of the Western world will create unprecedented changes in business, politics and societies.*

- *The aging of the U.S. population will present new challenges to marketers and managers.*

- *Immigration will force rethinking of one-size-fits-all management and marketing.*

- *Women in business will rise in numbers, and even more rapidly in power.*

"Every night and every morn
Some to misery are born;
Every morn and every night
Some are born to sweet delight."
—WILLIAM BLAKE, ENGLISH POET

I N THE SECOND HALF OF THE 20TH CENTURY, TECH-
nology, freedom and education remade population
patterns in the developed and developing worlds
alike. Technology delivered the world's first safe, reliable contraceptives, which lowered fertility rates.
Technology also provided miracle cures for diseases, expanding life spans everywhere.

Education accelerated the diffusion of knowledge, sanita-
tion, nutrition and health care. In less than a half-century,
nations everywhere converted theoretical knowledge to widespread application. Higher standards of education, particularly for women, lowered birthrates in many countries.

In the U.S., education proved to be a pivotal engine of
business progress by raising both the educational attainment
and the business potential of women and minorities.

The expansion of freedom opened new opportunities at
work, enriching both the general workforce and the professions with the energy and enthusiasm of previously excluded
or marginalized women and minorities. The growth of freedom encouraged the unchaining of state monopolies and the
liberation of markets. Greater opportunities for economic and
political freedom attracted additional millions of immigrants to
the U.S, changing the demographic map forever.

Greater freedom opened opportunities for American women outside the home, further depressing birthrates. The rise of female executives and women-owned businesses brought new attitudes and issues to the workplace.

The problem for business is not the quantity, quality or availability of demographic data. Rather, the issue is how to sort through the data to identify the few critical trends.

In the developing world, freedom, education and technology raised living standards and lengthened life spans faster than at any time in history.

Each of these changes shifted power inside companies, countries and markets. Business, society's most pragmatic arm, responded to new opportunities and threats that are only just beginning to play out in the world of work.

Demographics, the scientific study of population statistics, give us a way to describe, quantify, and potentially to make sense of these trends in population. Demographics identify trends in birth and death rates, immigration, education, as well as population shifts from one region to another. Demographers routinely provide mounds of statistics, thousands of figures relating to everything from the number of master's degrees awarded by subject to life expectancy by race and sex and spending patterns by age of households.

In anticipating the future, demographics come as near to certainty as we get. Most projections of the future must assume a series of variables. In demographics, the biggest variable is already known—the people who will compose the American workforce and consumer population are already here and can be counted. Demographers can even give us reasonably accurate projections about the composition of those worker-consumer populations, including: where they will live, and how well educated they will be. The problem for business is not the quantity, quality or availability of demographic data. Rather, the issue is how to sort through the data to identify the few critical trends.

The trends listed in the next section are my candidates for the changes that are most likely to challenge American business in the next decade.

Falling Birthrates in the Developed World

Over the next 20 to 30 years, the U.S. will be the only large, advanced nation that will add population. Japan, Germany, France, Italy, Russia and others will lose population. The U.S. will add some 2.5 million people a year, on average; more births than deaths will account for about 60% of the gain, and immigration for about 40%. Even so, the U.S. will be growing far more slowly than in the recent past, from 274 million at 20th century's end to 298 million people in 2011.

There is no modern precedent for this kind of change. Governments and businesses alike have traditionally assumed an expanding population except for periods of war or pestilence. More people traditionally meant bigger markets and a plentiful supply of workers. Now most of the Western world must build strategies on the premise of shrinking population.

According to conventional wisdom, this deceleration of population growth means that any business growth strategy in the U.S. must include the more rapid assimilation of immigrants as workers and consumers. Another key strategy must focus on even faster substitution of human labor by technology. That will mean further mentalization of work, requiring still higher educational attainment in the U.S. workforce. A third strategy will center on accelerating the growth of production and sales in the developing world, where population is still growing rapidly. (Chapter Three presents a more detailed discussion of this strategy.)

Europe and Japan will be confronted with even more urgent choices. If Europeans want to keep their economies and social services running at the present pace, they will have to lower their traditional barriers to immigration. European countries "will face the wall," says Joseph Chamie, director of the United Nations' population division. "They either bring in migrants or they are going to decline in size."[1] Germany, for example, will have to import 500,000 people a year to keep its population at 1995 levels. How practical is that kind of growth in nations traditionally reluctant to absorb immigrants?

Today, the conventional wisdom and the proposed responses to demographic change just described are firmly rooted in the experience of the agricultural and industrial ages and are based on a *quantitative* approach. That wisdom dictates this formula: More people equal bigger markets, more workers and more production, whereas fewer people equal less consumption, fewer workers and less production. That formula almost automatically narrows the choice to immigration or stagnation.

Qualitative rather than quantitative policies would focus on growth through development rather than on just expanding by the numbers as in the past.

However, the advanced nations could choose instead to pursue 21st century *qualitative* policies, which would open a wider, more creative range of options. Qualitative rather than quantitative policies would focus on growth through development rather than on just expanding by the numbers as in the past.

For example, today strong vested interests in the West resist exporting factories as well as increasing trade and imports. Support for such positions might gradually decline once it becomes clear that the alternative is more immigrant workers. Even in the U.S., historically the nation that has been most successful in absorbing immigrants, periods of rapid immigration have frequently been followed by periods of legal and social resistance to the absorption of new immigrants.

Qualitative-driven policies might also focus on developing still underutilized pools of potential workers. Such an approach could lead to concerted efforts to use technology and education to improve work opportunities for people in inner cities and rural areas as well as for women who prefer to work for an employer from home.

Fewer people might also make it possible to improve the quality of education and health care services. Certainly, the quality of both services has been strained in the West under quantitative pressure to extend their benefits to more people. It can be argued that a reversal in population growth would present an unexpected opportunity for improvement without a dramatic increase in costs.

The Graying Baby Boom

P art of the pressure on health care services arises from improvements in health technology, better education and greater freedom from backbreaking toil and life-threatening scourges. These three advances have dramatically extended life spans in the U.S.[2]

Americans in the 55-to-64-year-old group who are still in the workplace will increase by a stunning 56% in the first decade of this century. This cohort's share of the workforce will climb to 13. 3% by 2008 (up from 9.6% in 1998). Baby-boom women, the first generation of women to take up full-time work outside the home en masse, are moving into that age group, causing much of the increase.

Looking at this so-called age wave through the marketing telescope reveals that in the early 2000s, people over age 50 will grow fastest in numbers and purchasing power. Although they accounted for only 25% of our population at the 20th century's end, they already controlled half of our disposable incomes and 75% of financial assets. This shift will accelerate significant changes already under way in employment and marketing.

Until recently, years on the job were shrinking as a result of voluntary and forced early retirements. Now, labor force participation by men aged 55 to 59 is projected to creep up to 79% by 2006 (from 78% in 1996). Even that small gain is good news for the economy. It signals that a decades-long trend toward early retirement may be coming to an end, as businesses begin to trim early retirement incentives.

Many people want to work longer because they enjoy handling the growing number of mental jobs created by technology and education. Others will stay on the job because they don't think they have enough money for a worry-free retirement. For one reason or the other, nearly 70% of U.S. workers today expect to work for pay in retirement, according to a 1999 survey by the nonpartisan Employee Benefit Research Institute.

If past patterns hold, these older workers will be more loyal to employers. They will have better people skills and be less likely to take sick leave than younger workers. Investment banker Peter G. Peterson, who wrote a book on aging (*Gray Dawn: How the Coming Age Wave Will Transform America and the World*, Times Books, 1999), says that keeping people at work means overturning traditional views of age. "An entire stereotype will have to be reversed," he writes, "along with all the institutional rules and habits of thought that perpetuate it."

Businesses that today are still pushing 55-year-old employees out the door will try to keep older workers on the job, at least part time. A phased-in retirement will become more common. Even today, as the shortage of skilled workers becomes more intense, companies are frequently rehiring former employees to work part-time on a contract basis. Government and company benefits putting a premium on early retirement will be rethought.

For Aching Backs, Whirlpool Baths

On the marketing side, industries from automakers to soft-drink bottlers are already developing what *The New York Times* identifies as "a new generation of easier-to-use products specifically designed and marketed to a population that refuses to acknowledge the prospect of failing eyesight, hearing and dexterity." Boomers can choose to believe that life hasn't changed, adds *The Times*, "but the landscape of products is changing subtly around them," as manufacturers find ways to appeal to older consumers.

For aching backs, whirlpool baths with grip rails are replacing standard tubs. Shower stalls with seats are now routine. Lear Corp. has introduced a minivan refitted with larger controls, more legible instrument panels, and powered swiveling seats to help passengers enter or leave. Pepsi Cola is test-marketing a two-liter plastic bottle, called The Grip, that requires less hand strength. Wide-headed tennis rackets and large-headed golf clubs now dominate sales in their categories.[3]

The Hourglass-Shaped Workplace

As the number of middle-aged workers declines over the early 2000s, a countertrend will come to the forefront. For the first time in 25 years, the youth labor force—of 16- to 24-year-olds—will grow faster than the overall labor force. This shift suggests another strong argument for keeping the graying workforce in place. Older workers will be needed as mentors for the young.

This new hourglass-shaped workforce—a large, older generation at the top, a small, middle-aged group in the middle, and another large group at the bottom—will encourage business to offer more cafeteria-style benefits. Seniors will favor better health and pension benefits, while the younger group will look for bonuses and training in the latest technology. Firms that traditionally invest most of their training dollars in the young will have to redirect more of those funds to keep their middle-aged workers up to date.

From One Melting Pot to a Tossed Salad

L ured by the promise of greater freedom, immigrants will account for nearly half of U.S. population growth in the first two decades of the 21st century.

Hispanics will account for nearly 40% of our population growth. Every year some one million foreigners arrive here. Nearly half of them are Hispanics, many of childbearing age. By 2005, Hispanics will be the country's largest minority, about 36 million people, or 13% of total population. That will compare with 35 million, or 12.5%, of the population for African Americans.

Asians are the fastest-growing immigrant group. The number of Americans from countries like Japan, China, India, Vietnam and Cambodia will double between 2000 and 2020. This group will still be less than 6% of our population in 2020, but in terms of the sheer speed of increases, Asian Americans have everyone else beat.

Non-Hispanic whites are already a minority in New Mexico and Hawaii. Early in this century California will pass that milestone. Texas will follow by around 2015. Hispanics have already overtaken African Americans as the largest minority population on the Pacific Coast, in the Southwest and the Mountain States, as well as in much of New England.

Two-thirds of recent immigrants live in just 10 metropolitan areas: New York City, Los Angeles, San Francisco, Chicago, Miami, Washington-Baltimore, Houston, Dallas, San Diego and Boston. In contrast, only one in four native-born Americans lives in those areas. In New York City, at the past century's end, one of every three residents was an immigrant. Of those, nearly half had arrived since 1985.

While non-Hispanic whites will remain the majority until about 2050, the influence of minorities in the workplace will come much earlier. By 2030, most Americans under aged 18 will be minorities: Hispanic, African American, Asian and other. As early as 2006, minorities will fill one in four U.S. jobs. Stretch your definition of minorities to women and the numbers soar. In 2000, some 85% of new entrants to the workforce were women and people of color.

Education Propels Progress

Big advancements in education among minorities will translate into gains in jobs, incomes, homeownership and personal wealth in the early decades of the 21st century. By 2030, more than 90% of African Americans over 25 will have a high school diploma. That compares with 75% in 1997 and 50% in 1980.

By 2020, slightly more than 60% of the over-25 Hispanic population will have high school diplomas, up from 55% in 2000 and 45% in 1980. The surge in Latino immigrants from countries that lag behind U.S. educational standards tends to hold back the graduation rate for Hispanics as a whole.

Asian Americans age 25 or older already have an 85% high school graduation rate! Even more impressive is their college graduation rate—42%, compared with 26% for whites. Earning statistics once again document the power of education as an engine of progress. In 1998, Asian Americans had the highest median family income in the country at $42,250 a year, compared with $38,970 for whites, $26,630 for Hispanics, and $25,050 for African Americans.

Purchasing power (the combination of total size of a community plus its ability to spend based on income) will soar for Hispanics and African Americans in the years ahead. By 2000, Hispanics already represented a market of $350 billion a year. Current projections show that number climbing by 60% to 70% over each of the next two decades. Similarly, African Americans will see their purchasing power—now about $500 billion a year—climb by roughly 55% in each of the next two decades.

New Strategies Highlight Diversity

Inside companies, growth strategies will promote diversity as a competitive weapon rather than as a moral issue, particularly in the metropolitan areas listed earlier. In part this shift in emphasis will exemplify that time-tested American practice of making a virtue of necessity, but there are also indications that workforce diversity produces greater success in innovation.

Research by Harvard Business School professor David Thomas suggests that a multicultural work force produces a richer variety of possible solutions to problems. And, although cause and effect remains unclear, *Fortune's* "50 Best Companies for Asians, Blacks and Hispanics" consistently match or outperform the S&P 500 stock index.[4]

Religion Becomes a Bigger Issue

This changing mosaic of cultures in the workplace makes religion a far bigger concern for employers. Christianity is still the most common religion in the U.S., but workers adhering to Islam, Buddhism and Hinduism are growing in numbers. Religious discrimination charges already follow sexual harassment among the fastest-growing discrimination claims.

The Civil Rights Act of 1964 requires that employers "reasonably accommodate" religious preferences. Most cases involve company demands for work on the Sabbath or other religious holidays. However, Muslims have challenged company policies prohibiting beards and requiring women to wear company uniforms with pants.

Diversity Will Be the Norm in Marketing

Ethnic and racial diversity will become the norm in marketing for many parts of the country. That situation opens new sales, marketing and management positions to minorities. Companies will increasingly choose advertising and product selection to appeal to distinct communities. Insurance companies like New York Life, Metropolitan Life and Mony Life are already aggressively wooing high-profile members of immigrant communities to become agents.

Businesses will find hidden profits by catering to racial and ethnic preferences and by cultivating brand loyalty among new immigrants, many of whom are overwhelmed by the number and variety of products offered in their new country.

Successful businesses will reconsider who their customers are now and who they will be down the road. Already, more than one-fourth of U.S. consumers are nonwhite. By 2020 that proportion will be over one-third, and one in two children will be Hispanic, African American, Asian or American Indian.

The Gender Gap Closes

The growth of women's participation in the labor force will slow but will still exceed the growth of men's participation by 150%. By 2008, women's share of the labor force will reach 48%. More women will reach upper-level management. At the end of the past century, they occupied only 12% of the highest-level executive positions.

Women's higher rates of college enrollment and graduation will accelerate their progress. Over the past two decades the earning power of a college education has more than doubled, as the U.S. has shifted from primarily physical to mental work. In that period, the number of women earning college degrees surged by 44%. By 2008, women will significantly outnumber men in both graduate and undergraduate classrooms, according to the *Digest of Education Statistics*.[5]

The impact of this tide of educated women is already visible in companies everywhere. The number of women aged 25 to 34 in managerial and professional jobs increased by nearly

15% in the last five years of the 20th century, rising to a total of 5 million.[6]

Corporate America needs to hold on to this talented female resource pool to fill white-collar and managerial positions, particularly in the expanding service sector. As a result, competitive pressure will narrow pay gaps between men and women, opening more opportunities and providing greater flexibility in schedules and benefits.

Flexibility of schedule is a prime tool in recruiting and retaining talented women workers. Paul Klaasen, founder of the Sunrise Assisted Living chain and chairman of a task force on workforce preparation for the U.S. Chamber of Commerce, says that schedule flexibility is the least utilized, simplest, most efficient, and most productivity-increasing benefit an employer can provide.[7]

Corporate America needs to hold on to this talented female resource pool to fill white-collar and managerial positions, particularly in the expanding service sector.

Lang Group, Chartered, a Bethesda, Md., accounting firm, launched an outsourcing business through a strategy of workplace flexibility. When Lang takes over management of its clients' financial departments, it often staffs positions with skilled women who have left the workforce full-time to be with their children. There is a good supply of such talent among young mothers who want to work two or three days a week.

Flexibility at work also increasingly means providing good child care. A few vanguard companies like Hewlett-Packard and Dayton Hudson have created on-site schools for working parents. Nearly all the Fortune 100 companies now offer their employees a dependent-care spending account, according to Hewitt Associates. Some 8,000 companies provide on-site child care services, up from 1,000 in 1986, says Burud & Associates, a California research firm.[8]

The next round of benefits geared primarily toward women's needs will focus on elder care. Women in the workforce are more likely to be primary caregivers of elderly or infirm parents. The number of employers offering elder care hotlines and referral services is sure to grow. The pressure will mount on employers and government to provide paid family leave to care for old folks as well as babies.

Women-Owned Businesses Will Multiply

T hanks, but no thanks," say the growing number of women who are leaving the corporate world to start their own businesses. Part of the reason is that businesses lag in providing more opportunities for women to reach the executive suite. Of women who formed businesses in the past 10 years, 22% cited a corporate "glass ceiling" as a reason for starting their own firms, according to a study by the National Foundation for Women Business Owners (NFWBO) and Catalyst, a women's issues research firm in New York.[9]

The size and scope of this demographic pattern will grow in the next decade. The stereotype of businesswomen as owners of mostly small retail and service firms will continue to fade. Growth of women's businesses between 1992 and 1999 was strongest in construction, wholesale trade, transportation, communications, agriculture and manufacturing, according to NFWBO. Women won't just own *more* companies, but they'll own *bigger* companies as well. As more women-owned firms start tapping the equity market, the size of women-owned businesses will soar.

Summary and Conclusions

T echnology, education and freedom have reshaped both the American and the world workplace in terms of customers, workers and expectations. Slowing growth in the U.S. population will produce an "hourglass" workforce— more graying boomers at the top, a shrunken middle cadre, and a large Internet generation at the bottom.

The U.S. will fare better than other Western nations and Japan largely because of the traditional U.S. openness to immigration. Japan and Europe, in contrast, must liberalize their immigration policies or face economic and social stagnation. A third option is to reverse traditional habits of thinking and exploit the developmental options created by smaller populations. By necessity Japan and Europe must decide first. Thus U.S. policymakers and businesses will have the opportunity to analyze and refine policies the basis of the experience of others.

Whatever the choices, demographic debates will dominate the politics of all developed countries for the next 20 to 30 years. Political battles over Social Security and Medicare are only the beginning. We will inevitably have "a politics of great turbulence," says Peter Drucker, because neither political parties nor countries are really prepared to deal with an issue that cuts across ideological lines. For example, is keeping workers on the job longer a liberal or a conservative policy?[10]

Shortages of skilled workers in the U.S. will prompt more companies to establish subsidiaries or alliances in developing nations where both population and education standards continue to rise. In the U.S., the divide between technologically educated "haves" and "have-nots" will widen, creating tensions. Efforts to elevate performance of school systems and to develop more company-sponsored education are critical to maintaining internal stability as well as U.S. living standards.

America's capacity to absorb and Americanize immigrants remains one of our greatest competitive strengths. Other underutilized resources (minority and female workers and managers) will become more prominent in the next decade. Partially by necessity and partially by evolution, progressive businesses will see diversity less as a moral and regulatory issue and more of a dynamic competitive advantage.

Meanwhile, as the next chapter discusses, more businesses, large and small, will be seeking opportunities beyond our borders, in rapidly expanding global markets.

The Global Frontier

KEY CHAPTER THEMES

- *Beyond economic globalization*

- *Three types of cross-border economic activities*

- *Widening global perspectives*

- *Accelerating global income and demand*

- *The case against globalization*

- *The influence of changes in behavior on globalization*

> *"The merchant has no country."*
> —THOMAS JEFFERSON

> *"Interdependence re-creates the world in the image of a global village."*
> —MARSHALL McLUHAN, CANADIAN EDUCATOR AND AUTHOR

SSESSING GLOBALIZATION REQUIRES A NARROWLY focused and a wide-angle lens. The narrow focus sees globalization primarily as an economic phenomenon; the broader perspective considers deeper social implications as well.

Amazingly for a term that is so widely used, there is no precise, generally agreed upon definition of globalization. Indeed, the World Bank has noted that the meanings attached to this term seem to be increasing rather than narrowing, "taking on cultural, political and other connotations in addition to the economic."[1]

Our differing understandings about what is really happening contribute to making globalization one of the most charged issues of the day. Turn on the evening news or public affairs programs and you will find extreme opponents insisting that globalization continues to impoverish the poor, enrich the rich and devastate the environment. With equal fervor, supporters contend that the globalization of opportunities is creating a high-speed elevator to universal peace and prosperity. Who has the better case?

Using a narrowly focused lens, let's begin with the most common, or core, sense of globalization—the indisputable fact that a rapidly rising share of economic activity now takes place among people and companies in different countries.

The World Bank identifies three primary forms of cross-border economic activities:

International trade. Exports and imports are growing rapidly in nations around the world. In the developed countries, for example, foreign trade as a proportion of total economic activity rose from 27% in 1987 to 39% in 1997.

Foreign direct investment (FDI). Total investment in one country by firms based in another country more than tripled, rising to $610 billion (U.S.) in 1998, compared with $192 billion (U.S.) in 1988.

Capital market flows. Savers, especially in the developed world, increasingly diversify their portfolios to include foreign assets such as foreign bonds, equities and loans. Meanwhile, borrowers increasingly turn to both domestic and foreign sources of funds.

Any serious discussion of the effects of globalization must consider these three forms differently. Each raises distinct issues and has distinct consequences. Generally, the evidence suggests that in trade and FDI, "the payoffs for economic development and poverty reduction tend to be large relative to potential costs or risks," the World Bank says. Liberalization of capital market flows, however, "can sometimes foster boom-and-bust cycles and financial crises with large economic costs."[2]

An Evolutionary Trend

Throughout human history, widely scattered populations have gradually become involved in increasingly complex economic relations. A more developed form of economic globalization—one we would recognize today—flowered in the late 19th century, as the rich European nations expanded foreign trade through their colonial empires. However, this peak was reversed in the first half of the 20th century, a time of growing protectionism, national and great power strife, world wars, revolutions, and massive economic and political stability.

In the past 50 years, the tide has again flowed toward greater economic globalization and relations have become more tranquil, compared with those of the previous half-century. Institutions like the General Agreements on Tariffs and Trade (GATT; today the World Trade Organization) provide a framework of rules and procedures for countries to manage their commercial policies.

As part of a general shift toward greater reliance on markets and private enterprise, governments have reduced policy barriers to greater international trade and investment. Among the most striking examples of this trend are China's sweeping economic reforms beginning at the end of the 1970s, the peaceful dissolution of communism in the Soviet bloc at the end of the 1980s, and the steady growth of market-based reforms in democratic India in the 1990s.

Even today the evening news is full of sound and fury of opposing nations and even tribes. Yet that same evening news shows us how significantly and rapidly our perspective has widened.

The rush toward greater globalization has significance well beyond economics. Economics is only one aspect of the expansion of human perspective over time, from a narrow focus on family, to an ever more inclusive view of clan, tribe, feudal system and nation-state, and now to a global view.

To be sure, there have been countless reverses in this expansion of perspective followed by new initiatives and still more setbacks. Even today the evening news is full of sound and fury of opposing nations and even tribes. Yet that same evening news shows us how significantly and rapidly our perspective has widened. In looking at the news, remember that as late as 1940, significant portions of the American people—perhaps even a majority—insisted that the U.S. had no stake in a fierce war that pitted Germany and Italy against France and Britain. Now we debate our proper role in conflicts in areas that used to be considered far to the periphery of our interests—in Bosnia, Africa and the Mideast.

Global Bargain Hunters

This shift in perspective influences us all personally, especially members of a younger generation. Today's young, cosmopolitan businessperson sees every stranger, regardless of national origin, as a potential customer, supplier, employee or partner. Innovative companies now routinely look for solutions beyond their national borders. When the Olive Garden, one of America's largest chains of Italian restaurants, wanted to enhance the culinary sophistication of its nearly 500 units, it opened a cooking institute to train its chefs—not in the U.S., but 20 miles outside Sienna, Italy.[3]

When we shop, we all search for bargains and quality from the global market—for our autos, shoes, shirts, suits and vacations. Global shopping is more than an American phenomenon. In East Asia, the craze for Japanese popular culture and products, especially among young people, "is unprecedented in its scope and size," according to *The New York Times*. In South Korea, Japanese-style cafes and teahouses are replacing American fast-food restaurants and European-style coffeehouses. In Hong Kong, newsstands can't stock enough Japanese fashion magazines. In China, Singapore, Indonesia, the Philippines and Thailand, thriving markets move bootleg copies of Japanese music, movies and merchandise.[4]

Today's young, cosmopolitan businessperson sees every stranger, regardless of national origin, as a potential customer, supplier, employee or partner.

Social and economic globalization is driven by—and in turn contributes to—the forces of technology, education, freedom and demographics. Technological progress reduces the cost and difficulty of transporting goods and services. It speeds the communication of information and ideas between countries. Formal and informal education makes distant nations and cultures more familiar and accessible. Greater freedom liberates flows of investment and capital while facilitating travel between and among nations. Changing demographics creates huge new markets in Asia, Latin America and Africa just as populations decline in the West.

Accelerating Global Income and Demand

The next 10 years will see even faster growth in living standards and consumption around the world. You can sense the accelerating pace in the following figures: The U.S. doubled output per capita in 47 years beginning in 1839. Starting in the 1880s, Japan took 25 years. The pace quickened after World War II. Indonesia doubled its output in 17 years, South Korea in 11 and China in 10.[5]

This success extends beyond material output. A reasonable guess would put worldwide life expectancy at about 30 years in 1900. By the late 1990s, life expectancy worldwide averaged 65 years, more than a doubling of life spans in one century. The developing nations shared in the bounty created by the "health explosion" around the world. The gap between life expectancy in rich and poor regions narrowed from 25 years in the early 1950s to around 11 at century's end.

The Pessimists Were Wrong

Only a couple of decades ago, reports like "The Limits of Growth" and "The Population Bomb," by Paul Ehrlich, predicted an end to progress on "Spaceship Earth." By this time, the volume of new mouths was supposed to swamp our capacity to feed, clothe and protect them.

The pessimists overlooked the fact that resources are no longer fixed so much as they are the creation of human ingenuity. Again and again in human history, we have developed substitute or improved materials to replace those that are in short supply. This amazine adaptability of the human mind will continue. For example, Knight Kiplinger, editor-in-chief of *The Kiplinger Letter* and Kiplingerforecasts.com, predicts: "Long before the world's petroleum reserves run out, biotechnology will havedevised countless ways to substitute plant and animal substances for petrochemical feedstocks in the making of plastics, fuels and lubricants." What the pessimists overlooked with their focus on population growth in relation to *existing* resources, says *The Wall Street Journal,* is that every newborn child comes equipped "with not only a mouth but a mind."[6]

To be sure, success has generated new problems and exacerbated old ones. Population in the developing world continues to grow, increasing urban overcrowding, pollution and crime. And, despite an incredible half-century of progress, some 2 billion of the world's 6 billion people still live in dire poverty. In a wired world of instant communication, such a serious imbalance creates a constant threat to stability.

Some 2 billion of the world's 6 billion people still live in dire poverty. In a wired world of instant communication, such a serious imbalance creates a constant threat to stability.

That said, accelerating economic progress is clearly expanding political freedom, economic security, education and modern conveniences for billions of people in the developing world. One important product of this change is a newly energized global "middle class" with rising expectations, aspirations and purchasing power.

For many Western consumer industries, this opportunity comes along just as they face slowing growth in domestic markets because of demographic trends. The opportunity is two-sided. Developing countries can respond more quickly to the rising aspirations of their expanding middle class only by participating more fully in the global market.

Despite such obvious advantages, there is strong and even understandable resistance to the rapid expansion of the global market. However strong the opposition, the information technology revolution makes defending a commercial fortress nation more difficult.

Not that threatened interests won't try. Lands' End, the Dodgeville, Wis., mail-order retailer, set up shop in Britain in 1991 and Germany in 1996. Before long, the company learned that its Web site had run afoul of a German law banning marketing gimmicks such as an unconditional lifetime guarantee—one of the company's key selling points. The German authorities contended that the cost of the guarantee was hidden in the sales price and was therefore illegal under German laws protecting consumers.[7]

Seizing New Opportunities

The more skillfully governments and vested interests try to block global electronic commerce, however, the higher the price they are likely to pay in their cost of living and the dynamism of their economy. Rather than resist the force of globalization, some nations are seizing the opportunities to leapfrog from the agricultural to the information age. The Philippines lagged far behind in the Asian boom of the 1980s. Today, the products of its recently established technology companies account for more than 70% of the nation's exports.

In the 1990s, Ireland shook off the twin demons of poverty and despair to become "the most dynamic, successful, fastest growing nation in Europe," says *Fortune*. "What struck me most forcefully," says the magazine's Rob Norton describing a 1997 visit, "was a single statistic: Ireland's GDP [gross domestic product] per capita was about to surpass Britain's."[8]

Barring unexpected reversals, the opening of new markets in developing countries means that the volume and diversity of world trade will soar in the new century.

Foreign investment, especially high-tech manufacturing, has been one of the mainstays of Ireland's transformation. The Intel factory in County Kildare, the company's biggest outside the U.S., will employ 4,000 people once construction is completed on a $2 billion extension. When the facility opened in the early 1990s, many of the senior engineers were returning Irish immigrants. After two centuries of losing people through immigration, Ireland today is a net importer of people.

Barring unexpected reversals, the opening of new markets in developing countries means that the volume and diversity of world trade will soar in the new century. In recent times, U.S. export strength has been built on high-priced capital goods and other business-to-business transactions—jet liners, computers and scientific equipment, for example. More recently, hard goods have been joined by a surge of consumer products. Levi's, Disney and McDonald's are worldwide rather than national brands.

Getting closer to these new customers will encourage the transfer of still more Western production plants, raising living standards in the developing world still further. To compete, U.S. companies will be continually challenged to upgrade their skills and asset base, raising the productivity of U.S. industry.

The Case Against Globalization

With all these benefits, how good is the case against globalization? Critics contend that the rapid growth of international trade increases world poverty, worsens inequality between and within nations, and creates "a race to the bottom" in environmental standards. Also, globalization's opponents harbor a deep distrust of multinational corporations. For each charge, critics muster compelling anecdotal evidence to support their case. Recent studies, however, give even stronger ammunition to those *supporting* expansion of the global marketplace in goods, services and ideas. The sections that follow outline some of the findings of these studies.

Economic Growth and Poverty Reduction

Critics accurately note that global progress on poverty reduction has been painfully slow even as global trade has accelerated. The number of people living on $1 (U.S.) a day or less fell only slightly from 1.3 billion in 1990 to 1.2 billion in 1998. Behind those grim global totals, however, are extremely uneven regional differences, which add a different perspective to the argument.

Poverty fell dramatically in East Asia, whose 1.8 billion people represent over a third of the population in the developing countries. During the 1990s, East Asia was the world's most rapidly growing region. Yet, between 1990 and 1998, East Asian economies created the largest and fastest reduction in poverty in history, according to the World Bank.

During that period, the percentage of people living on $1 or less a day in all of East Asia fell from 27.6% to 15.3%. To be sure, improvements in living standards in just one huge country, China, accounted for a major portion of that improvement, but there was significant improvement elsewhere in the region, too. Even *excluding* China, the poverty rate for East Asia fell from 18.5% to 11.3%.

Still, critics can argue that even if per capita income rises, that famous rising tide will not in the end lift all boats, but World Bank studies challenge this argument. Indeed, the Bank says "recent work suggests that higher average incomes in a country are generally associated one-for-one with higher incomes for the poor."[9]

International Trade and Inequality

Macro statistics, however, seem to bolster the critics' case. The distribution of per capita income between countries has become more disparate. For example, in 1960, the average per capita GDP in the richest 20 countries was 15 times the average in the poorest 20 countries. Today, that gap has widened to 30 times, because the rich countries on average have grown faster than poor ones.

However, greater openness to trade is unlikely to explain why poor countries on average have grown less quickly than rich ones. Poor countries that are open to trade have grown "slightly faster than rich ones," and a lot faster than poor countries that remained closed to foreign trade, the World Bank reports.[10]

Globalization and the Environment

All this growth must inevitably lead to more industrial pollution and environmental degradation, other critics argue. This, of course, is an argument against economic growth in general rather than against globalization specifically. Further, many developing countries are stepping up the fight against pollution at much lower levels of income than the rich countries did at the same stage of development.

In Indonesia and the Philippines, for example, pilot projects based on public disclosure of information about factory pollution have significantly reduced industrial pollution. China has stabilized or improved its average air quality in large cities since the mid 1980s—the same period in which the country experienced both rapid growth and increased openness to trade and investment. A study of steel production in 50 countries found that open economies led closed economies in the adoption of cleaner technologies by wide margins.

Critics also contend that developing countries will keep their environmental standards low to attract foreign industries in what they call "a race to the bottom." Yet no evidence exists to prove that the cost of environmental protection has ever been a determining factor in foreign investment decisions. Far more important are issues such as the cost of labor and raw materials, the existence of transparent regulations, and protection of property rights.[11]

Growing Power of Multinational Corporations

Today's noisy outbreak of hostility against multinationals is only the latest round in a boom-and-bust cycle in the reputation of the global corporate giants.

In the 1950s, multinationals were often seen as missionaries, extending the benefits of what was then called "American management" to eagerly receptive businesspeople overseas. In the 1960s and 1970s, the giants were denounced for their size, irresponsibility and monopolistic practices. In the 1980s, they were dismissed as clumsy dinosaurs, too big and plodding to matter in an entrepreneurial world. In the 1990s, they were again hailed as the great instruments of modernization, bringing foreign capital, technology, know-how, and hope of higher living standards to people around the world. Now the pendulum is swinging back again.

Size and speed of growth have made multinationals a highly visible symbol of globalization. If multinational corporations were national economies, 50 of them would be among the largest nations in the world. "Even in rich, well-run countries, their sheer size can seem threatening," *The Economist* notes. In Ireland, cited earlier as a beneficiary of globalization, "foreign firms account for almost half of the country's employment and two-thirds of its output."[12]

As with any group, individual firms can and do abuse their strength. Still, *The Economist* adds, "as a class the multinationals have a good story to tell." For example:

In the rich world, foreign firms pay better than domestic ones and create new jobs faster, according to figures that have been published by the Organization for Economic Cooperation and Development (OECD).

This is true even in many poorer countries. In Turkey, for example, foreign firms pay wages that are 124% above average, and their workforces have been expanding by 11.5% a year, compared with 0.6% in local firms.

Multinationals also provide a principal conduit for new technologies. Seventy percent of all international royalties for technology involve payments between parent companies and their foreign affiliates.

No matter how strong or logical the case for globalization, opposition—vocal, persistent and dedicated—will surely increase. Doubts extend far beyond the pony-tailed protestors who disrupted the December 1999 Seattle meeting of the World Trade Organization. Still, the existing and potential benefits of a global economy are too tangible to cast aside, no matter how loud the protests. As a result, the future appears to offer evolving reform rather than a reversal of direction.

Changes in Behavior

Reform will probably bring significant changes in behavior. There are already indications, for example, that the World Trade Organization may behave in a much more multinational style than the American and European hegemony that critics say has dominated the organization in the past. Although that will not be an easy transition, it could produce a more globally popular balancing of priorities—for example, between the demands of rich countries that want greater protection for intellectual property and the poor nations that want still greater access to rich markets.

Also, public opinion will probably drive changes in behavior among the more progressive and pace-setting multinationals. No corporate leadership that is really paying attention can ignore how public attitudes are changing. The Millenium Poll on Corporate Social Responsibility included interviews with more than 25,000 typical citizens across 23 countries on six continents. The survey, conducted by Environics International Ltd., in cooperation with the Conference Board and Business Leaders Forum, showed the following:

Two in three citizens want companies to go beyond their traditional social responsibilities of making a profit, paying taxes, employing people and obeying all laws.

In the view of those surveyed, there are now 10 areas of corporate social accountability that rate higher than contributing to charities and community projects. These areas include protecting health and safety of employees, protecting the environment, and never participating in bribery and corruption.

Fully half of the population in the countries surveyed now pays attention to the social behavior of companies, and two in five consumers reported either rewarding or punishing companies in the previous year on the basis of their perceived social performance.[13]

Summary and Conclusions

Whatever the pace of reform in the process, globalization represents a major evolutionary step in human perspective. Throughout history, changes in perspective that challenge the existing order have always engendered opposition, and the history of technology offers many such examples. The loom and the steam engine were once viewed as instruments of the devil. Mass-market credit instruments like home mortgages were once seen as destroyers of thrift and responsibility. The opening of the economy in India was viewed by many there as a return to colonialism. The evolution of democracy was fought by European monarchs and aristocrats.

Rising expectations are driving globalization. For that reason alone, despite the opposition, the tide of globalization will not be substantially reversed. Its benefits far outweigh its costs, even though specific sectors and communities will be severely damaged. Consumers want wider, cheaper choices. Intellectuals want an expanded network of ideas. Business searches for profit in global markets and international technologies. Investors seek new growth opportunities over the horizon. Nations have learned that greater security can be achieved collectively rather than alone. Especially in developing nations, some citizens may wish their countries to escape "foreign influence," but a growing number understand that they can't afford to pass up the advantages of foreign investment, technology and ideas.

Globalization is not just an economic or commercial phenomenon. It is a social evolution bringing individuals, organizations, nations and cultures closer together. Given this importance, every organization should take the present and potential effect of globalization into account in formulating its strategy.

Business Evolution

KEY CHAPTER THEMES

- *Accelerating change reflects a largely invisible evolutionary process.*

- *Successful businesses reflect and adapt to that evolutionary process.*

- *Successful adaptation requires that businesses energize one or more of five key components.*

- *Successful positioning requires keeping all five components in alignment with each other and with societal evolution.*

"Life is the continuous adjustment of external relations." —HERBERT SPENCER, 19TH CENTURY BRITISH AUTHOR

ECHNOLOGY, FREEDOM AND EDUCATION ARE RESHAP-ing our world. The previous chapters showed how these three forces interact with population shifts and changing global perspectives to create new patterns of business activity. Those patterns influence what, where and how business sells. The changed patterns also dictate new strategies for recruiting and retaining talented people.

Fully understanding the changes around us requires more than identifying the five forces discussed in the previous three chapters. Anticipating the future requires gaining a broader understanding of how societies and businesses actually evolve.

A broader perspective recognizes that business evolution reflects—rather than causes—developments in society. If we extrapolate current economic trends without gaining a better awareness of the context in which those trends operate, our perspective remains limited.

Author's Note: In this book I have adapted a recent theory of societal development to business development. This societal development theory is the work of Garry Jacobs and Robert Macfarlane, my frequent consulting and writing partners, and political scientist Harlan Cleveland. For further information about their work, see the Preface (page xvii) or visit their Web site at www.mirainternational.com.

Aspiration Shapes Economic Projections

In the 1980s, experts projected existing trends to predict that Japan would tower over the rest of world business by early in the 21st century. Thirty years of disciplined effort gave the Japanese an aura of economic invincibility. Adding to this mystique, their success had produced huge surpluses of capital.

Surplus cash can be absorbed for growth of existing activities. It can be invested in new and higher levels of activity, or channeled into speculative investments. Great excesses in speculative investments create dangerous economic risks. The roaring Japanese economy of the late 1980s was created by a brilliant export-led strategy that overshot its ambition to catch up with the West. The existing Japanese economic model lacked the capacity to absorb the country's huge savings surplus. Without a new national aspiration, surplus funds flowed heavily into speculative investments.

The difference between Japan and South Korea is not the degree of structural reform, but the degree of vision.

As the Japanese economy strained and then stalled in the early 1990s, conventional wisdom concluded that the key to recovery rested on making structural changes, such as modifying the traditionally close relationships between Japanese banks and major industrial firms. Certainly, structural changes are important and are needed in Japan, as they are in the U.S. However, structural changes by themselves are not the answer.

Arguably, Japan has accomplished more restructuring than all other East Asian countries combined. Compared with the situation in 1988, the country is far more open in its disclosure of financial information and in its opportunities for foreign firms. If structure were the problem, why are there not better results?

The rapid recovery of other East Asian countries from the financial crisis of 1997 offers a clue to the true nature of Japan's challenge. As with Japan, leading economists prescribed radical structural surgery for victims of the Asian economic flu. Further, they predicted that recovery would require 5 to 10 years of hard labor. Yet, in less than 2 years, with structural changes still in their infancy, South Korea again achieved near double-digit growth.

The difference between Japan and South Korea is not the degree of structural reform, but the degree of vision. South Korea is still playing catch-up. Its direction is clear. The energy of its people is fully engaged, regardless of structural obstacles. Japan, in contrast, has enormous underutilized potential. It has abundant human energy, productive skills, technology, organizational capacity and money. Those resources need a new national ambition and a channel for productive employment.

Aspiration Determines, Technology Fulfills

Projecting technological innovation without a context of societal aspiration is similarly risky. Today, every businessperson would rank the Internet at the top of developments reshaping business. The deeper truth is that the Internet's electrifying growth is far more than a technological expansion; it is also an expression of the aspirations of society to expand individual freedom.

Test that thesis by imagining that the Internet was developed and generally available in the Soviet Union at the height of the Cold War. An impossibility to imagine? For that matter, it strains credulity to imagine the Internet in 1950s America. The aspirations and priorities of both societies were clearly so different.

The economics and culture of the Internet feel very American today, because the Internet so clearly reflects American values and aspirations even though many of its technical innovations came from other countries. For a start, the Internet reflects ingredients of the American entrepreneurial climate. Those ingredients, says *The New York Times*, include "venture capital financing...a deregulated business environment, and a culture that celebrates risk-taking, ambition and getting very, very rich."[1]

Culturally, Net technology also reflects late-20th-century American society. It tends to be "informal and individualistic ... decentralized and hard to control," *The Times* continues. Fareed Zakaria, managing editor of *Foreign Affairs*, adds, "The Internet is profoundly disrespectful of tradition, established order and hierarchy, and that is very American."

These underlying societal aspirations rather than the technology itself have slowed acceptance of the Net in countries like France and Germany. The political values of those countries support more regulated economies. The countries also value social cohesion more, and diversity less, than America does. In time, of course, the Net's interaction with those societies will influence societal aspirations, eventually creating a far more global-looking, less predominantly American, society in cyberspace.

Young Tom Edison Learns a Lesson

Technological entrepreneurs fail when they get too far ahead of society's aspirations. As a young man, Thomas Edison wanted to convert his knowledge of telegraph technology into a practical, profitable product. He invented an apparatus to record votes in legislative assemblies instantaneously. To Edison's amazement, potential customers in the Massachusetts legislature and the federal Congress reacted with horror. Instantaneous counting of votes closed too many opportunities to bribe, cajole or persuade legislators to change votes. "Young man," they told him in Washington, "if there is any invention on earth that we don't want down here, it is this."[2] Edison learned the lesson. Thereafter, he concentrated on applying technology to meet society's aspirations.

Even inside companies, adoption of new technology depends on a company's aspiration. Any business today can buy a computer system to streamline its activities, but making full use of the new software requires changes in virtually all operating procedures. One company with an aspiration for continuous improvement readily adopts the technology and makes the procedural changes. Other companies in the same industry postpone the adaptation or, worse yet, spend millions on the system and then fail to exploit its benefits. Months or years later, the threat of competition—or a new CEO with different aspirations—will make acceptance of the technology seem obviously easy.

For country or company, the principle is the same. Aspiration determines direction. Technology fulfills.

Growth or Development

Aspiration also influences how a company grows, develops or stagnates. Because *growth* and *development* are closely related, many businesspeople use the words interchangeably. Montreal retailer and entrepreneur John Banks defines the distinction using the example of coaching his salespeople: "When we help the salespeople by updating their sales materials, we are promoting their growth. We are helping them to close more sales. When we encourage them to change their attitudes toward the customer, we are promoting their development."

It is the same for the company, Banks continues. "When we concentrate on growth, we focus on ways to sell more product to existing or new customers. We increase our advertising or add more salespeople. When we concentrate on development, we ask what we need to do inside the company to serve our customers better. We improve our speed of response. We expand training, not only our salespeople but our back-office people as well."

Growth is a multiplication of existing activities at the same level of organization. A company grows by opening new branches or franchises. Another way to grow is to expand the range of product choices in a given category. An industry grows when new companies enter its field, creating more sales. Individual managers grow when they get promoted to run bigger units.

Where growth is quantitative *expansion*, development is qualitative *enhancement*. Companies develop by elevating values such as quality, customer service, and respect for people. An industry develops when a consolidator organizes smaller, disorganized units into a more cohesive, cost-effective, competitive entity. Individual managers develop when they add new knowledge, skills or attitudes that expand their personal competence and self-confidence.

Walton Stinson, a successful Denver entrepreneur, says that the challenge for any business is to find the resources to invest in both growth and development. Part of the problem arises when business leaders fail to understand that growth and development are separate strategies. Stinson, who has founded and headed several organizations of small businesses, adds, "From a practical point of view, even the smallest businesses must make some investment in development."

Symptoms of lagging development are not always apparent. Any slippage in growth shows up quickly in a company's sales volume or in market share reports. However, a company's visible energy is one reliable indicator of its level of development, John Banks believes. A lack of development shows up as "boredom in the company," he says. "Development by its nature releases more energy. It's more inspiring. While growth is certainly exciting, when I see people or companies develop, they seem to be expressing a higher level of energy." The fabled, around-the-clock energy of the dot-coms stems at least in part from the fact that both the companies and the individuals are developing at such a rapid rate.

The fabled, around-the-clock energy of the dot-coms stems at least in part from the fact that both the companies and the individuals are developing at such a rapid rate.

For a more personal example, think of the surge of energy you felt the last time you acquired a new business skill. Keeping focused on development is understandably difficult in a rapidly expanding economy. The opportunity to expand units or sales is attractive and immediate. The challenge of development sometimes feels like trying to rebuild the jet plane while flying it through turbulence. Yet at no time has a focus on development been more important.

Business reflects society. U.S. society is going through an intense period of development. Organizations that invest energy in development have a far better chance of staying in tune with society. They will more easily discover the paths to growth.

A look backward at three entrepreneurs illustrates how developing a company in alignment with changing societal values can lead to rapid growth:

Ray Kroc didn't invent either fast food or franchising but he elevated the values of quality and consistency for both. As a result, McDonald's became the gold standard of food franchises.

Walt Disney rode a more affluent society's hunger for better entertainment and used four developmental values—safety, courtesy, show and efficiency—to transform the dingy amusement park industry into a worldwide giant.

William Randolph Hearst caught a wave of expanding literacy in the early years of the 20th century. He created or revamped publications to feed a new appetite for easy-to-read information. Newly literate millions, many of them immigrants, purchased his products. From two papers in 1895, his empire expanded over 40 years to a high of 28 major newspapers, 18 magazines, several radio stations, movie theaters and his own wire service.

Surplus Energy for Growth or Development

For either growth or development, a company must have available more energy than what is required for survival. A society in a desperate war consumes its available physical or mental energy for survival. The same is true of a business on the brink of bankruptcy. Neither has much surplus energy for further development.

The initial source of energy in a business flows from the entrepreneur's aspiration for personal advancement, service to others, or both. If the entrepreneur's aspiration sparks sufficient effort and if that effort is sufficiently in harmony with society's direction, the business generates enough energy for an initial take-off.

Growth brings more physical, mental, and even psychic energy into the company. Entrepreneurs recruit new people with higher knowledge and skills, raising the physical and mental energy in the company. Entrepreneurs expand the technological assets, elevating human physical energy into systemic mental energy. They transmit to their employees their own enthusiasm for the product and their commitment to the customer, expanding the available pool of psychic energy.

To grow, a company channels this surplus energy into doing more of the same activities. To develop, the company invests a portion of its surplus in raising its activities to a higher level of skill, organization, speed or other values to match the evolving direction of society. Growth requires greater physical energy to do *more*. Development requires greater psychological energy to do *better*.

The Creation of Higher Levels of Organization

The institutions of society (business, government, the military, education, science and the arts) all represent organized channels through which energy is distributed according to a society's priorities. From the beginning, the U.S. has supported education as an important priority for societal development. Accordingly, the U.S. has organized and funded education at higher and higher levels of more and more complexity. In 1870, only one doctoral degree was conferred in the U.S. In 1999, American universities awarded nearly 46,000 academic doctorates.

Once a new or wider organizational channel is available, pioneers seek to exploit it. In business, our acclaimed pioneer is the entrepreneur. Few entrepreneurs actually create a whole new model of business organization. Fred Smith, founder of FedEx, and Thomas Edison, creator of the research laboratory, are exceptions. However, the hundreds of thousands of jobs created by more traditional U.S. entrepreneurs over the past 20 years are testimony to the power of opening new and more complex channels of organization. The growth provided by an innovative organizational structure like franchising is a prime example.

Until 1899, Coca-Cola was sold only through soda fountains, by the glass. In that year, two men from Chattanooga attending a baseball game came across a soft drink that was sold in a bottle. They approached Asa Candler, who owned Coca-Cola at the time, to suggest that he sell Coke in bottles. Candler was not interested but agreed to give the two men a perpetual franchise to sell bottled Coke virtually throughout the U.S. Candler awarded the franchise for $1. Legend has it that even that dollar was never paid. If so, it was the best dollar Coca-Cola never made—"a master stroke" as *Fortune* called it.[3] This was the beginning of the company's franchise bottling system—the granddaddy of all franchising—consisting of independent bottlers whose entrepreneurial spirit has carried Coke to the four corners of the world. Today, Coca-Cola and its subsidiaries operate in 200 countries. Following the franchising model that the company pioneered, bottling and distribution operations are, with some exceptions, locally owned and operated by independent businesspeople who are native to the nations where the operations take place.

> **Once a new or wider organizational channel is available, pioneers seek to exploit it. In business, our acclaimed pioneer is the entrepreneur.**

The franchise system adopted by Coca-Cola in 1899 has formed the basis for many entirely new industries. The fast-food business actually began in 1921, when White Castle opened its first hamburger stand. The company had the right idea but not the system. White Castle never sold a franchise. Sixty years later it still had only 175 units. If it had not been for the franchise system, there might be only 175 McDonald's restaurants instead of more than 25,000 in about 120 countries. Ray Kroc opened his first McDonald's franchise in 1955, and within five years he had surpassed the level reached by White Castle over a half-century.

The power of the franchise organizing system stems from the entrepreneurial initiative associated with private ownership combined with the name, expertise and experience of the parent company. The system has transformed the way retail business is carried out in the United States and around the world. Adopting an organizing system that is already prevalent in a field enables an entrepreneur to compete with leaders in the industry. Adapting a system to a new field enables a company to become a leader of the industry.

Five Channels for Corporate Energy

The critical corporate task in the next decade is to balance qualitative development and rapid growth in a climate of immense opportunity and accelerating change. Entrepreneurs who start a successful business have an intrinsic advantage. If their concept is right, they are closely aligned with societal direction at the moment they open for business. Also, they do not have to deal with the clogged systems, obsolete skills or bureaucratic encumbrances that sometimes slow their more established competitors.

In time, of course, success will multiply the challenges. With rapid growth, informal one-to-one direction will cease to be practical. As people are added, the entrepreneurs can no longer rely on rudimentary policies, procedures and systems. Competition, as well as those new shareholders acquired through the IPO, will require the entrepreneurs to be more disciplined. However, they will still be far ahead of the curve for as long as they can keep their company developing in tune with society.

Leaders of established companies can find new paths to growth and profit by looking more deeply inside their companies for untapped reservoirs of creative energy.

However, the American economy, as distinct from the American stock market, draws its greatest strength from millions of companies that were not founded yesterday. In that pool we find established midwestern metal benders, far western auto dealers, northeastern food wholesalers, eastern supermarket retailers, southern contract manufacturers, southeastern contract retailers, exporters and importers, professional services firms, publishers and dozens of other categories.

For these established companies, the challenges of developmental renewal are more complex. However, leaders of these established companies can find new paths to growth and profit by looking more deeply inside their companies for untapped reservoirs of creative energy. Specifically, each of the five engines listed below provides a field of potential creativity and profit. Elevating performance in any of these components—or better yet in all of them—is a sure path to releasing higher creativity, productivity, profitability and growth.

A healthy business expands or abandons functions, structures and activities as it evolves with society. As society has engines of progress (technology, freedom, education, demographics and globalization) companies have their own engines. Individually and collectively, the productivity of these engines determines how well a company can stay positioned with societal evolution. Whatever its size, market or product, every business has underutilized assets in the form of these five engines or components. Each of these components represents a channel for the effective and creative redistribution of corporate energy. The five are:

1. Market: The full array of social requirements and desires that create the market for business, as well as the tools and techniques that the company uses to serve society's needs. Successful businesses have traditionally focused on serving the customer. The opportunity today is to anticipate future needs.

2. Products and services: The profusion of technical applications, products and services that business uses or provides to serve its market. The force of the technological innovation discussed earlier opens extraordinary opportunities in this component today.

3. People: The potentially limitless strength created by the knowledge, skills and attitudes of the workforce available to business to deliver products and services to its market.

Higher educational attainment, a shortage of skilled people and the rapid mentalization of work are creating the potential for exciting innovations in this critical component.

4. Organization: The structures, systems and vehicles for communication and coordination inside the company and inside the arena in which business operates. The driving forces together are rewriting the rules of traditional organizational theory. Information-technology enthusiasts refer to the rapid productivity gains expected from technological progress inside the high-tech sector as the New Economy. As the information sector has spread to other more traditional industries, the term New Economy loses meaning. A recent study by two

Federal Reserve Board economists reports that the "noninformation technology" industries have contributed more to gains realized through technology investments than has the computer industry.[4] Any company can benefit by lifting its organization component to a higher level through use of information technology, making the terms Old Economy and New Economy even more meaningless.

5. Capital: Financial and other nonhuman assets available to business to support its activities. Availability and flexibility of sources of capital, key ingredients in the boom of the 1990s, will be even more important in the decade ahead.

New Opportunities in Every Component

The driving forces identified in the first three chapters of *Business 2010* create new opportunities in each these components. For example, look at how three of those forces—technology, education and freedom—are redefining opportunities within each of the five business components.

The Effects of Information Technology
Information technology (IT) has responded to our societal aspiration for faster service. That interaction converted speed to a higher value in every component.

MARKET. In the market, customers demand instant response—instant coffee, instant communication, overnight delivery. In 1915, the American transcontinental telephone system could handle three simultaneous voice calls. A generation later, AT&T developed a coaxial cable handling 480 calls at once. By the 1980s, individual Telstar satellites had enough capacity for nearly 100,000 telephone links. New forms of transmission coming on line can handle 1 trillion bits per second, enough for three centuries of a daily newspaper.[5]

PRODUCTS AND SERVICES. The World Wide Web rapidly revolutionized the technology for producing many products and services. In publishing, seemingly overnight, newspapers, bookstores, book publishers, radio and television networks, record producers and software distributors all faced new threats and opportunities. The annual product update is becoming passé as more companies figure out ways to download their product improvements directly to customers.

ORGANIZATION. Through information technology, organization has evolved to higher levels in industry after industry. Just-in-time-inventory technology enabled retailers like Wal-Mart to cut costs and prices. Online networks helped companies pool resources. For example, the National Transportation Exchange, Inc., in Downers Grove, Ill., helps trucking company drivers and dispatchers find cargo in range of their trucks. NTE fills empty rig space, making driver time more productive.

PEOPLE. Although experts argue over details, information technology has clearly made people more productive. Macroeconomic Advisers, a St. Louis forecasting firm, says improvements in technology have raised the productivity level so sharply that the U.S. economy should be able to grow at 3% a year for the next decade without significantly adding to inflation.

CAPITAL RESOURCES. Information technology expands the availability and reduces the cost of the capital resources on which business depends. Businesses avoid long-term telephone or Internet contracts with full confidence that lower costs are on the way. Despite sometime disruptive swings in individual commodities, overall lower commodity prices from metals to plastics are now the pattern, as technology speeds the availability of competitive prices and quickly identifies new sources of supply.

The Effects of Advancing Education
Another driving force—advancing education—creates opportunities and challenges in every component.

THE MARKET. Greater awareness created by formal and informal education multiplies a desire for wider, more individualized customer choices in the market component. The "I'll have it my way" mentality spreads from burgers to BMWs. Higher levels of education fuel and support customers' demands for better, safer products.

PRODUCTS AND SERVICES. Higher levels of education create a demand for more complex, smarter products and services. More companies are adding an educational component to their services. Stockbrokers become "financial advisers." Home Depot opens a store a week. Its competitive advantage is the home repair education provided by its salespeople.

ORGANIZATIONS. Organizations that used to depend on physical energy depend on mental systems created and operated by better-educated people. Reengineering any organization structure for faster customer service requires trained workers on the front line.

Complex businesses today depend more on *teams* of educated professionals. Twenty years ago business problems were more likely to be passed from one "silo" of experts labeled *marketing* to another labeled *product development*. Many companies today are staking a big piece of their future on a strategy known as cross-selling, that is, offering a diverse mix of a company's products and services to the same customer. To be successful, cross-selling depends on ad hoc organizations of experts built around a customer's needs. This development has helped spark a boom in teamwork training.

PEOPLE. Better-educated people seek more mental and less physical challenges on the job. Thirty years ago, business depended on the expertise acquired by key people over a 20-year career. On-the-job experience was the training norm. Businesses today depend on people well educated in disciplines like finance, marketing, and research and development. The drain of educated and skilled workers from old style to newer, high-tech-based companies illustrates the premium paid for education in business today.

CAPITAL RESOURCES. Education expands both the variety and availability of all resources, including capital. Using IT, highly educated engineers in Germany can update a manufacturing line in China. Distance learning online gives the entrepreneur with a high school education access to the financing knowledge base of today's MBAs. Rising education permits more individual choices among benefit plans for employees, opening the way for better allocation of resources by companies.

The Effects of Expanding Freedom

A third driving force—expanding freedom—unleashes competition and creates more choice in every market and inside every company.

THE MARKET. In the market, greater freedom from regulation expands competition across and between industries. Choice has transformed customers from the kings of yesterday to the absolute monarchs of today, and fickle monarchs at that. Price points are exposed everywhere on the Net and in the media. Top companies learn that a premium brand is invaluable only as long as it is not linked to too high a premium price.

PRODUCTS AND SERVICES. The societal aspiration for greater freedom endorses entrepreneurial products and services as never before. Parents boast of children creating new products at an unknown high-tech company. A generation ago they bragged of offspring in management training programs at GM or Sears.

As women exploit their new freedom of access to executive suites, entrepreneurial companies expand services from day care to housecleaning. The fashion industry reinvents its products to accommodate the new freedom to express yourself by "dressing down" at work.

ORGANIZATION. Freedom invades the organization structure by spawning new structures like self-directed or continuous improvement teams. Both depend on granting greater freedom to front-line workers. As choice expands customers' freedom, companies like Wal-Mart and Southwest Air reorganize around distribution channels rather than product lines or market segments. The "Channel Champion," the new job at the center of the new structure, ensures that the company has faster information about customer preferences and that it introduces the appropriate value-added benefits, such as 24-hour phone access, ahead of the competition.

PEOPLE. Inside companies, intellectual assets have replaced physical assets as the prime competitive weapon. Human knowledge is the most strategic asset in any enterprise, the source of all creativity, innovation and economic value. As a result, there is a new premium on attracting and retaining talented people. Expansion of flexible schedules and telecommuting reflect the greater physical and mental freedom of today's workplace. The new sense of self-realization at work actually encourages the kind of job-hopping that was a career killer only 20 years ago.

CAPITAL RESOURCES. Freedom from regulatory restraint permits capital resources to flow toward areas of greatest potential, nationally and internationally. New, freer standards for judging companies value mental assets more than physical. Want to start a shoe factory today? Forty years ago, you would rent space, buy equipment and raw materials, and hire workers. Nike built a worldwide brand while doing few of those things. It outsourced production to its suppliers, reserving its human and physical capital to elevate its skills in design and distribution. The suppliers financed the capital necessary for production.

Summary and Conclusions

The accelerating change around us arises from a largely invisible process. Successful businesses evolve in reflection of that process. Societal aspiration, a never-completed revolution of rising expectations, is the hidden driver of change in societies and in business.

Societies or companies embrace innovations, including technological innovations, quickly or slowly, depending on the power of the aspiration the innovation supports. A society valuing greater freedom for individuals will seek and support innovations that advance that freedom. A company valuing continuous improvement will find the resources to advance to the next level of performance.

Societies create higher levels of organization to channel the surplus energy. In business, that surplus energy flows through five channels or components: the market, product or service, organization, people and capital. Each component is critical to the success of any enterprise. All components must be in reasonable balance to keep a company positioned for success in a changing environment.

The five forces of change discussed earlier (technology, education, freedom, demographics and globalization) are reshaping the boundaries of every business component. Although all of these boundary shifts create opportunities or threats for specific business organizations, their influence varies widely with the industry and the positioning of individual companies. (This issue is discussed in greater detail in the next five chapters). Keeping any component in alignment with forces of change requires a conscious effort to develop, not just expand that component.

Every business planning team should assess where its company, and its five components, falls today within each of the trends highlighted in the next five chapters. Some of these trends may be inconsequential to a particular business, while others may have a dramatic effect. No trend should be dismissed until the team has thought through all of the implications it may have for the business in the next 10 years. Some trends, not particularly important today, may loom far larger on the horizon tomorrow.

In light of those trends, the team must ask, *How strong—that is, how well developed—is each of the company's five components?* Answering that question, the team will quickly uncover previously unseen opportunities and threats. The next five chapters explore that question as it applies to each component, or engine of business. Chapter 10 includes a list of key, open-ended questions each team to consider in reviewing the company's strengths and opportunities to improve in each component.

Five Keys to Profit and Productivity

ART ONE IDENTIFIED FIVE FORCES OF CHANGE—technology, freedom, education, demographics and globalization—and described the new environment in which business now seeks to achieve productivity, profit and growth.

Part Two—the next five chapters—explores how leading companies are responding to the changes described in Part One. Any company in any industry can usefully adapt many, if not all, of the strategies for success outlined for each major component of business.

Chapter Five looks at the market, the key component of business success defined by customers' rising expectations. Chapter Six analyzes technology, which includes products and services, and the tools and techniques companies use to produce what they sell. Chapter Seven looks at the dramatic changes now unfolding in organization—the network of structures, systems and accountabilities created by companies to improve the speed and efficiency of their operations. Chapter Eight describes changes in capital and other nonhuman resources, as business redefines traditional concepts of limits. Chapter Nine explores the implications of a world in which people have become the resource most in demend for business success.

For sustained success, every company must keep these components aligned with the forces of change and in reasonable balance with one another. This part describes how to achieve this goal.

The Market Rules

KEY CHAPTER THEMES

- *New opportunities to expand existing and new markets*

- *Six strategies to stay better connected with the market:*
    1. *Exploit the power shift toward consumers.*
    2. *Individualize products and services.*
    3. *Discover new ways to build customer loyalty.*
    4. *Provide more targeted information.*
    5. *Shift from planned time to real time.*
    6. *Follow the demographics.*

"Business is going to change more in the next 10 years than it has in the last 50."

—BILL GATES, CHAIRMAN OF MICROSOFT

F AST. SMART. CONNECTED: THEY'RE THE FORMULA for success in a leap-*before*-you-look market.

Businesspeople have always focused on the market. Street peddlers in Babylon certainly arranged their wares to entice potential customers, and an exciting new Web site is only the latest spin on an ancient skill.

What's new, however, is the speed at which markets move in unexpected directions. Ten years ago, companies charted changes in customers' needs and desires in months or years. Now, new plans, price quotes, or requests for bids fly through cyberspace at the click of a mouse. For all companies, that speed creates urgent, new priorities: respond faster, keep adding value, and treat your customer as an individual. Customers who find your service slow or unresponsive can easily type in the name of a competitor who may be more in tune with today's requirements.

Instant availability of information adds another dimension to speed. Nineteenth-century science and inventions created an expectation of continuous progress through expanding knowledge. It quickly became second nature to measure progress quantitatively. As early as 1816, prison, temperance and school reformers in Boston and Philadelphia published statistical surveys to bolster their demands for reform. By the 1830s, businessmen regularly employed double-entry bookkeeping to keep their accounts in a more systematic way. The American Statistical Society was founded at the end of that decade.

Early in the 20th century, the pursuit of business success through the numbers became "scientific management." By mid century, American business had adopted the quantified approach to information in market research, production engineering and financial analysis.

What's new is that information has become broader and deeper than ever. Most important, it's more widely available. Any desktop computer provides quicker access to better information than General Motors enjoyed a generation ago. Long, ponderous market studies are out. The new definition of smarter marketing depends on continuous connection with new and potential customers, while more advanced models anticipate customer desires.

Having the right information faster is a start toward smarter marketing, but maintaining market leadership requires careful focus and constant connection across companies and between companies and markets. This chapter focuses on strategies to stay better connected with the market. Chapter Seven looks at the effect of connectivity inside companies.

Market refers to all existing and potential customers for a company's products or services, including all the tools and techniques that companies use to understand and better serve their customers.

Unprecedented Opportunities

The forces of change discussed in the first four chapters have combined to open unprecedented opportunities in the market component. Freedom expressed politically creates an explosion in democracy. Freedom expressed economically keeps expanding choices in the marketplace. Simultaneously, education raises aspirations and awareness of opportunities for a better life. Technology lowers the barriers between haves and have-nots, between customers and suppliers, between price and availability. Demographics changes the profile of customers in almost every industry selling directly to consumers. Globalization creates stunning new market threats and opportunities.

These accelerating engines pulling together will propel the global consumer boom for at least the next 50 years. It will take that long before the world even begins to exhaust the expansion of comforts, acquisitions and possessions that energized the U.S. population after 1950. Starbucks Coffee, for example, now operates 3,000 outlets but is planning to push that number to 20,000, mainly through expansion overseas.[1]

Meanwhile, in the U.S., sophisticated technology opens the way to the kind of customization of products and services that was once limited to royalty. The customer is truly becoming the king, with all the escalating desires and capriciousness that were once the prerogative of monarchs.

The sections that follow list six key strategies to help any company to take full advantage of the unfolding riches in the newly energized markets at home and around the world.

Market Strategy #1: Recognize the New Balance of Power in Every Marketing Thought and Action

If you're still not used to it, get used to it in a hurry: The market rules. The traditional balance of power between producers and customers is now reversed. In the not so distance past, producers controlled the flow of information to customers. Suppliers had the best data about costs, prices, quality, competition and availability. Now all that information—and more—is readily available to consumers. Their range of options for price, selection and availability widens every day, putting producers and suppliers of all types of merchandise increasingly on the defensive.

Currently, customers weary of shopping for the best price often pay more than the lowest price available, but technology erodes this equation every day by lowering customers' search and other transaction expenses, in terms of both time and money. Today's search engines are the organizers of the Internet; tomorrow's engines will give personalized advice on customers' selections, creating a new set of challenges for manufacturers. How, for example, will "value-added" be defined in a world where both a better price and customized advice are a mouse click away?

The burgeoning wireless Internet will add a new dimension to this challenge. OracleMobile.com, a subsidiary of Oracle, now permits consumers to select information they want to receive on their cell phones. If your flight is late or a favorite stock drops below a prearranged level, automatic alerts are sent out.

Other new services are raising the stakes in comparison-shopping. Debating whether to buy that stereo receiver? Punch in the barcode number on your cell phone, and suppliers are ready to provide independent information about the product, including a list of lowest prices and details on how to order.

New Transparency

Online auctions have brought new transparency to the purchasing of goods and services, one of the most time-consuming processes in industry. The explosion of business-to-business (B2B) Internet exchanges permits groups of companies to buy supplies (such as car parts) or sell products (such as airline or other travel tickets) in direct online auctions between buyers and sellers. These Internet exchanges have thus far gone through three phases, notes *The Economist*. The first phase saw firms such as General Electric and Wal-Mart gain big savings in procurement time and costs by simply moving to buying online. Suppliers could immediately see, and feel the pressure of, their competitors' low bids. Next came third-party exchanges—independent firms bringing together many buyers and sellers to create a genuine independent market. In 1999, one such organization, FreeMarkets.com, auctioned more than $2.7 billion worth of industrial parts, raw materials, commodities and services online. The company estimates that it saved purchasers 2% to 25% on those orders. The third phase has seen industry giants getting together on their own to create their own multiple-company online

To be sure, the auction economy has not repealed the adage "Buyer beware." And would-be suppliers may suffer "winner's curse."

markets. For example, in February 2000, Sears, Roebuck and France's Carrefour announced a retail consortium that will bring together $80 billion of annual purchases.[2]

GM, Ford and DaimlerChrysler have created a similar supply network that will also feature online auctions. Suppliers that want to sell to these companies must bid online in an open market. Marriott and Hyatt agreed to form a similar Internet auction company to supply the hotel industry with everything from bath soap to electricity. Transora.com, which was announced in June 2000, created a packaged consumer goods exchange backed by 49 major manufacturers, including Coca-Cola, Procter & Gamble, Unilever and Sara Lee.[3] Forrester Research, an independent Cambridge, Mass., firm that analyzes the future of technology change and its effects on businesses, consumers and society, projects that the value of this type of online group purchasing will reach $1.3 trillion by 2003.

Buyer Beware

To be sure, the auction economy has not repealed the adage "Buyer beware." "Winner's curse" still occurs online when a would-be supplier, in the heat of excitement, agrees to provide a product or service at too low a cost. Collusion on either side of the auction fence is another risk. Bidders can work as partners to price most others out of the market before the high bidder drops out, leaving the winning bid with the partner. Or sellers can employ shills to drive up prices.

These risks cannot mask the basic power propelling this new model of buying and selling. The technology-driven access to the latest information made product comparison far easier, forcing products that once competed on special features or brand image to compete on price. The inevitable outcome of this seismic change is already easy to see: an increasingly competitive marketplace in which it is difficult to raise prices. With pricing so competitive, gaining a better market position by adding a valued service like better information remains the most accessible path to sustaining profit margins.

One advantage of this shift in the balance of business

power is a more efficient, and therefore more productive, economy. The flip side is the rising threat to producers who depend on profits created by inefficiencies. For years, companies in the metalworking field depended on increasing prices to "cover" inefficiencies in purchasing, scrap and reworking. Now that costs and prices are far more transparent—and more competition is coming from companies overseas—these companies have been forced to accelerate their efforts to improve quality and efficiency at lower cost. They have also been required to provide more accurate and up-to-date information to their customers. This example, multiplied across dozens of industries, has helped create a far more productive economy. Finding replacement profits in a very productive economy "is a very hard life," says Intel Corp. Chairman Andrew Grove, because raising prices is less and less an option.

The challenge of that hard life puts a premium on attracting and retaining managers who can find new sources of profit in a world where the customer rules. "I think managers will have double reasons for existence," says Grove, "because we will have to figure out how to earn profits that replace the profits that some of the change has sucked out of the world."[4]

Now, all effective market strategies will accept accelerating price pressure as a continuing reality, which puts an even higher premium on efficiencies in production and finding new definitions for value.

Market Strategy #2: What Have You Done for Me Lately?

Traditionally, marketing managers respond to competitive pressure by turning up the volume of their advertising. Although new technology provides exciting new tools for marketers, there are plenty of signs that customers are tuning out.

A time traveler from 50 years ago would be astonished by the expansion of advertising and marketing messages in our homes and public spaces. This growing intrusiveness reflects an escalating conflict between marketers and consumers, with technology the weapon of choice, notes *Wall Street Journal* writer Jonathan Kaufman.[5]

Marketers use the technology of television to shotgun their commercials into people's living rooms. An average hour of prime time TV now contains 15 minutes and 44 seconds of commercial time. Consumers fight back with remote controls to mute the TV and VCRs to fast-forward through commercials. "The wheel has been considered the greatest invention of all time," says syndicated columnist Dick Boland, "but the remote has to be in second place."

Marketers have counterattacked by inserting their products into shows and implanting their messages into the backgrounds of televised sporting events. Between 1995 and 2000, the number of sports stadiums with brand names rose from 6 to 50, reports IEG, a research company that tracks corporate sponsorships.[6] Taking a page from the TV playbook, companies now offer "free" Web information and services in return for viewing ads when we download from their sites.

The assault on consumer attention has gotten so bad that some experts predict a growing demand for what Phillip Kottler, professor of marketing at Northwestern University, somewhat facetiously calls "designated market-free zones."

Predictably, consumer resistance is mounting. People arm themselves with caller identification to slow the telemarketing offensive, and use computer-filtering software to evade e-mail spammers. Or they simply tune out.

The assault on consumer attention has gotten so bad that some experts predict a growing demand for what Phillip Kottler, professor of marketing at Northwestern University, somewhat facetiously calls "designated market-free zones." We will pay to take vacations in such camps "to be cleaned out of brand assault," Kottler suggests.[7]

Strategies more closely aligned with changes in the market will lower the volume of generic noise in favor of more attention to individual customer choice. More and more businesses are employing software that looks at customers as individuals and then delivers what they would like.

More Manipulative Than Ever

When the software or its users get it wrong, however, marketing seems more manipulative than ever. Amazon.com regularly recommends to customers a list of new books they might like on the basis of previous purchases. Amazon recently recommended a new book to an author friend, which was, in fact, a book he had just published! Yet, when the system works, it empowers individuals still further.

Focusing more on individual customer needs increases the emphasis on marketing that is based on information and solutions. Focusing more on individual customer needs increases the emphasis on marketing that is based on information and solutions. Travel agents can no longer compete by providing airline schedules and reservations, because online "reservation agents" have taken over that function for many customers; however, the market for customized information about travel and recreation is expanding. Similarly, HMOs are diversifying into more comprehensive preventive services, such as diet, exercise and stress reduction. Universities increasingly are teaming with businesses to offer education and training modules custom-tailored to businesses' needs.

A New Expectation for Brands

"The central problem for consumers is shifting from getting a 'good buy' on a standardized commodity to deciding precisely *what* they need," says former Labor Secretary Robert Reich, now a professor of economic and social policy at Brandeis University. This development changes brand management strategies forever, adds Reich. "Yesterday's highly valued brand name came attached to a standardized product customers could count on. It was always the same, exactly what it was advertised to be." Tomorrow's brand offers customers more than a promise that they are getting what they got last time. Successful brands of the future will provide "a trusted guide to what's new."[8]

Already, some of today's highest-value brand names (including Dell Computers, Oracle, Merrill Lynch, Amazon, Cisco and Anderson Consulting) no longer stand only for specific products or services but for continuing, individualized solutions.

The classic mission statement answers three key questions: What business are we in? Who is our customer? What do we offer of value? Each of those questions must now be elevated to a new level in keeping with the changed expectations of customers. It is no longer enough for a company to say, "We are in the trucking business," or, "We are in the shipping business," for example. Rather, a business must specify the *solution* it offers. For FedEx, the solution was overnight delivery. Expanding the definition of what the customer values leads any supplier beyond the actual product into intangibles like customer service and rapid response.

Conversations, Not Monologues

In the future, the most successful marketing will engage the customer in more of what appears to be a conversation, rather than talking at the customer in a monologue. The conversation will be solution oriented rather than hard sell; it will ask the customer "What do you need?" and "What do you care about?" instead of telling the customer, "I have what you need." Tying those rising trends together will foster the expansion of "cause-related marketing." In this approach, companies use advertising dollars to sponsor or support activities that address issues of importance to their customers.

For example: Cisco Systems effectively combined an event—the first Internet Age "We Are the World" concert—with a legacy Netaid Web site. Netaid.org uses the Internet to enable people to take action on extreme poverty around the world. The concert, broadcast simultaneously from London, Paris and New York in October 1999, reached the largest radio audience in history. The Web site, which features the Cisco logo on every page, has raised $8 million for the Netaid endeavor.

Empowering customers is the primary business challenge of the next 10 to 15 years, says management expert Tom Peters. Empowering customers, Peters explains, means providing choices on how "to customize your products and services—to meet their specific needs."[9]

Strategy #3: Customer Satisfaction Is a Promising First Date, but Customer Loyalty Is the Real Relationship

Excitement about the New Economy persuaded some businesspeople that customer loyalty was as dead as Japanese Quality Control Circles. Customers by the tens of thousands seemed to be abandoning brands they had supported for decades in favor of dot-com upstarts.

New Economy media hype, however, disguised a central fact that emerged when dot-com profitability problems caught the attention of Wall Street. The ever-receding profitability of the dot-coms stemmed in considerable part from the large marketing budgets they were having to maintain to get customers and earn their loyalty. "If there is one element of the dot-com experiment that can be declared a categorical failure, it's [the] attempted creation of the instant company," says *Fortune*. "Except in a handful of cases (Amazon.com being the most notable), huge up-front ad expenditures failed to translate into big sales, leading to customer acquisition costs as much as four times higher than those of offline competitors," according to McKinsey & Co.[10] After the dot-com crash, it certainly seemed an appropriate time for another look at that old-fashioned idea of customer loyalty.

Although many companies accept low customer loyalty as a fact of business life, some companies have always profited by hanging on to customers longer than their competitors. In the life insurance industry, policy persistence is the best single measure of policyholder satisfaction. Northwestern Mutual, of Milwaukee, Wis., had a persistence rate of just under 96% in 1999, among the best in the industry. It can't be entirely unrelated that the company's 1999 financial results were so strong. The company accrued policyowner dividends of $3.1 billion, paid in 2000. That distribution represented more than 20% of the policyholders', ordinary life dividends distributed by U.S., legal reserve, life insurance companies. With one-half trillion dollars of life insurance in force, Northwestern is the nation's largest provider of individual life insurance. Statistics like these have put Northwestern Mutual at the top of *Fortune's* annual list of "Most Admired Life Insurance Companies" for 17 consecutive years.

A Wrong Way to Increase Profit

One thoughtful view of customer loyalty comes from Frederick F. Reichheld, a senior management consultant at Bain & Co. in Boston. Companies pay too little attention to hanging on to customers because of the model that dominates business thinking today, says Reichheld.[11] That model dictates that only profits determine whether a business is performing well.

Rigid adherence to this model can lead to short-term profits not by creating customer value, but by destroying it. Cut research and development and training budgets. Reduce quality standards and critical support functions. Pay your talent less than competitive wages. Any of these actions can increase short-term profit margins. All of them risk taking value away from customers.

To be sure, this is an old idea. In the 1940s and '50s, Peter Drucker identified creating customer value as the most important function of any business. Even before that, Henry Ford noted: "Business must be run at a profit—else it must die. But when anyone tries to run a business solely for profit—then also the business must die, for it no longer has a reason for existence."

The Power of Complaints

Most businesses by now have learned the value of good customer service. Just to stay competitive, most companies have implemented policies, procedures, training and systems to ensure good (or at least to avoid bad) customer experiences. Even so, companies have been losing the loyalty wars, according to Reichheld. Bain's figures show that, on average, a U.S. company loses half its customers in five years, and half of its employees in four. Other studies support this trend. One survey in the appliance industry showed customer satisfaction ratings of more than 90% for most manufacturers, but the corresponding loyalty rating even for the best barely reached

50%.[12] Xerox has identified customer loyalty as the single most important ingredient in determining its long-term financial success. Its commitment to customer loyalty led to in-depth customer studies tracing the relationship among various levels of satisfaction and customer loyalty. One study showed that *totally* satisfied customers were six times as likely to repurchase Xerox products within 18 months as *merely* satisfied customers.[13]

While losses in the early stages of an Internet relationship are higher, profit growth accelerates at an even faster rate in future years.

The purpose of an effective customer service system should go far beyond helping just one customer at a time. A customer who complains often tests a company's commitment. True, some customers are jerks, but the vast majority of complainers are decent people who have been abused by a company's systems or people, or both. As customer service expert Chip R. Bell notes, a customer from hell is critically different from a customer who's been through hell. Companies that assume the latter point of view reap rewards of priceless feedback about their operations. Best of all, that advice is free![14] This approach contrasts sharply with the view in many companies that a complaint is an isolated incident rather than a symptom of an underlying problem and an opportunity to improve.

Success Through Loyalty

In the average company, loyalty is dead, says Reichheld. Bain & Co. a decade ago first documented the relationship between profit and customer retention over a period of years. The company study, carried out with Earl Sasser of the Harvard Business School, analyzed the costs and revenues derived from serving customers over their entire purchasing life cycle. The study showed that, in industry after industry, the high cost of acquiring customers makes many customer relationships unprofitable in their early years. Only in later years, when the cost of serving customers falls and the volume of their purchases rises, do relationships generate big returns.

In most businesses, satisfied customers spend more money

over time. In addition, established customers take less sales support time, energy and money. Established customers typically pay more than new customers, who often must be attracted by introductory offers, discounts or special coupons. Referrals from existing customers are the cheapest, yet most effective, form of marketing.

This is a sobering analysis for companies who live or die on the Internet. When Bain applied the same methodology to analyzing customer life-cycle economics, Reichheld says, "We found classic loyalty economics at work. In fact, the general pattern—early losses followed by rising profits—is actually exaggerated on the Internet."

At the same time, Bain's studies offer some definite encouragement to Internet companies that are stepping up their efforts to improve company loyalty. While losses in the early stages of an Internet relationship are higher, "profit growth accelerates at an even faster rate" in future years. In apparel e-tailing, for example, repeat customers spend more than twice as much in months 24 to 30 of their relationship as they do in the first six months. Also, because it is relatively easy for Web stores to extend their range of products, they can offer more and more different kinds of goods to loyal customers. Evidence so far indicates that Web customers tend to consolidate their purchases with one primary supplier as part of their daily routine. This trend is particularly apparent in business-to-business Internet sales.

Market Strategy #4: Build Relationships With Customers Through Targeted Information

Dell sells about 40% of its daily sales volume online, but Dell still welcomes your order by phone so that the human order taker can tell you about things you did not know you needed. For some 20,000 large customers, Dell has created individual Web pages that give each customer information about any order. Even for a smaller business, ordering perhaps 50 computers a year, the company will set up one of these Premier Pages in three or four minutes over the phone.

Dell also takes its information show on the road. "Dell on Wheels," the company's 18-wheel, specially equipped traveling showroom, has stopped in 50 cities to show customers, particularly small-business customers, its latest technology. Dell is betting that the bond it is forging with its small-business customers will be unbreakable by the time they are big enough to be noticed by IBM or Compaq.[15]

> **Dell's current strategy is to use its powerful, one-on-one relationships with customers to sell them a wide array of other products.**

Dell's efforts to build stronger customer relationships reflect intensifying competitive pressure. Not so long ago, Dell was happy to be a hugely successful retailer of low-cost, mail-order computers. Now yesterday's hot product has become a commodity. In 1999, sales of desktop PCs in the U.S. declined 3.5%, while sales in Europe grew by only 20%. Dell's annual sales growth, which averaged 60% in the 1990s, has slowed to about half that pace. Dell's current strategy is to use its powerful, one-on-one relationships with customers to sell them a wide array of other products, including digital cameras and office equipment.[16]

Strengthening customer relationship through better information takes many forms. Microsoft purchased Firefly Network in 1998. Microsoft made the acquisition to speed its delivery of software and services that conform to emerging privacy standards as agreed upon by the World Wide Web Consortium Platform for Privacy Preferences. Firefly's products—Firefly Passport, Firefly Office, and Firefly Catalog—allow end-users to create profiles of information to be provided to specific Web sites. The sites can then provide content in accordance with users' profiles.

Increasingly, news services seek to individualize their customer service by tailoring clipping services and bulky market reports. Dow Jones Interactive, *The Economist,* Bloomberg Business News, Dialog-Nexis, Kiplingerforecasts.com and others package a wealth of information that their subscribers can download according to their interests.

Such moves are instinctive for retailers. Now, heavy manufacturers are learning how to reinforce their customers' loyalty through faster, more personal online information and attention.

No one buys million-dollar, electricity-generating turbines by phone, much less online. Yet General Electric Power Systems has opened a Web-based information tool. This "turbine optimizer" enables a power-company turbine operator to compare current performance of its GE turbine with that of similar GE models everywhere in the world.

The optimizer will then show the operator how to improve the turbine's performance and to calculate the value of the resulting savings. Naturally, the tool lets the operator schedule a service call to make the suggested improvements. In addition, Power Systems provides customers with useful information at the customer's special Web site.[17]

Market Strategy #5: Jump the Clock Forward From Planned Time to Real Time

Effective businesspeople instinctively choose speed as a marketing strategy. The "Sundowner Rule" is part of the culture at Wal-Mart. The idea was founder Sam Walton's twist on the adage, "Why put off until tomorrow what you can do today?" The working principle at Wal-Mart is that every customer request gets same-day service.

People feel a power surge anytime they execute priorities without delay. General Electric CEO Jack Welch, a longtime advocate of speed as a competitive weapon, makes the case like this: "Speed exhilarates and energizes. Whether it be fast cars, fast boats, downhill skiing, or a business process, speed injects fun and excitement into an otherwise routine activity."

In business, Welch argues, "speed tends to propel ideas and drive processes right through functional barriers, sweeping bureaucrats and impediments aside in the rush to get to the marketplace."[18] After adopting speed as a value in the mid

1980s, GE cut production time for its locomotives in half, from 92 days to 46.

The modern economy runs by a beat of time that used to be measured in days, then hours, and now seconds. "It's no longer about the big beating the small, it's about the fast beating the slow," says Larry Carter, chief financial officer of Cisco Systems.[19] Bill Gates defined the unfolding era when he called his recent book *Business @ The Speed of Thought.*

When FedEx opened its doors in 1971, competitors were baffled by its prices. In delivery services, you charged by weight or size. FedEx strangely thought that it could charge for speed. A decade later, as the speed of delivery service accelerated, just-in-time inventory management swept through American manufacturing. By 1999, Dell could boast that parts lingered an average of only eight hours in its factories before leaving as finished PCs.

Multiply speed of manufacturing and delivery by today's connectivity of communications and a new dimension is created. In 1984, only 8,000 fax machines were sold, mostly to law offices. Five years later, annual sales totaled 2 million machines. The start of an even faster boom in e-mail addresses was six years away.

One fax machine alone is useless; add another one somewhere else and you have a new, but limited, communication tool. Add millions more in a year and you create a powerful network that can connect the globe. By the end of the 1980s, Chinese students protesting in Tiananmen Square instantly faxed reports of repression to sympathizers in the U.S. The Internet is now dwarfing the network created by faxes. The Computer Industry Almanac estimates that more than 717 million people worldwide will use the Internet by the end of 2005.

The IBM Speed Team

Forward-thinking companies have been aware of the power of fast product development for some time. A study by McKinsey & Co. in the 1980s showed that high-tech products that came to market six months late but on budget earned 33% less profit over five years. In contrast, coming out on time and 50% over budget cut profits by only 4%.[20]

IBM became a symbol of the slow-moving corporate culture in the late 1980s and early 1990s. Now IBM is on the move, aiming to imitate the speed and agility of its start-up rivals. IBM's 100,000-person information-technology staff recently created a temporary "Speed Team" dedicated to reducing product time to market.

The Speed Team tapped company leaders with a record of pushing projects through ahead of schedule. The leaders set a six-month limit to the team's operation. Short-term priorities focused on"speed bumps," steps in the process that could be accelerated or even eliminated entirely. Longer-term fixes were to take no more than 90 days. "The Speed Imperative," as IBM calls it, is not about doing the same things faster and for longer hours. Rather, says Steve Ward, IBM's vice president of business transformation and chief information officer.

IBM's Speed Team values: strong leaders, team members who are speed demons, clear objectives, a strong communication system, a carefully tailored process and a speed-oriented timetable.

"We're really about getting people to change the way that they do things, about blowing up the process and discussing ways to avoid speed bumps."

After reviewing many successful fast-moving projects, the team found six common characteristics, according to *Fast Company* magazine. It then created its list of Success Factors for Speed: strong leaders, team members who are speed demons, clear objectives, a strong communication system, a carefully tailored process (rather than a one-size-fits-all approach) and a speed-oriented timetable.[21]

The Speed Team learned the importance of getting everyone involved. It held online "town hall meetings" to ask for ideas about problems and opportunities to improve. E-mail and other electronic media were used to explore possibilities and to bounce ideas off other team members. Face-to-face meetings were used to keep the momentum strong.[22]

Other tradition-bound companies are also using speed-to-market as an energizing weapon. Thomas O. Ryder arrived at *Reader's Digest's* Pleasantville, N.Y., headquarters determined to remake the staid publishing company into a nimble, Web-wise publisher and marketer. The new CEO discovered that the company required nearly a year to develop direct mail campaigns to sell the company's products. Ryder broke tradition by outsourcing work previously handled in-house. Predictably, long-time employees resisted overturning decades of standard procedure, but Ryder and John Klingel, his new circulation director, kept pushing back. *Reader's Digest* now develops direct mailing campaigns in 13 weeks.[23]

A New Perspective on Time and Space

For awhile in the late 1990s, the drive for faster responsiveness was summarized by the jargon phrase "Internet Time." Popularized with the Silicon Valley slogan "You have to run on Internet Time—or die," the concept's adherents persuaded themselves that Internet Time meant that everything had to run 7 to 10 times faster than basic business time. How they came up with that measurement was never clear. "The Internet folks have been running way ahead of us, like a hunter's hound chasing a fox," says *USA Today* technology columnist Kevin Maney. "But, eventually, they and their wagging tails have to wait for us hunters to catch up, and we can only ambulate through technological change so fast." Even though, "Internet time seems destined to become another quaint mind-set from a specific moment in history," Maney adds, "major technologies often do change our concept of time."[24]

In 1801, when Thomas Jefferson became president, information took six weeks to travel from the Mississippi River to Washington, D.C. People expected that it would always be like that. In 1861, when Abraham Lincoln moved into the White House, information moved almost instantaneously by telegraph, but only from one point to another. By 1963, an estimated 68% of the U.S. population knew of President Kennedy's assassination within a half-hour. During the Gulf War, we could see combat half a world away as it happened. Clearly, Americans who lived in the eras of Jefferson, Lincoln and Kennedy and who have lived in our own era have seen time and distance from different perspectives. So, while Internet time may soon be a forgotten phrase, faster, more responsive information will be a growing expectation among all types of customers from here on.

Toward Internet Economy 2.0

It's a safe bet that in five years, today's speed limits will seem slow. Internet Economy 1.0 is now accelerating into a faster model—Internet Economy 2.0, according to International Data Corp., a leading provider of market data and analysis to builders, providers and users of information technology. The millions of new Internet users coming online in the next few years will be "far more demanding and far less patient" than today's relatively patient users," says IDC's eBusiness Advisory Research Service Group vice president Sean Kaldor.[25] They will expect to operate ever more exclusively in "real time."

> **In managed time, companies run like buses, with specific routes and schedules. Real-time organizations are more like taxis, responding to a customer waving an arm or calling in.**

The notion of operating in "real time"—or gathering information, making a decision and acting almost instantaneously—came of age with the widespread use of the computer, a machine defined by speed. Real time means the computer can actually keep up with the job, processing input with no delay in output. Now we have real-time scheduling, real-time analysis, real-time auditing: The use of the term has expanded in the business world to mean *more* than fast. It means get the answer and act on it now! And as computers get faster, real time accelerates.

Stephen Haeckel, an IBM strategist, likens the difference between managed time and real time to the difference between a scheduled service and an on-demand service. In managed time, companies run like buses, with specific routes and schedules. Real-time organizations are more like taxis, responding to a customer waving an arm or calling in.[26] In the post-PC, wireless world, real time is faster yet.

There's big money to made—or saved—in switching from

planned time to real time. Experts estimate that the average fast-food restaurant can increase sales by $54,000 a year simply by improving the efficiency and speed of a drive-through window by 10%.[27] Alcoa says that switching to real-time systems helped reduce inventories by more than a quarter of a billion dollars while increasing sales by almost $1 billion in 1999. The key was providing a steady stream of real-time data while enabling workers to make corrections on the spot.[28]

Time to Think

With all this speed, do we risk losing something important like time to think? A *New Yorker* cartoon captures the present mood well. It shows a man answering the phone, "No, I don't have four seconds to talk."

Real-time decision-making still requires slowing down long enough to think—ahead. The quality of real-time decision-making reflects the quality of the advance thought that precedes it.

Effective real-time decision-makers must:

- **Get the basic framework right,**
- **Be able to explore available alternatives rapidly, and**
- **Be willing to decide without delaying for one more fact.**

To casual observers, doing all this looks like leaping before you look. However, first looking carefully and then leaping fast is a more apt description.

Getting the fundamental framework right is often the most difficult challenge for today's fast-transaction managers. Building a solid framework requires anticipating where your market is heading next. Answering that question has never been more difficult, yet there is no time for paralysis by analysis.

That's where thinking through and then regularly rethinking the fundamentals discussed in this book will pay off for any manager. Consider what effects each of the following will have on your business:

- **Technology**
- **Rising standards of education**
- **Changes in demographics**

- **Globalization of markets**
- **Changing expressions of freedom among your customers**

Depending on your answers to these questions, what do you think your current customers will want next? Can you then project emerging needs in potential customers? Perhaps most important, do you have in place a team that shares your vision of the evolution of your market?

When you sense where your market is going, what segments you want to keep or abandon, and what value you propose to sell, then—and only then—are you truly ready for real-time decision-making. The rest of your preparation to increase responsiveness should focus on techniques that anyone can master:

Surround yourself with teams of speed demons, and make sure the teams have clear goals congruent with the basic framework you have chosen.

Use the latest technology to communicate: instant messages, teleconferences, videoconferences and software tools to control the key factors that spell success or failure in your business.

For maximum speed, shift every possible decision to the point closest to the customer. To get a bank balance, you used to have to go to the bank and ask the teller. Now you can call and get your answer by phone. Or, if you are a manufacturer subcontracting to another firm and you wanted to change your specifications or order, you used to have to go to a "boss" three levels up from where you work was being handled. The boss then had to go look at the job on the floor, make a decision and call you. Now, depending on the degree of complexity and cost involved, in many companies it is the worker on the floor who makes that decision and tells you on the spot.

Respect your business processes. Follow them when they help; revise them quickly when they slow you down.

Set continuous improvement targets for speed. There is always a better, faster way to do anything.

Market Strategy #6: Follow the Demographics to New and Expanding Markets

As was discussed in Chapters Two and Three, shifting demographics are opening unprecedented market opportunities in the U.S. and abroad. Customers everywhere have a different look, speak a different language and value different priorities. Those companies that react quickest seize an important advantage.

Wal-Mart has always been agile in following demographic signals overlooked by competitors. In becoming the world's largest retailer, the company avoided the suburbs and targeted smaller, underserved rural areas. That same alertness—and willingness to ignore conventional wisdom—now points to new directions driven by changing demographics, such as the rapid growth of the Hispanic market.

On May 20, 1998, Wal-Mart opened Store No. 2568 at Panorama Mall, the first Wal-Mart within the city limits of Los Angeles. In keeping with the company positioning, signs in the store display such familiar messages as "Always low prices. Always." However, at Panorama the signs actually read, "Siempre precios bajos. Siempre." While most Wal-Marts feature a McDonald's, the Panorama store includes a Mis Amigos Mexican restaurant and snack bar.

The opening was "definitely something new and unique for Wal-Mart," says assistant manager Javier Rincon. The company signaled its commitment to the community through cause-related marketing. It linked its opening to a Los Angeles Police Department gang prevention program. Wal-Mart gave $34,000 to the LAPD program plus more than $15,000 to other community organizations and causes.

Panorama City responded by making the new store one of the most successful Wal-Mart launches ever. Sales on opening day exceeded projections by 20%. More than 43,000 customers passed through the check-out lines in the first week. An average of 9,500 customers have bought something at the store every day since it opened.

Internet entrepreneurs also have been quick to seize the

opportunity created by changing ethnic demographics and have combined it with technology. EthnicGrocer.com CEO Parry Singh launched the site after hearing a relative complain that her husband wouldn't accompany her on a long drive to an Indian grocer where she could buy pickles and curry. Singh, a graduate of Northwestern University's Kellogg Business School, saw the potential in bringing convenience to this market. Overall, ethnic populations spend $64 billion a year in North America. Now, in addition to Indian food, EthnicGrocer.com offers Chinese and Latin American foods, spices, recipes, cooking utensils and household items.

Working Woman Barbie

The expanding role of women in the workplace suggests other opportunities. Mattel, Inc., in partnership with *Working Woman* magazine, brought out Working Woman Barbie in 1999. The doll comes equipped with a miniature computer and cell phone, as well as a CD-ROM with information about understanding finances. Appropriately, Working Woman Barbie faces tough competition in the marketplace. Late in 1999, two California entrepreneurs introduced the Smartees line of dolls. Among the members of this family are Ashley the Attorney, Emily the Entrepreneur, Destiny the Doctor and Jessica the Journalist.[29]

Generational demographics open other opportunities. Sony Corp. hopes to capture the attention of the Generation Y younger crowd with its new line of digital music devices. Meanwhile, live entertainment companies like Cirque du Soleil and Ringling Brothers try to lure more upscale, older customers by offering the opportunity to watch a circus performance while sipping champagne and dining on fancy foods.

Growth in the African American Market

Among the biggest opportunities come from the growth in African American spending power. Some companies like McDonald's and Coca-Cola have marketed effectively to blacks for decades. Ford has long sponsored programs for African

American dealers, franchisers, suppliers and distributors. Other alert retailers are now opening stores in Harlem, long a focal point of the African American community. The area now boasts such upscale names as Starbucks, the Disney Store, Gap and the Body Shop.

In 1999, American Express opened 20 "diversity learning centers" for individual investors in minority communities. The target for this effort is the U.S. African American population of 31 million, which has $500 billion in total annual income and a pool of investments that has quadrupled in two years to $13.6 billion.[30]

Perhaps the most intriguing aspect of this investment potential is the opportunity to put it to work in minority markets in the U.S. Nathan Chapman Jr., a Baltimore financial entrepreneur and mutual fund manager, argues that instead of looking for opportunities in Asia, Latin America or Africa, investors can get the same growth and diversification from a U.S. "emerging" minority market. As an added selling point, Chapman notes that this market avoids political and currency risks. The idea may be catching on, reports *Fortune*. Aetna added Chapman's DEM (Domestic Emerging Markets) Equity fund to the list of 100-plus mutual funds it offers its 2 million 401(k) customers. In addition, Aetna has created its own domestic emerging-markets division to sell financial services.[31]

While African American marketing efforts tend to focus on a single group, Asian Americans are more effectively addressed as separate nationalities. Charles Schwab & Co., for example, produces separate marketing brochures for Cantonese- and Mandarin-speaking Chinese, Mandarin-speaking Taiwanese, Taiwanese-speaking Chinese, and clients originally from Hong-Kong. This tailored approach lets Schwab speak to present and potential customers in a more intimate and individualized manner.

Global Demographics

While demographic-driven opportunities at home are formidable, they will be dwarfed by potential sales in the rest of the world. After all, the U.S. population of 270 million represents only about 5% of the world's 5.7 billion potential consumers.

Today, about 20% of world output is produced and consumed in global markets. Within 30 years, this total will rise to 80%, according to McKinsey & Co.[32] "As such markets emerge in food, healthcare, telecommunications, the mass media, accounting and many other industries, the profit opportunities will be reckoned in the hundreds of billions of dollars," McKinsey adds. "Companies will have access to the most talented labor, the largest markets, the most advanced technologies, and the best and cheapest suppliers of goods and services."

Before counting on all those potential profits, however, companies should note one important McKinsey caveat. In this unfolding cornucopia, "every business will have to compete with the best, and integrating markets are volatile and uncertain."

Brainpower and New Wealth

As already noted in Chapter Three, all this international integration of markets is the latest acceleration of an old pattern of human history. Now, technology is driving the next wave of change.

Wealth creation traditionally grew from efficiency and economies of scale in the production of goods and services. A bigger steel mill or auto plant was once the key to outproducing and outperforming your competitors. Today, size and location matter far less, and the smaller high-tech company running on brainpower often has the competitive advantage. India's new generation of software engineers who are creating a whole new industry is only one example.

U.S. Companies Positioned to Win

Fortunately, American companies are well positioned in the emerging battle for world markets.

Distance across two oceans was once a barrier to Americans in world trade, but accelerating technology has steadily pushed down the cost of connecting with customers overseas. The cost (in inflation-adjusted dollars) of a three-minute phone call from New York City to London dropped from $245 in 1920 to $9 in 1950 to 78 cents in 1999. Meanwhile, from 1950 to 1999, the cost of air travel fell from 68 cents a passenger mile to 12 cents.

Government policies still form a crucial backdrop to corporate international success. However, since the end of the Cold War, leading corporate players like General Electric, IBM, and Cisco Systems have been the drivers of global change. Household names like Manpower, Mobil, Citicorp, Gillette, Avon Products, Xerox and McDonald's now have more than half their assets outside the U.S.[33]

According to the Center for the Study of American Business, at Washington University in St. Louis, a U.S. company is number one worldwide in 17 industries. A host of companies including Coca-Cola, Colgate-Palmolive, Hewlett-Packard, Proctor & Gamble, Texas Instruments and 3M now get at least two-thirds of their sales from overseas markets. Perhaps even more significant, among the top 10 companies in *Fortune*'s worldwide most-admired list, only one (Sony) is not American.[34]

Smaller Companies and the Overseas Market

The time is also ripe for small businesses to expand their horizons overseas. Already, about 97% of U.S. exporters are businesses with fewer than 500 employees. All you really need to go global is a computer server and the ability to receive credit cards, says Mark Rosen, director of strategic alliances at the Small Business Administrations Office of International Trade. Small companies can make initial contacts with foreign businesses over the Internet, often through trade portals sites that connect them with potential overseas trading partners.[35]

Summary and Conclusions

The growth of the information economy has altered but not repealed the basic principles of effective marketing. Understanding—better yet, anticipating—customer desires remains at the heart of any effective marketing strategy.

What has changed are the range and depth of customer expectations and the speed with which these higher aspirations are spreading. People who for generations were content with— or at least accepting of—their lot in life now want more of the comforts, conveniences and luxuries enjoyed by "the rich." Over the coming decades, freedom, education and technology will accelerate this "revolution of rising expectations."

Carried by a wave of demographic change, this revolution is now opening market opportunities that barely existed a generation ago. At home, the growing spending power and wealth of minority groups will change how and where companies prospect for sales.

Opportunities internationally will dwarf the growth of new U.S. markets. Exports to China alone will rise by about $4 billion a year through 2005. Lower tariffs and no quotas will encourage more U.S. small businesses to join the China trade. Exports to China from American small and midsize firms will probably hit $10 billion by 2005.

One principle must never be lost amid all this change, however. In the Old Economy or New, customer loyalty is what pays the bills this month and next year.

Another irrevocable change is the power of new technology to deliver to customers what they want, when they want it and how they want to receive it. This capability puts a premium on speed. You will get exactly the car you want built for you in 14 days. You'll also get better information and solutions packaged with your products and services. From here on, the race to see which competitor pleases the customer the most will intensify even as competition becomes more transparent.

For most companies, all this will represent a big stretch. As later chapters discuss, organization structures must be overhauled and rebuilt. Employees from the shop floor to the executive suite must acquire a host of new skills. Technology must be upgraded. Vast sums of capital will be needed to keep technology rolling, to explore new markets, to keep up with customer expectations.

One principle must never be lost amid all this change, however. In the Old Economy or New, customer loyalty is what pays the bills this month and next year. Cool marketing or cutting-edge technology will never be enough to turn butterfly customers jumping from one Web site to another into true profit spinners. Sooner or later—and increasingly sooner—shareholders always demand a return for their money. Then, survival and growth will hang on one issue and only one issue: the capacity of a company to find and deliver value to profitable customers.

The Vast Profit Potential of Expanding Knowledge

KEY CHAPTER THEMES

- *Rising aspiration liberates a worldwide market for products and services.*

- *New knowledge revolutionizes production.*

- *Accelerating services fuel an unprecedented growth in productivity and jobs.*

- *These trends set four priorities for business:*
    1. *Redefine value.*
    2. *Add intangibles.*
    3. *Aim for perfection in quality.*
    4. *Upgrade mental-level production.*

"Knowledge is power."
—SIR FRANCIS BACON, ENGLISH STATESMAN AND PHILOSOPHER

"The newest battleground in world trade won't be manufactured goods, farm products or fuel, but something you can't even see or touch—services."
—KNIGHT KIPLINGER, EDITOR-IN-CHIEF, *THE KIPLINGER LETTER* AND KIPLINGERFORECASTS.COM

K NOWLEDGE AND SERVICE ARE TWIN PATHS TO profit in an unfolding revolution in products and services.

In the 1990s, the U.S. economy expanded more rapidly and continuously than most experts predicted. Even in retrospect, the cause of this expansion stirs debate. Some see demographic changes as the root cause while others cite the increased productivity created by the information-age economy. According to this thesis, we have entered a new economic model in which nonmaterial resources, inherently less limited than material resources, drive the economy.

Rising standards of education, expansion of democratic principles and growing globalization all have their advocates as primary or secondary contributors to a prosperity that caught even the most experienced economists by surprise. (One noteworthy exception is the Kiplinger organization, which accurately forecast the major elements of the 1990s boom in 1986 with *The New American Boom*, and again in 1989 with *America in the Global '90s).*[1]

As was argued in earlier chapters, each of these developments represents an important but partial explanation. The market for products and services in any country reflects the sum total of the aspirations of people in that market. When confidence rises, companies and individuals produce more, spend more and invest more. That situation, in turn, leads to boom times.

The experience of the 1990s will, in time, seriously challenge the dogma that developed economies can grow by only about 3% annually without serious inflation. In 1999, before the Federal Reserve put on the brakes, the U.S. economy was growing at an annual rate of 5.8%, on top of 5.7% and 6.5% increases during the two previous years. Unemployment was nearing historic lows. Inflation was asleep. The political debate shifted to what to do with unexpected surpluses in government revenues rather than how to deal with deficits. It couldn't be happening, according to traditional economics, but it was.

If this "new model" can be traced to any single event, the most likely candidate is the end of the Cold War. For 40 years the U.S. economy operated on a semi-war footing maintained with vast amounts of our productive and research capacities. The threats posed by that struggle encouraged the expansion of a larger centralized government, which absorbed still more resources. Some of the brightest minds of at least two generations devoted their energies and working careers to ensuring American success in this vast and critically important national effort. The sudden, unexpected lifting of a great psychological and resource burden ignited American optimism and faith in the future. That release of energy, supported by all the important forces discussed earlier, fueled the unexpected boom.

Rising aspirations for a better, more comfortable life, not just in the U.S. but around the world, have liberated a worldwide market for goods and services. At the same time, rising expectations coupled with changes in demographics and new technologies have rearranged the positioning of virtually all products and services.

Knowledge Revolutionizes Production

One continuing force driving this change is an accelerating rate of expanding knowledge. Rapidly expanding knowledge revolutionizes production in every age and in every field.

Eighteenth-century Enlightenment gave birth to the modern vision of man dominating the natural world through knowledge and reason. Visible results included a period of scientific experimentation and the Industrial Revolution, which started in the English Midlands in the 1770s.

Mechanization of production through application of knowledge quickly gave birth to rising expectations and unprecedented prosperity. Between 1780 and 1860, British income per head doubled. As a new nation with an optimistic view of the future, the U.S. eagerly adopted the new manufacturing and transportation technologies. By 1900, the U.S. produced enough economic surplus to devote 18% of its workforce just to creating and distributing knowledge in office jobs. That percentage kept rising all though the 20th century. By 1970, the U.S. could afford to have as many people working in offices as in our factories and farms combined. That growth was one reflection of the shift in our labor force toward more knowledge work—a trend that continues to accelerate. For example, between 1996 and 2006, the number of database administrators, computer support specialists, computer engineers and systems analysts will double. In contrast, precision production jobs will grow only 7%.

Mechanization of production through application of knowledge quickly gave birth to rising expectations and unprecedented prosperity.

The power of knowledge to transform production is a worldwide phenomenon. New agricultural knowledge created a Green Revolution, lifting crop production to previously undreamed-of levels in India and elsewhere. The introduction of computers changed manufacturing processes in industries throughout the world.

In 1973, Daniel Bell named the emerging era when he called his seminal book *The Coming of Post-Industrial Society*. Bell noted that, from here on, "what matters is not raw muscle power, or energy, but information." Bell's insight grows truer every year. We are accumulating knowledge and information at a dizzying rate. Scientific knowledge doubles every decade. Our pool of business information expands even faster.

Pioneers Reap the Richest Rewards

Two significant technological revolutions undergird today's knowledge explosion. The communications revolution overcomes distance as a barrier. Meanwhile, computers accelerate the speed with which we organize and distribute knowledge. These twin forces are creating the so-called Information Age. Regions and producers who most quickly and effectively stay on top of these technologies reap the richest benefits.

The introduction of electricity early in the 20th century provides a parallel insight into today's extraordinary opportunity. When Ezra F. Scattergood became chief electrical engineer of Los Angeles in 1909, he set out to make California the first "all-electric state," notes historian Paul Johnson. By 1924, 83% of the homes in California had electrical wiring, versus 24% nationally. Nationally, the cost per kilowatt-hour averaged $2.17. In California it was $1.42. The state boasted one of the first, all-electric transport systems—the Pacific Electric, which ran for 1,164 miles, tying together 42 incorporated cities and towns within a 35-mile radius of central Los Angeles. The huge, thundering electric engines are gone now, familiar only to fans of early movies because they appear in many Keystone Kops and Laurel and Hardy short films. However, the Los Angeles freeways even today follow Pacific Electric routes. Cheaper power helped turn Southern California into the world center of the new movie industry.

The introduction of electricity early in the 20th century provides a parallel insight into today's extraordinary opportunity.

Low-cost electricity fueled the continuing California boom through the 1920s and difficult '30s. It gave the state a powerful infrastructure advantage for war production in World War II and for the subsequent growth of the economy.

Further north, in Seattle, J. D. Ross, a Scattergood disciple, preached the virtues of cheap electricity the way some business leaders tout the virtues of cheap computing today. Ross was right. By the 1930s, Seattle had more electric ranges than any other American city. A few years later, its electrical base enabled it to share in the wartime industrial expansion, laying the foundation that today makes it a center of the U.S. aviation and high-tech industries.[2]

The Roots and Projected Growth of the Technology Revolution

Even with the backing of visionaries, electrification took decades. Today's pace of technological progress just doesn't *seem* far faster than that—it is. Now almost all knowledge workers in the U.S. have networked personal computers on their office desks. Fifteen years ago, such networks were rare. In the early 1990s, the Internet was cutting edge technology; now it is routine. Households that account for two-thirds of the purchasing power of the domestic economy were expected to have home connections to the Internet by the end of 2000. The pace of change toward more accessible, faster information technology continues unabated. By 2010, Web-enabled information appliances—personal digital assistants, intelligent automobile options, wireless phones—are expected to outsell PCs by a factor of 10 to 1.[3]

The accelerating impact of the information revolution spawns a far greater and wider technology revolution in a dozen fields, says management professor William E. Halal. A decade ago, Halal launched the George Washington University (GWU) Forecast of Technology and Strategy. The Forecast tracks about 100 emerging technologies in fields such as transportation, medicine and farming. Periodically, the Forecast gathers expert panels to predict when each technology will most likely enter the mainstream in the next decade. In selecting its 10 potential breakthroughs (see box), the experts attempt to identify not just technological breakthroughs, but developments that will have significant economic potential and social impact.

Halal argues that the speed-up in technology rests on at least three related trends, all linked to information technology:

1. Scientists and engineers worldwide are using sophisticated information networks to share their work much more quickly.

BOX 6-1 The Top 10 Emerging Technologies

The George Washington University Forecast of Technology and Strategy in June 2000 selected the 10 technologies listed below as the most likely candidates for important breakthroughs in the next decade.

1. Portable information devices. The GWU panel of experts forecast that these appliances, which combine the computer, the Internet, television and the telephone, will be used by at least 30% of the population in developed nations by 2003.

2. Fuel-cell technology. Toyota, Ford, and DaimlerChrysler plan to introduce fuel-cell autos by 2003–04, although the cars are still likely to be experimental. Despite the high potential of a breakthrough in fuel cells, many technical and economic obstacles remain before such a sophisticated technology will be commercially viable for common use.

3. Precision farming. Satellite data sent directly to a tractor's computer controls the amounts of irrigation water, seed, fertilizer and pesticides to optimize land production yard by yard. Today, farm equipment manufacturers sell precision farming systems on standard tractors as an optional

extra. The GWU panel projects that in 10 years all farmers will use this technique, which offers a viable way to increase crop yields on limited farmland.

4. Mass customization. Dell Computer provides people with the precise machine they want, delivered in three days, at a discount. (Mass customization is the tailoring of a mass-market product to individual customer needs, as compared with mass production, which is the manufacture of exactly the same product for a mass market.) As Dell recognized early, the Internet makes it far easier to get customers to participate in this kind of transaction.

5. Teleliving. Even now, homes, autos, and offices are being wired into linked, intelligent networks that work together. Companies are already embedding 4 billion chips every year in everything from coffee makers to Cadillacs. Increasingly, wireless networks will link disparate electronic devices.

6. Virtual assistants (VA). The GWU expert panel envisions a smart program stored in your PC or portable information device that monitors your e-mail, faxes, messages, computer files and phone calls. Eventually, this virtual assistant could take over routine tasks like writing a letter, retrieving a file, making a phone call or screening people.

7. Genetically altered organisms. While resistance to genetically modified (GM) food appears to be increasing in the West, alleviating hunger globally will require improved yields in crop and animal production. The GWU expert panel forecasts that in the next decade more nations will opt to risk dangers to gain the benefits of plants that resist disease, grow faster, produce their own fertilizers and contain more nutrients.

8. Computerized health care. The health care industry has lacked the interconnected hardware and software for the type of major computerization that has changed business operations over the past decade. All that could change as more integrated computer systems improve medical record keeping, prescription fulfillment, monitoring, self-care and almost all other facets of medicine. Smart chips in a more computerized health care system can provide a complete record of patient history from birth, replacing the paperwork that invariably seems to get lost when patients transfer from one provider to another. Computerized diagnostic systems can exceed the knowl-

edge available to many physicians.

9. Alternative energy sources. Carbon-based fuels will continue their dominant role in industrial societies, but alternative energy sources will probably increase from 10% of all energy use at present to 30% by the end of the decade. Included in this forecast are wind, geothermal, hydroelectric, solar, biomass and other alternative energy sources. Technological advances are bringing down the costs of alternative energy sources. In 1998 the cost of wind and hydroelectric power approached that of oil, coal and gas.

10. Smart, mobile robots. Robots today lack sensory devices and sophisticated artificial intelligence systems. The GWU panel estimates that by the end the decade, robots will be commercially available to perform more sophisticated factory work, run errands, do household chores and assist people with disabilities.

Source: William E. Halal, "The Top 10 Emerging Technologies: Researchers at George Washington University Forecast Coming Technological Breakthroughs," originally published in the July–August 2000 issue of *The Futurist.* Used with permission from the World Future Society, 7910 Woodmont Avenue, Suite 450, Bethesda, MD 20814; 301-656-8274; 301-951-0394 (fax); http://www.wfs.org.

2. In every field, researchers can now use far more powerful computers and instruments.

3. As industrial work yields to knowledge work, the sheer number of researchers in every field is expanding rapidly.

The pace of innovation in information will accelerate even faster in the years ahead, according to Halal's Forecast panels. For example, they project that optical computers, operating on light waves rather than electricity, will replace current computer technology within 20 years at the most. The GWU panels estimate that, as chip circuits shrink to one molecule wide, today's computer technology will reach its limit in a decade or so and be able to miniaturize no further. The optical computer, using light—the fastest known power in the universe—is likely to be the next major evolutionary step. One thousand times faster than today's electronic models, optical computers may be commercially available by 2015.

Much of the infrastructure for computing with light is already in place. Fiber-optic cables provide high-speed transmission lines, lasers serve as modulating devices and CDs allow high-capacity optical storage. At present, Halal says, more than 3,000 companies are hard at work trying to create optical computer breakthroughs.[4]

Accelerating Services Fuel Our Job Growth

The acceleration of services is another force reshaping the patterns of what and how we buy and consume. This change has fostered nearly as many myths as there are theories behind our recent astonishing growth. One fact is indisputable, however: The service sector is now our greatest engine for job creation.

More than 30 years ago, Peter Drucker identified a major trend in the American economy: Increasingly, organizations were creating new jobs far faster for people who manipulated knowledge than for people who manipulated physical things such as industrial machinery. Now, this growth of service jobs—in fields such as insurance, the media, government, public affairs, publishing, securities trading, education, leisure activities and health care—dominates our economy.

Twenty years ago, people feared this shift, warning that we would end up as a nation with no jobs except service jobs like flipping burgers and cutting hair. I remember the astonishment of a friend who retired 15 years ago to Southern California after a long and successful manufacturing career in the Midwest, who commented, "Nobody out here *makes* anything, but they all seem to have plenty of money." While attitudes have evolved slowly, most business leaders now fully understand that offering an intangible service can create as much economic value as producing a tangible product, and sometimes even more.

What has occurred since then is not so much a decline in agricultural and manufacturing jobs as an acceleration of service jobs. Between 1975 and 1996, the total number of U.S. jobs in agriculture and manufacturing remained fairly steady. However, during that period the American labor force grew by slightly more than 60%. Virtually all the new jobs were in the service sector.

Changing societal aspirations account for much of this shift. Aspiration does not decline when people meet their basic needs—for food, shelter and security. A whole new level of wants and desires kick in. As your level in life rises, look how much larger a share of your income goes to entertainment, travel, and services to improve your health, to provide better education for yourself and your family, or to make your life more comfortable or pleasant.

Purists may deplore this all-too-human tendency for needs to escalate. They may even embrace a simpler style of life—a choice that most of us in an economy of abundance can look upon with indulgence and perhaps even admiration as long as it remains a distinctly minority choice. High-pressure urban professionals seeking to unwind by taking a vacation in a bucolic area provide a good illustration of this dichotomy in our thinking. As one such vacationing professional said to me: "I love it here, the way everybody is so centered, so laid back.

I'd move here tomorrow except the service is so slow."

Despite contrary evidence, some critics still argue strongly that the shift to service jobs is harmful because too many service jobs are low-pay, low-benefits, low-skill dead-ends. In fact, the accusation of physical drudgery, low skill requirements and barely subsistence wages can be leveled as accurately at many manufacturing factories and farms in the U.S. and abroad.

Contrary to the low-skill, low-pay argument, some of the fastest-growth sectors of the service economy require high skill and offer high pay.

Contrary to the low-skill, low-pay argument, some of the fastest-growth sectors of the service economy require high skill and offer high pay. These include jobs for software engineers, technical support staff, financial analysts, scientific researchers, marketers, logistical experts, educators and medical practitioners.

Even within the manufacturing and agriculture sectors, many of the new jobs rise above physical drudgery. These new agricultural and industrial jobs are service-related, support positions such as sales and customer service, research engineering, and the programming and maintenance of sophisticated machinery.

Services: More Exponential Growth in Productivity

The historic advance from land-based agriculture to machine-based manufacturing produced exponential growth in human productivity, employment opportunities, incomes and living standards. We are already seeing that the move from machine-based manufacturing to information-based services represents the next important evolutionary step at home and abroad.

The physical barriers that constrain both manufacturing and agriculture count for far less in services. Work, employment, money and accumulated wealth are all expressions of human productivity. In agriculture, human productivity is traditionally tied to and limited by land. In industry, the traditional limiting factor is the capacity of mechanical processes. In services, human energy relates to and releases the energy in other humans. The fact that human energy is virtually unlimited suggests that the further evolution of services will continue to generate higher living standards and more abundant employment in every society. It also suggests that as the traditional industrial and agricultural sectors become more linked with the information and service sectors, the traditional sectors, too, will create new opportunities for growth and higher living standards although their net employment of people relative to services will continue to decline.

To understand the job growth that will continue to come in services, let's look at three important service-sector industries—education, health care and tourism.

The Education Job Engine

Employment in education soared in the 20th century but has yet to approach a saturation point in any country. Since 1900, the number of teachers in the U.S. has grown fivefold. Between 1994 and 2005, total employment in noncollege teaching positions is projected to increase by nearly 30%; for college teaching positions, the projected increase is 18%.

Behind this growth is an increase in the number of school-age children and a mounting demand for qualitative improvement in education. Experienced teachers are now in such demand in San Francisco that the city is building federally subsidized apartments for teachers who can no longer afford Bay Area housing.[5] The push for quality shows in macro classroom numbers as well. From 1960 to 1995, the average student-teacher ratio in the U.S. dropped from 26.4 to 17.

Internationally, the growth of education as a job machine is poised for a spectacular takeoff. Student-teacher ratios in many developing countries are 60 or 70 to 1. Given the rising demand for education as well as projected demographic growth in these countries, just reducing the ratio to anywhere near the U.S. level would create millions of new jobs, with resulting increases in incomes and living standards.

The Health Care Boom Ahead

In coming decades, modern health care, now available to less than a quarter of humanity, will be another fast-growing service activity. Between 1980 and 1995, the number of people employed in the U.S. health care industry nearly doubled (from 5.3 million to 9.3 million). In the last 25 years of the 20th century, the ratio of nurses to population doubled.

Even after assuming the growth of computerized health care in the years ahead, demographic trends will fuel even faster increases in health care jobs. As the baby boom ages, average life expectancy will rise from 79 years to 84 for women and 74 to 80 years for men. The demand for assisted-care lodging and other geriatric medical services will increase rapidly. The biggest generation in our history will have the political clout to ensure that government policies and expenditures support this demand.

Once again, the potential growth of jobs in the developing world is more striking yet. The ratio of physicians to population in Western Europe is roughly 10 times as high as the ratio in India, 40 times as high as that in the Philippines, and 50 times as high as that in Bangladesh. Bringing those ratios up throughout the developing world will create millions of new jobs in the health care industry alone.

Achieving such phenomenal growth in education and health care jobs can be accomplished without the supply and demand limitations imposed by agriculture and industry. The key factor in the growth of these service industries—human resources—is available in great numbers in every developing country. Given the will, the technology to leverage that resource is readily available.

The Expanding Global Leisure Business

The tourism and hospitality industry is already among the largest sources of global employment, yet the scope for future expansion is enormous. Increasingly affluent societies, and particularly their healthy, wealthy retirees, will create new jobs relating to leisure, entertainment and travel.

Examples include more jobs in hotel, restaurant, resort and

club management; travel planners and tour guides; airline operations people; film and music production; golf course design and maintenance; live entertainment management; and sports management. In the U.S., employment in the entertainment and recreation industries has tripled since 1975. Employment in retail food-service establishments grew by 50% between 1980 and 1995.

Production Amid the Shift From Physical to Mental Technology: Four Priorities for Business

Expanding knowledge and service are overriding themes in the ongoing revolution in what is bought, sold and paid for around the world. One basic challenge for producers of goods and services today is to stay on top of the accelerating shift from physical to mental technology. This transformation changes the way producers must organize, as well as the requirements for recruiting, retaining and motivating a 21st-century workforce, that is, harnessing the energy of human resources. The chapters that follow will focus on organization, capital and people. This chapter, however, focuses on the implications of the change to mental technology on how companies produce, distribute, and sell products and services.

For every product the new question is, What knowledge or information does it convey, either inherently or indirectly? For every delivery system or channel—whether it is direct mail, an individual salesperson or the Internet—the key question is no longer just what product will we deliver, when and at what cost, but also how can we provide better, faster, more complete service to support that product?

Given the magnitude of these changes, every product or service development and marketing team must ask four basic questions:

1. **Have we rethought our definition of value?** If we are delivering a product with no distinction except price, we have become a commodity producer, the toughest possible position to

defend in a market in which pricing is becoming increasingly transparent. We need to ask, What else, beyond the product itself, does the customer consider of value?

2. **How can we add more "intangible" value to our product or service?**

3. **In building quality into our product or service, are we keeping up with—or better yet anticipating—customer expectations?**

4. **How well do our products, services and production systems reflect the accelerating shift from physical to mental technology?**

The remainder of this chapter discusses how a few representative companies are answering these questions today.

Rethinking Your Definition of Value

Michael Dell, founder of Dell Computers, says we are all now redefining value. "There used to be value around inventory; now there's value around information." Dell's point is that many businesses still tie up large amounts of their assets in inventory to ensure that they can handle a rush order from a key customer. Traditionally, they considered those huge inventory costs as a business necessity or perhaps even as a competitive advantage in dealing with customers. Also, large inventory surpluses were often the result of inefficiencies in the production processes. With today's more transparent pricing, however, customers see no reason pay for inefficiency or for the costs of financing, producing and storing all that surplus inventory. That leaves the supplier with higher costs and lower profit margins.

Dell operates with six days' worth of inventory, compared with about 60 days for its competitors. That practice translates into faster service for customers, because Dell has used more effective information to narrow the gap between what the customer wants today and what is on hand at the moment to fill the order.

Dell is able to control its inventory by using information technology to stay in close touch with suppliers who provide its components. Technology enables the whole Dell production system, including suppliers, to operate in "real time" rather than the older model "planned time," represented by stacks of inventoried component parts waiting for orders to come in. Also, because the value of computer components declines over time, Dell does not have to charge the customer for parts purchased earlier at higher costs.

The new principle, says Michael Dell, is "an inverse correlation between the quality of the information you have and the amount of inventory you need." That is, the higher the quality of the information you have, the less inventory you need. Too many businesses still tie up assets anticipating things that may not actually happen, says Michael Dell. "If they had a system that was customer-demand driven, they would be much more efficient in their assets." Put another way, intellectual assets now trump physical assets. Not all physical businesses are thereby doomed, however, but any business that was originally built or predicated on physical assets must now reconsider its basis. Just being physically close to your customer is no longer an automatic advantage, for example. We will still go to nearby restaurants we like for a good eating or social experience. However, five years from now, how many of us will stand in line at a drugstore to buy embarrassing items?

If you are going to continue in a physical business, says Michael Dell, "you've got to deliver something that is more valuable than can be delivered online."[6]

'A Fundamental Rethinking of the Nature of Disease'

Rethinking value can prompt a company to reinvent itself and create a new vision of its future. That's been a continuing theme at Medtronic, Inc., the Minneapolis company Earl E. Bakken and his brother-in-law founded in Earl's garage in the mid 1950s. The company began by repairing medical electronic equipment for hospitals and research labs. The first month's sales were $8. Then, in 1957, Earl patented the first wearable external heart pacemaker. Two years later, the company helped develop the first implantable pacemakers.

By the mid 1990s, Medtronic was selling nearly $2 billion worth a year of a product line built on pacing technology, but including other types of medical devices. By the end of 1999, the company had sales of $5 billion, and its 24,000 employees served physicians and patients in 120 countries.

In January 2000, Medtronics chairman and CEO Bill George announced a "new vision for Medtronic." By 2010, he said, Medtronic aims to become "the world's leading medical technology company, providing lifelong solutions for people with chronic diseases." The new Medtronic strategy clearly grows out of trends discussed in this book: rapid technological change, aging populations, rising expectations for a better life, a better-educated public, and international opportunities.

The source of that new-found power for patients? Abundant information via the Internet and the expectation that people will have greater influence in managing their health.

Focusing on how such changes would affect Medtronic's future persuaded the company's leaders to redirect its product strategy. Today, George explains, "Medtronic products treat patients in relatively late-stage disease . . . as a series of acute events." With its new focus, Medtronic will provide products for more holistic treatments "from wellness through diagnosis to the treatment of advanced disease."

Medtronic Vision 2010 is based on the premise that health care in the new century "will be radically transformed by the rising power of the patient and the consumer." The source of that new-found power? Abundant information via the Internet and the expectation that people will have greater influence in managing their own health. Already health care information sites are among the Internet sites most frequently visited on the Internet.

One way that Medtronic will seek to capitalize on this change is by enhancing the "direct connectivity" between patients with chronic disease and their specialists. Medtronic is joining Microsoft and IBM in a project to connect patients at home with cardiac physicians' offices around the world via a secure Internet connection. As now envisioned, a monitor-transmitter would download information from a patient's cardiac device even while he or she slept at home. In effect, the system would provide a house call over the Internet.

What's required, says George, "is a fundamental rethinking of the nature of disease itself and the organization of health care to address the diseases that are prevalent today...." Today's primary-care system is well equipped to handle a wide variety of acute diseases, but the system is not nearly effective enough in disease prevention, especially in addressing the needs of the whole person—body, mind, heart and spirit.

The next real revolution is neither genetic therapy nor bioscience, important as they will be, George insists. What will most shape the future of healthcare—and Medtronic— is *empowerment of the patient*.[7] By focusing on the changing expectations of patients, Medtronic is redefining the value it provides to its customers.

Adding 'Intangibles' to Your Product or Service

Politicians lament the declining importance of manufacturing jobs in our economy. Businesspeople, however, should understand this decline as the inevitable and healthy result of economic development. We don't complain today that 3% of the American workforce can produce all the food we need and then some. Americans in the future won't look back with nostalgia to a time when most of our working people were employed as manual workers in factories.

"Every offer [of service] has both a tangible and intangible economic value," according to consultants Stan Davis and Christopher Meyer of Ernst & Young's Center for Business Innovation.[8] For example, the tangible value of that high-end multimedia entertainment center you purchased from a specialty audio-video dealer is the physical entertainment center itself. The intangible value consists of the service and information provided by the technicians who came to your house to set it up in exactly the right place for the best possible performance. You might have received the same tangible value by purchasing the same or similar entertainment center from a large super store, but you probably would not have received the intangible value. You would most likely have had to put the pieces of the entertainment center in the back of your car at the store's loading dock and have had to try to figure out the instructions for putting it together from the manual at home. The key question for any supplier today is how to identify and deliver an intangible value that will win customers while still selling at a competitive price.

Davis and Meyer see a "meltdown of all traditional boundaries," in which products and services are merging. They note that product cycles are a fraction of what they used to be because of rapid obsolescence through advances in technology. When selling the same product to the same customer every six months, the consultants ask, doesn't the business begin to qualify as a service business? For example, computer software updates are now delivered over the Web ready for customers to download. By traditional definitions, is that a product or a service?

"The intangible portion of the economy has grown quietly, altering how we see the world without calling too much attention to itself," Davis and Meyer continue. In their book *Blur: The Speed of Change in the Connected Economy*, they note that intangibles now appear in four forms:

1. **Services,** which have dominated the economy for decades, are the most familiar. They include everything from barbers to brain surgeons.

2. **Information,** including specialized knowledge in databases about customers' likes and dislikes as well as comparative information on how to get the best price for that appliance you are thinking of buying.

3. **The service component of products,** which includes after-sale service and the opportunity to create the product you want through computer simulation.

4. **Emotions,** the intangible that Davis and Meyer define as "the trust and loyalty that people feel for a brand, the prestige conveyed by a label, the attraction exerted by a celebrity. . ." endorsement of a product.[9]

IBM Shifts to Services

This intangible portion of the economy is now growing much

faster than the market for physical products. Throughout the 1990s, companies were repositioning the value they offer to their customers to respond to this change. A cornerstone of IBM's remarkable recovery is its emergence as the world's largest provider of information technology (IT) services, rather than primarily as a manufacturer of office products.

In 1999, IBM's customers bought new IT service contracts worth more than $38 billion. Meanwhile, Big Blue's backlog of IT service engagements (work the company will do and be paid for in 2000 and into the future) grew by 18%, to more than $60 billion. In 1999, IBM's revenue in e-business services alone increased by 60%,

The key question for any supplier today? How to identify and deliver an intangible value that will win customers while still selling at a competitive price.

to more than $3 billion.[10] IBM's service business has evolved from consulting with customers about which computers and software to purchase, to advising corporate clients on how to establish and maintain their e-commerce businesses.

Alliances are a major part of IBM's strategy to expand its reach into information technology services. In June 2000, the company signed deals with eight Internet consulting companies to provide technology and support for businesses building wireless Internet services for mobile e-commerce.[11]

Home Depot's Personalized Strategy

Home Depot, a retailer of products for building contractors and the do-it-yourself market, recently added a service component to its sales strategy. Small contractors, who are Home Depot's most valuable customers, now get a password to log on to a site full of valuable information and solutions. For example, when builders enter details of their jobs, the Web site tells them what materials they need, how to schedule the work and what difficulties they may encounter.[12]

The company even offers loans for up to 10 years to help customers pay for its goods. Starting in the fall of 2000, credit lines from $3,000 to $30,000 were available in all 900 Home Depot stores in the U.S.

Services Take Off at GE Aircraft Engines

Adding services can sometimes help a company overcome business setbacks in traditional products. GE Aircraft Engines decided to enter the service business in the early 1990s amid cutbacks in defense spending and a recession that hurt commercial customers. Pressure mounted as some commercial airlines filed for bankruptcy. Surviving airlines wanted more value and longer life from the engines they had already purchased.

Welch's initiative turned the company away from the "wrench-turning game" toward providing services to help customers become more productive.

The push to services accelerated in 1995 when GE's CEO Jack Welch urged all senior executives to optimize their service potential. Before then, product development was the main job of GE's huge corps of engineers and scientists. According to CEO Jack Welch: "The best and brightest of these wanted to work on the highest-thrust jet engine, the fastest medical scan or the leading-edge electrical turbine design. Product services consisted of less exciting maintenance of our high-value machines—turbines, engines, medical devices and the like."

Welch's initiative turned the company away from the "wrench-turning game" toward providing services to help customers become more productive. In 1995, when the initiative was launched, GE derived $8 billion a year in product service revenues. In 2000, the figure was projected at $17 billion.[13]

Selling Convenience

Convenience is another popular intangible. We are all pressed for time, and we favor those businesses that make it easier for us to buy. We also favor those that provide useful auxiliary services, particularly services we find unpleasant. Today you can hire pet sitters, house sitters, party planners, closet organizers, yard workers, personal fitness trainers. The nation's largest maid service companies—Maid Brigade, Inc., in Atlanta; the Maids International in Omaha, Neb.; Molly Maid in Ann Arbor, Mich.; and Merry Maids in Memphis, Tenn.—are all expanding. "There is so much business out there, most of our [franchise] owners have waiting lists for customers," says Molly Maid President Linda Burzynski.[14]

Kodak has an online service called PhotoNet. Pay an extra few dollars when you drop off your film and the next day when you get your prints back, your photos will also be posted at the PhotoNet Web site. You can then download the images on your PC, send them to friends as e-mail attachments, or use them to decorate greeting cards, coffee mugs, T-shirts or other trinkets.

Traditional grocery chains were built on price and one-stop shopping. Now new e-retailers such as Peapod, Inc., or Grocer.com enable consumers to transfer themselves with a click to their favorite market's front door. These virtual stores usually promise delivery in 24 hours within a half-hour window. In providing this convenience, these entrepreneurial companies were following a clearly defined social trend. An *American Demographics* survey of the "top 10 most-dreaded chores" found that 65 percent of Americans strongly disliked grocery shopping.[15]

The Internet also offers traditional retailers new ways to feature a higher level of convenience. 1-800-Flowers was built on the convenience of placing same-day orders by phone for bouquets, gift baskets, plants, and balloon arrangements. The company created an interactive division as early as 1992. It established its presence on America Online in 1994, and created its own Web site the next year. 1-800-Flowers's online reminder service uses sophisticated technology to alert customers to upcoming birthdays and holidays.[16]

Bookseller Barnes & Noble is also using the Internet to make one of its established marketing tools more convenient for customers. For some years, the company has brought crowds to its stores by offering free author lectures. The company is now working with powered.com. to offer free Web-based courses to bring people to its site and encourage them to buy its books and other products.[17] Powered.com, formerly not.Harvard.com, was established in 1999 to create private-label universities for organizations seeking to attract more e-commerce customers.

Retail Imitates the Net

Meanwhile, retail life is aiming to imitate the 24-hour, seven-days-a-week Internet. In March 2000, 13 of Washington, D.C.'s Home Depot stores went round-the-clock. Also in the capital, seven of Kinko's eight photocopy stores are open day and night. Super Kmart stores also are staying open 24 hours. Some experts predict the coming of the 24-hour shopping centers. To be sure, there is a price to be paid for the round-the-clock lifestyle. "The big question becomes 'When does work end and play begin?' You feel like you are always on," says Cathy Rusinko, who teaches classes on management in the 21st century at Philadelphia University. "In one way or the other, I'm bemoaning all this," Rusinko told *The Washington Post,* "but on the other hand, when I want to go to Home Depot at 11 P.M., or the supermarket or Kinko's at midnight, I'm almost indignant if these places aren't open.[18]

Retail developers have also picked up signals from consumers that they want a speedy shopping experience, not the entertainment and browsing often associated with enclosed suburban malls. Drugstores are opening free-standing stores with drive-in windows in inner-city locations. Movie theaters, a key component of many enclosed malls, are choosing sites away from malls to build multiplex facilities offering tiered, stadium-type seating.

Developers will not sit still and watch their customers leave. To facilitate their customers' shopping, they will latch onto the "streetscape" trend that is already part of downtown revival and create new "suburban downtowns." Inward-facing malls built 20 to 30 years ago today typically house the clusters of big-box stores meant for browsing. With the new emphasis on convenience, these malls will be overhauled to provide more open air, new signage, and new entrances to let customers skip the whole mall experience and rush to their destinations quickly.[19]

To be sure, other developers are seeking to trump pure convenience by combining that value with another customer aspiration—bigger and better entertainment. In a state that boasts Mount Vernon, Monticello and a host of Civil War battlegrounds, Potomac Mills, situated in Prince William County, is quickly becoming Virginia's biggest tourist attraction. In

1999, the Mall attracted 24.3 million visitors, a third of them from more than 50 miles away. The same developer, Mills Corp., opened the $230 million Arundel Mills project near Baltimore in November 2000.

We want to be "so compelling that people would pay admission to get in," says Mills Corp. chairman Laurence C. Siegel. Among the attractions, Bass Pro Shops features fishing demonstrations in its huge fish tank. Sun & Ski Sports offers rock climbing. The Nascar "speedway" features simulators. A 24-screen movie complex evokes the early days of movie theatres. The mall provides a variety of food service—everything from fast-food restaurants to white-tablecloth establishments with outdoor dining.[20]

The Southwest Airlines Advantage

Southwest Airlines has sold convenience as a benefit to its customers since its maiden flight in 1971. The company introduced self-ticketing machines in 1979. By 1995, Southwest offered ticketless travel systemwide. The Southwest Rapid Rewards frequent-flyer system creates a competitive advantage by increasing the convenience of a benefit now offered by virtually all airlines. It awards points based on the number of trips taken, not miles flown. Award tickets are fully transferable—to anyone you choose. There are few blackout dates when ticket recipients can't use them. The program received the travel industry's 1998 "Best Award Redemption" for the ease of earning and using Rapid Rewards Tickets.

Keeping Up With—or Anticipating—Rising Expectations of Quality

In barely more than a decade, American consumers have compelled companies to shift from a search for excellence to the pursuit of perfection.

In a slower-paced, less-demanding world, keeping up with the competition was a serviceable standard. Today, as the race to better quality at lower cost enters a new dimension, the old target defines mediocrity.

Whereas the old business slogan was, "If it ain't broke, don't fix it," today's slogan should be, "If we ain't fixed it lately, it's liable to break." Thus, there remains a role for continuous improvement programs such as "Kaisan," a system originating in Japan that offers techniques for continuous incremental improvement of production processes in accordance with suggestions from front-line employees. Another program growing in importance is "ISO 9000," the international quality system that measures a company's adherence to specific procedures and standards. However, as pressure on margins increases, any system that defines quality strictly by conformity with standards established *inside* the company can no longer guarantee success in the marketplace or ensure an improvement on the bottom line. The old question was, Did we produce and deliver this product or service in conformity with our standards? Today's question is, Did we produce and deliver this product or service in conformity with the customer's expectations?"

The built-in limitation of most quality programs is that they focus too heavily on internal improvements, particularly improvements in making and delivering products and services. Customer expectations today go far beyond the effective delivery of a quality product. Too often, even good companies settle for 98% conformity to an internal production standard without realizing that the other 2% of performance is what really annoys the customer and reduces customer loyalty. That last 2% may be a four-hour delay in a delivery that an impatient customer awaited at home. It might be a delay in a follow-up service call to fix a small glitch in an expensive piece of machinery—a delay caused by a technician who neglected to bring the right part.

Companies like Motorola, GE, Honeywell and Polaroid have become strong proponents of a system known as Six Sigma. The goal of this management strategy goes beyond just improving quality. It aims to improve *profitability*, even though improved quality and efficiency are immediate by-products.

"Six Sigma is about asking tougher and tougher questions until we receive quantifiable answers that change behavior," according to Mikel Harry and Richard Schroeder. Harry is founder and CEO and Schroeder is president of the Six Sigma Academy, Inc., in Scottsdale, Ariz.[21] Sigma, taken from a letter in the Greek alphabet, is used in statistics as a measure of variation. Harry gave the name to the methodology he developed and helped deploy at Motorola in the late 1980s.

Companies undertaking Six Sigma relentlessly question every process, number, and step from design to delivery while aiming for a "Six Sigma performance target": 3.4 defects per million "opportunities."

Companies undertaking Six Sigma relentlessly question every process, number, and step from design to delivery while aiming for a so-called Six Sigma performance target: 3.4 defects per million "opportunities," which is quality-control language for the individual steps that go into producing and delivering a product or service. That's more than just an escalation of traditional quality standards. It's a whole new dimension. Consider: Achieving a performance level of 3.4 defects per million opportunities translates into products or services that are 99.9999999% defect-free—or near perfection. By way of comparison, a product that is 97.7% perfect *still* allows for 308,538 defects per million opportunities.

In their book *Six Sigma: The Breakthrough Management Strategy Revolutionizing the World's Top Corporations* (Doubleday, 2000), Harry and Schroeder use this everyday example to illustrate the demands of the system:

If wall-to-wall carpet in a 1,500-square-foot home were cleaned to the three-sigma level, that would equal 66,800 defects per million opportunities, or about the level of quality provided by many typical companies. Looking at this three-sigma-level job on your carpet, you would see that about four square feet of carpet (the carpet under your average-size recliner chair) would still be soiled. In other words, a three-sigma level would lead to a good number of disgruntled customers. If that same carpet were cleaned to the Six-Sigma level, the soiled area would be the size of a pinhead—virtually invisible."[22]

Today's demanding customers are satisfied only when they receive the near-perfect value they expect. When an organization reaches the Six-Sigma level, it can be 99.99966% confident that it is delivering a product or service that meets the customer's expectations.

GE and Six Sigma

GE CEO Jack Welch, no particular fan of other quality programs, fully embraced Six Sigma starting in 1996. Since then, the company has applied the system to most aspects of its business—designing, producing and delivering products as well as billing and other follow-up interactions with customers. The system's heavy emphasis on defining customer expectations has reduced costs while lifting quality throughout GE.

"We quickly moved from complaints to chocolates and praise," said one GE Capital executive.

The system has been particularly helpful as the company has moved into more Web-based applications. For example, GE Appliances in 1999 decided to set up a Web-based system to arrange delivery of GE products to people who bought them at Home Depot. Intuition suggested that customers would put a high value on having their new appliances delivered within 24 hours. However, Six Sigma focus groups showed that customers assigned little value to this fast delivery.

"Six Sigma eliminated any perceived need for evening deliveries, next-day deliveries, Sunday deliveries, all sorts of costly things we had wrongly thought would be important to customers," says Michael P. Delain, GE Appliances quality manager for local delivery service. Instead, the company learned that as long as delivery took place within the promised time window, customers cared most about how they were treated by installers and delivery people. That discovery, in turn, led to training for installers and delivery personnel on people skills.[23]

GE estimated that the quality gap between where it started in 1996—at about three sigma—and Six Sigma was costing the company as astonishing $7 to $10 billion in profit every year. That figure was the estimated cost of quality errors inside the company resulting in scrap, reworking of parts, correction of transactional errors, inefficiencies and lost productivity. GE went at the task with typical energy, commitment and cash. In 1997 alone, the company trained some 60,000 people—more than a quarter of its workforce—in the new system. By 1998, GE had invested $500 million, but that cost had already been offset by more than $750 million in savings.[24]

Service companies can learn from the experiences of early Six Sigma adopters like GE. One division of GE Capital kept trying to improve its response time to queries from institutional clients seeking information about the company's annuities services. It answered some queries in less than a day, or even within a couple of minutes, but it took as long as 65 days to respond to others. Division officials wanted to accelerate the response time to a satisfactory level for *all* customers, regardless of the nature of the question. In barely four months, Six Sigma teams pushed the response time to 24 hours or less for all queries. "We quickly moved from complaints to chocolates and praise," said one GE Capital executive. The chocolates came from one of the division's previously most critical customers.[25]

Six Sigma and Smaller Companies

For the moment Six Sigma programs are mostly the province of larger manufacturing companies in the U.S., but in view of the program's success to date, that situation will surely change. A report in the *Toronto Globe and Mail* predicts that companies around the world "will be falling over themselves to adopt GE-style Six Sigma" because of the improvement in profits for companies that have adopted this system.

Small to mid-size companies supplying Six Sigma giants will also be under increased pressure to adopt the system or lose their contracts, because their customers will depend on the total quality of parts provided by the suppliers. As for smaller companies that insist they are too small for Six Sigma, Harry and Schroeder respond that carrying out a Six Sigma project in a large company usually consists of a series of smaller projects within individual divisions that are similar in many respects to smaller stand-alone companies of similar size.[26]

Scaling Up From Physical to Mental Technologies

I n mid 1999, IBM CEO Lou Gerstner described the new dot-com companies as "fireflies before the storm—all stirred up, throwing off sparks." However, he continued: "The storm that's arriving—the real disturbance in the force— is when thousands and thousands of institutions that exist today seize the power of this global computing and communications infrastructure and use it to transform themselves. That's the real revolution."

That revolution is now shifting into high gear, and it is forever changing the way companies, particularly large companies, buy, sell and account for products and services. Some examples:

CISCO'S use of the Web has shortened the time needed to close its quarterly books from 10 days four years ago to 1 day now. Financial data that used to take weeks to gather and verify is now collected automatically as a part of everyday business.[27]

HEWLETT-PACKARD saved $75 million when it moved some personnel functions onto an internal Web site. The company's in-house tech team uses an HP-built "agent" to keep tabs on where human resources are needed.[28]

MERCK & CO. has shown how a giant company can use Web friendly corporate infrastructure to elbow aside an Internet start-up. The company's Merck-Medco unit runs a large mail-order pharmacy network and administers drug benefit plans for 60 million workers. Today, says *Forbes Magazine,* Medco is "clobbering the competition. Every week it processes 80,000 online prescriptions, raking in $8.5 million in revenues—about what PlanetRx.com sells in a quarter."[29]

SUN MICROSYSTEMS needs about 6,000 new hires a year to support its rapidly expanding sales, product development and support efforts. Sun recruiters are searching in a talent pool where competition is particularly intense. Sun lists openings on its internal intranet and uses bonuses to encourage employees to suggest candidates. In 1999, about 41% of new hires started with referrals from current workers. Sun's home page features a helpful resume builder for job seekers. Those prospects unwilling to submit a resume can simply register with an online matchmaker service called the Sun Agent. Sun Agent will then alert job seekers when a suitable job becomes available.[30]

Now that the early excitement about "e-tailing" has cooled somewhat, the power of the Internet to market business products and services has come more sharply into focus. Some 72% of Internet trading in 1999 was business-to-business (or B-to-B), a figure that is projected to increase to 87% in 2003, according to International Data Corp. A report by the Commerce Department, "The Emerging Digital Economy II," notes, "By 2006 almost half of the U.S. workforce will be employed by industries that are either major producers or intensive users of information technology products and services."

The Third Stage of Net Evolution

In May 1999, Intel's Andy Grove made a statement that in two sentences captures the next stage of Internet evolution. "In five years time there won't be any 'Internet companies.' All companies will be Internet companies."

The Internet is now rapidly evolving into a third stage of evolution, according to a report by the investment banking and trading firm Bear Stearns. The first stage was the Internet's creation by the Department of Defense. The second stage—its infancy—was its commercialization by companies like Amazon.com and Yahoo. The current stage is widespread deployment among leading corporations everywhere. "Beyond that stage," says Bear Stearns, "will be its deployment in virtually every commercial organization in America.[31]

That rapid deployment will include the use of sophisticated new personal digital assistants (PDAs), which are quickly becoming as necessary as pagers and cell phones in the business world. These PDAs (also mentioned in the previous chapter) will undergo radical advances in form and function over the next few years. Prices are falling so fast that technology budgets—and individual wallets—will not be greatly strained by the cost of purchases, upgrades or replacements.

Today's PDA is a small, palm-sized computer useful for storing appointments, phone numbers, notes and other data. It often has rudimentary word processing, spreadsheet and database capabilities. Many PDAs use wired and wireless modems to share information from either the Internet or company intranets. However, despite their reduced costs and handy size, PDAs still lack the sophistication of notebook computers.

Already, personal digital assistants are becoming an integral element in the business strategy to create "enterprise networks."

Already, PDAs are moving beyond electronic substitutes for jotting notes on paper. They are becoming an integral element in the business strategy to create "enterprise networks." Sophisticated enterprise software applications from Oracle, SAP and others can now tie together an entire corporation's information sources and then distribute them over the Internet or company intranets. PDAs increasingly will tap into these enterprise networks via wired and wireless links, thus allowing employees outside the office to retrieve and share data, track billings and expenses, and coordinate their schedules.[32]

It's More Than Information Technology

While information technology captures the imagination—and the headlines—other aspects of the technology revolution will have a major impact on how business produces products and services.

Maytag, for example, is using advanced technology to create a value-added sale. In the early 1990s, the company began building newly designed, more expensive washing machines, refrigerators and vacuum cleaners that used new technology and carried fancy features that helped them stand out in the crowd. It was a risk to market premium-priced machines in a market that views such products as a commodity.

However, rather than turning consumers off, Maytag's products were an innovative hit—and sales took off. In 1998, the Iowa-based company posted the best showing of its 106-year history, as sales rose 19% to $4.1 billion and net income climbed 56% to $281 million. In adopting this approach, Maytag was returning to a value that made its brands popular many decades ago—selling an innovative product for which the company could charge extra money.[33]

Here Come the Mechanical Men

Amid excitement about information technology, we don't hear much about robotics these days. Yet robots represent another fast-moving mental and technological process that has the potential to change the way we do business in the next decade.

Japan took an early lead in this technology. Some experts speculate that progress in the West has been slowed by an ancient distrust of manufactured men. After all, Frankenstein started out to be an ideal man and ended up a terrifying villain. However, economics represents a more likely root cause. The worker shortage reached critical proportions in Japan far earlier than in the West.

Whatever the reason, in 1997, Japan used 277 robots for every 10,000 people working on manufacturing lines, according to the International Federation of Robotics in Geneva, Switzerland. In the U.S. the proportion was just 50 robots for every 10,000 people.[34]

A Japanese consortium has already produced "3P," a life-like robot that can walk, wave, shake hands, go up and down stairs, and pick things up. Members of the consortium—Panasonic, Mitsubishi, Hitachi, Honda and several leading universities—plan to hook the 3P to powerful fiber-optic networks controlled from a central location. That will change robotics forever. Each robot can be freed of its own internal super computer, enabling it to be smaller, lighter and cheaper.[35]

The New Materials Frontier

Technology is not only driving how products are manufactured and delivered, but it is changing what raw materials are used to make them. "There is no simple product today—

whether made of metal, wood, glass, concrete, plastic or any other substance—that will not be made from some entirely different material 20 years from now," says Knight Kiplinger, editor-in-chief, *The Kiplinger Letter* and Kiplingerforecasts.com.

Researchers working with advanced technology are aiming to design and build new materials, molecule by molecule. Using computers, the researchers are extending the boundaries of materials science into new fields such as "computational chemistry"—the use of computers in the analysis of chemicals. Also on the technology frontier is "molecular nanotechnology," the effort to manufacture complex devices inexpensively by controlling the arrangement of individual atoms that make up that device. The possibility of maneuvering things atom by atom is expected to materialize in 15 to 30 years. If so, it will revolutionize not only manufactured products but the processes used to make them.

As these new sciences mature, manufacturers will custom-order precisely the materials they need from chemical companies, which will custom-build the materials for just the right combination of characteristics—flexibility, resistance to heat or corrosion, or enormous strength with minimal weight.

Find that difficult to believe? Forty years ago, says Kiplinger, people could hardly envision tennis rackets made of plastic and carbon fibers, stovetops made of glass, golf clubs made of titanium, synthetic lumber extruded from a hot dough of hardwood sawdust, and grocery bags formed from shredded polyethylene. Yet all these products exist today.[36]

Summary and Conclusions

We are living in an era of convergence. Markets are converging. Distinctions among market distribution channels are more arbitrary. Products and services are no longer separate, but integrated, categories. Global competition turns once impregnable brands into commodities that increasingly sell on price rather than collecting a premium for their name recognition.

Yet for product and service champions there remain basic

principles that must always be observed and regularly addressed. The old product manager strategy sounded like the sheriff in a 1940s western movie: "They went thataway." In this late and sometimes lamented model, the product and service people studied the demographics, listened to the focus groups, watched the competitors, and hired marketing gurus to interpret the changing landscape. Then, after long—usually too long—deliberation, they followed the customer, and frequently the competition, "thataway" by introducing a "new and improved" product or tweaking an old service.

Today's model might also be compared to another, more proactive, sheriff in the old westerns: "Head 'em off at the pass." The key to today's product and service success lies in *anticipating* customer aspirations earlier than the competition does.

In a world of upheaval, how can one possibly anticipate something as apparently fickle as customer aspirations? To answer that question, look at the fundamentals stressed in this book and, specifically, in this chapter:

■ **Customers are smarter today and will be even smarter tomorrow.**
■ **Customers have increasingly efficient tools to search for lower prices.**
■ **Customers want to be treated like individuals.**

As a result, you should:

■ **Add information to your product.**
■ **Use technology to cut your service costs.**
■ **Use technology to customize your service through better, more exact information.**

Keeping up with rising customer aspirations requires *externally* focused quality programs. Internal standards are useful as long as they mirror what the customer wants today. Too often they reflect a management bias toward what is easily measurable rather than the emerging "intangibles" that may be more important to customers.

"Six Sigma" is justifiably the rage today. This program carries the quality crusade to new levels of exactness. However, its biggest strength—and one that can be usefully adopted by any company—is its absolute insistence on determining first what really matters to the customer. From then on, the challenge is to align the measurements of performance with the customer's rising expectations: For faster service, for more complete service, for customized products, for better, more complete information, for convenience, for entertainment.

Yes, following this advice is hard, but it will get harder still, because the pace of aspiration is not slowing down. But there has never been a time when the rewards for success have been higher, or when the tools for achieving that success have been more readily available.

Toward "Uncentralized" Organizations

KEY CHAPTER THEMES

- *Organization: Humanity's greatest invention*

- *Converting human energy into performance*

- *Rethinking organization—five issues to consider:*
  1. Keeping pace with growth
  2. Adapting to new technology
  3. Designing for "uncentralized" thinking
  4. Adjusting to economic convergence
  5. Moving toward a global perspective

"None of us is as smart as all of us."
—WARREN BENNIS, AUTHOR, CHAIRMAN OF UNIVERSITY OF
SOUTHERN CALIFORNIA LEADERSHIP INSTITUTE

"Real sustainable advantage comes...from
the way a company's activities fit together."
—MICHAEL PORTER, AUTHOR, AUTHORITY ON COMPETITIVE STRATEGY

T HE END OF THE 20TH CENTURY PROMPTED FRE-
quent debates about humanity's greatest inventions. The sextant permitted the sailing of
uncharted oceans, and the printing press opened
the doors for universal education. The steam
engine ushered in the Industrial Revolution. The electric light,
the locomotive, the auto, the telephone, the air conditioner, and
the computer all played revolutionary roles.

The practical application of all these inventions depended
on a far older innovation. Without *organization,* however, these
inventions would have been rendered useless. It is organization—the capacity to bring together the physical and mental
energy of humans and then combine that human energy with
technology—that translated each of these breakthroughs into
a boon for humanity. In a company, organization encompasses
the structures, systems, and networks of coordination and communication that the company uses to stay attuned to changes
in its market and to deliver the right products and services to
its customers at a profit.

Growth is impossible without organization. What is the difference between the CEO of a $1 million company and the
CEO of a $1 billion company? The latter is not 1,000 times
smarter or more experienced than the former. The difference
is organization. It is the power of organization that permits
individuals to extend their capacity to perform thousands of

actions simultaneously, to accomplish work that would be impossible for one person or a small group. Archimedes said that with a lever long enough and a fulcrum to rest it upon, he could lift the earth. At its best, organization approximates the power of such a lever.

Competitiveness depends on how effectively companies organize themselves: how well they assign and monitor the tasks and responsibilities they give to individual managers, workers and suppliers; how effectively they coordinate available technology and other resources; and how smoothly and quickly they respond to customers.

Converting Human Energy Into Performance

In all fields of life, we rely on organizations, and the structures and systems that compose them, to convert human energy into higher levels of achievement. Educational institutions seek to achieve the organization and distribution of knowledge. Hospitals seek the cure and prevention of disease. Business seeks greater productivity, profitability and growth. The greater the capacity of a company's organization to release and focus the creative energy of its leaders and staff on the work at hand, the greater the company's potential for sustained achievement.

Think of your company early on a Monday morning as a vast pool of raw human energy. How usefully that energy is channeled by your company's structure and systems will determine your success this week and every week.

You can determine the effectiveness of your organization by answering questions like these:

- **Does the structure of your company clearly define who is responsible for what, or**
- **Do people spend valuable time and energy duplicating their work or squabbling about responsibility?**
- **How often does your company waste human energy when the right system could accomplish the same task in far less time?** For example,

are there well-defined, current systems for hiring, for ordering supplies, for defining and monitoring work?

Think of some recent problems that slowed the pace of
achievement where you work. How many of them could have
been avoided either by a clearer definition of
authority or by well-defined systems and procedures? The Six Sigma quality system
(described in the last chapter), which demands
scrutiny of all processes and systems, has liter-
ally saved GE billions of dollars in wasted
scrap, rework and lost productivity. In
essence, Six Sigma has enabled GE to achieve
a higher level of organization throughout the
whole company, increasing productivity by
avoiding the waste of time. That is the true power of organization: It organizes and optimizes those most precious human
resources: time and energy.

> **The true power
> of organization?
> It organizes and
> optimizes those
> most precious
> human resources:
> time and energy.**

The Basis of All Creativity

Human energy is the basis of all creativity. It is the fuel
that feeds the fire of inspiration. Read the biographies
of great business leaders, especially leaders who created great enterprises in their lifetime, and you will invariably
find references to their boundless energy.

Few individuals have created as much wealth for the world
as Thomas A. Edison. An indomitable worker, Edison frequently went days on end with only short naps. He produced
the equivalent of one patentable invention every two weeks of
his life—1,100 in all—giving birth to entirely new industries,
including motion pictures, the phonograph and recordings,
and the electric and household appliance industries.

Edison's genius for practical industrial organization gave us
the research laboratory, where teams of experts are brought
together to solve complex scientific and industrial problems.
The General Electric Co., which Edison founded, is today the
world's most valuable corporation in terms of shareholder value.

Continued on page 154

BOX 7·1 Converting Corporate Energy to Profitability, Growth and Quality

For some years, I have collaborated with Garry Jacobs and Robert Macfarlane, the founders of the consulting firm Mira International. Together we have used the accompanying illustrations (Figures 7-1A and 7-1B, on pages 152–153) to help senior managers think through the strengths and limitations of their companies as converters of human energy.

Figure 7-1A pictures a perfectly functioning business model—the ideal. I rush to add that my consulting associates and I have never found any company this perfect.

Figure 7-1B shows a malfunctioning business model. This illustration in particular invariably produces an "ah-ha" from any executive audience.

RAW ENERGY. Taking apart the elements common to both illustrations, consider first the energy initially available to any company, indicated by the arrows at the top of the illustration. This is the sum of all human energy available to the organization. It can be compared with the energy of a roaring river—powerful and yet diffused and unfocused, impressive but of little use for any specific purpose.

DIRECTION. The second step—labeled direction in the illustrations—captures, moderates and redirects the flow of the energy.

In a company, that direction can be autocratic, damming up and even, if the dam is too high, providing a powerful repression of the force of the flowing energy. However, when direction is artfully constructed, in tune with the environment, it converts the raw, initial energy into a focused force.

ORGANIZATION. The third major element in both illustrations is organization, the primary focus of this chapter. Organization defines the structures, systems and networks of coordination and communication that a company uses to stay attuned to changes in its market and to deliver the right products and services to its customers at a profit.

An appropriately designed organization efficiently transforms the human energy channeled by direction into an alert responsiveness—responsiveness to changes in society, to shifting customer desires and requests, to information acquired by employees. Using the analogy of the raw energy in the raging river, if direction is the dam, organization is the combination of hydroelectric generators and transmission lines that convert and carry the energy channeled by the dam, transforming it into useable power.

Organization encompasses everything from the system used to recruit employees, to the process of product research and development, to the procedures used to convey information from the executive suite to the shop floor and back again. Organization includes the decision-making processes that determine what and how capital equipment is purchased, what acquisitions are appropriate, and how employees are evaluated and compensated.

Organization functions as a strong—or weak—link between all other basic components of a company: market, products and services, people and capital.

PEOPLE. The fourth element on our energy conversion and dispersion illustrations is labeled people, the theme of Chapter 9. Included within this element are all the knowledge, skills and attitudes of the human beings who sell, produce and account for, or support a company's goals and objectives.

From the point of view of energy conversion alone, this people element can be compared with the electricity lines and appliances within an individual house or office. It is the energy contained here that converts everything that has gone before into actions that produce productivity, profitability and growth. An energy drain here can be as devastating—and often far more immediately visible—than any drain in direction and organization.

DISPERSION: A FAILURE TO CONVERT ENERGY. When an organization fails in responsiveness, we seldom think of the whole process of energy conversion. Our attention focuses instantly on the last, most immediate step in the process. That's almost always a person, usually someone on the front line: The sales rep who did not have the right answer. The customer service rep who lost the order. The engineer who misread the specifications. The accountant who was late with figures.

Yet the root cause of any failure in responsiveness can occur anywhere in energy conversion, just as it can in an electric power failure. Lack of clarity in direction dissipates energy, pursuing the wrong goals. Faulty wiring in organization causes key systems to sputter and fail. Failure to train people or help them understand corporate goals produces late, inadequate or wrong decisions.

The CEO of a Fortune 100 Company once summarized succinctly for me how one should react to any failure in corporate responsiveness. "Never waste time asking who messed up," he insisted. "Always start by asking where did our system fail?" While this is seldom the instinctive response, it is the right question to convert any failure into higher levels of responsiveness.

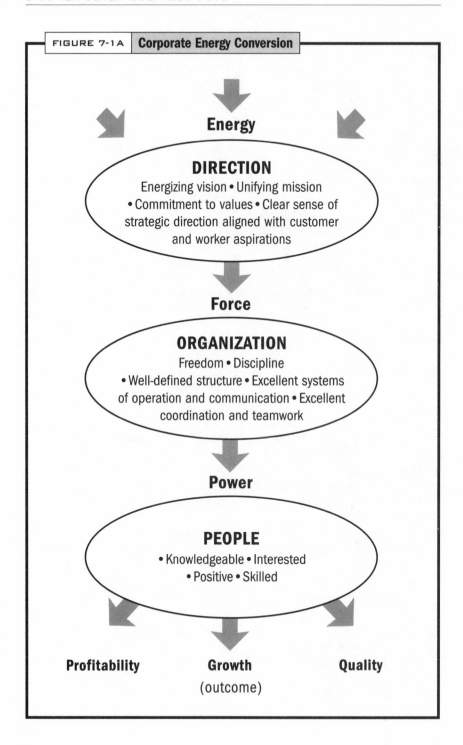

FIGURE 7-1A | **Corporate Energy Conversion**

Energy

DIRECTION
Energizing vision • Unifying mission
• Commitment to values • Clear sense of
strategic direction aligned with customer
and worker aspirations

Force

ORGANIZATION
Freedom • Discipline
• Well-defined structure • Excellent systems
of operation and communication • Excellent
coordination and teamwork

Power

PEOPLE
• Knowledgeable • Interested
• Positive • Skilled

Profitability   **Growth**   **Quality**
(outcome)

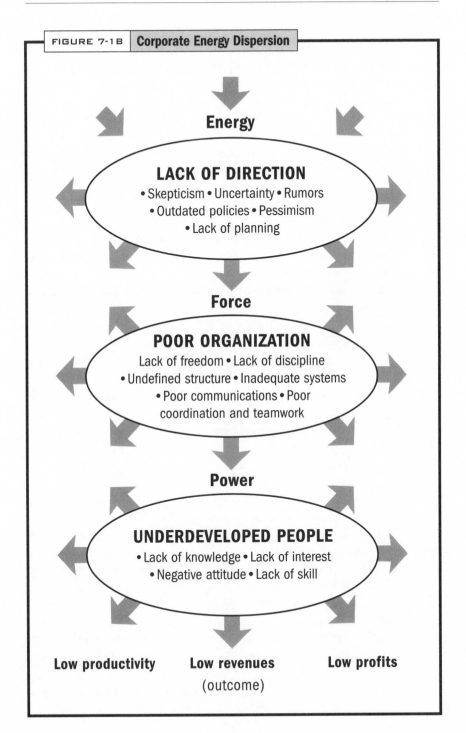

FIGURE 7-1B | **Corporate Energy Dispersion**

Energy

LACK OF DIRECTION
• Skepticism • Uncertainty • Rumors
• Outdated policies • Pessimism
• Lack of planning

Force

POOR ORGANIZATION
Lack of freedom • Lack of discipline
• Undefined structure • Inadequate systems
• Poor communications • Poor
coordination and teamwork

Power

UNDERDEVELOPED PEOPLE
• Lack of knowledge • Lack of interest
• Negative attitude • Lack of skill

Low productivity   Low revenues   Low profits
                          (outcome)

Edison's amazing physical and mental energy never flagged. When he was 60, *Cosmopolitan* magazine asked him to authorize a serialized autobiography. "When I go into senile decay I may consider the autobiographical scheme," Edison replied, "but as long as I can put in 18 hours daily, I don't want to waste time on it."

I don't expect to encounter many Thomas Edisons as I visit companies, but I always look for clues revealing the available level of human energy:

- **Do the layout and decor of the offices suggest that this is a place for purposeful work?**
- **Do people move briskly, with a sense of urgency?**
- **Does there seem to be an orderly flow of information and communication between people?**
- **Do the faces of people that I see in the hallways reveal a sense of confidence?**

Styles, of course, differ. Some companies are formal, some more relaxed. Some are quiet and others raucous. Geography matters, too. Travel in a single work week to an old-line southern bank, a midwestern metal-working company, and a high-tech Silicon Valley corporate headquarters, and you will feel the effects of different geographic and corporate cultures. But whatever the outward differences, successful companies invariably have a hum of human energy so palpable that you can almost hear it when you listen closely.

At Intel, I asked a senior executive what was the first thing he noticed when he came to the company. "Energy," he replied. "Energy is certainly one of the striking characteristics of this company and this industry." I heard a similar comment on a visit to a far older, East Coast–based pharmaceutical company, Merck: "There's an energy here," a senior executive told me. "Everybody feels it." Or as executive at Northwestern Mutual in Milwaukee put it, "There is "a kinetic energy that flows through all of us." What they feel is the power of the human energy available to the organization.

Feeling the potential of that power, of course, is not the same as converting it to achievement. (See the discussion and illustrations on pages 150-153.)

Organizations for Today:
Five Issues to Consider

There are at least five specific issues for business leaders to consider in designing or redesigning an organization that effectively channels human energy for achievement in today's marketplace. The balance of this chapter discusses these issues.

Organization Issue #1: Keeping Pace With Growth

The first challenge—an old one with a new urgency—is how to find ways to get the competitive payoff that comes with growth while preserving flexibility. In many respects bigger *is* better. A growing company has the resources—or can more easily get them—to launch more new products, attract more bright professionals, invest more in training or even acquire competitors.

By centralizing functions such as accounting, human resources or research, a growing company can develop the capacity to support a wider number of operating units. Company leaders can more easily divide work among specialists, bringing more focused expertise to every specific task. In theory at least, all these advantages add up to the once highly admired "economies of scale."

But bigger also has a price. Policies and procedures must be more uniform, often circumscribing creative thinking and action. Political negotiations among centers of power inside the corporation grow in complexity. Bigger traditionally means more hierarchy, which in turn slows decision-making, as approvals must move up the line two, three, or more levels.

Bigger is more likely to attract the attention of union organizers and activists who will seek to limit the company's flexibility in their areas of concern. Customers are often irate when workers, because of greater specialization, answer a request for information with an abrupt "that's not my job."

As a growing entrepreneurial company gets bigger, suddenly there's more to manage. Inventory that previously was handled in an informal, manual system begins to pile up. (The Dell system described in the previous chapter is still an exception among many rapidly growing companies.) The staff that used to work within the sound of the owner's voice have scattered to different buildings, perhaps in different parts of the world.

In the early days, the owner *was* the marketing department, as well as the customer service staff. Now, with more customers, extended markets and a more diversified product line, management of specialists has become a necessity and an added complication. The owner no longer decides how to coordinate marketing and production plans while driving to work; a geographically dispersed sales force must now communicate with the marketing department, the product line managers and the customer service people.

The growing adolescent company quickly captures the attention of outsiders—suppliers, regulators, venture capitalists, the media, perhaps even unions and Wall Street. This brings a host of new relationships to manage.

Growth and its attendant complexities are seen as a virtue, as the goal of any successful business enterprise.

DIMINISHING RETURNS SET IN. At a certain point, however, diminishing returns may set in. As the organization becomes more complex, important tasks sometimes misfire. Translating that innovative idea into a money-making application takes months rather than days, and the organization loses agility. Although its bigness is still valued, a certain envy develops for smaller, faster competitors—those tiny idea factories that seem to be having all the fun.

This decline after achieving bigness is not inevitable, but it is common. Already about half the companies on the Fortune 500 list of 1980 are gone. Some have been replaced on the 500 list by newer companies that are more attuned with the market, such as Microsoft. Others have been acquired by more successful giants and are now either entirely gone or live on as divisions of their more successful acquirers. RCA, for example, is part of GE.

An adaptable organization is a critical factor in successfully keeping up with the rigors of growth. Yesterday's structure and systems will creak and groan under the pressure of rapid expansion. Although most business leaders would agree in principle, many still take organization too much for granted when they make plans to expand product lines or enter new markets.

When working with business groups, I often ask them to identify the five most important components of their business. The first four always come quickly—market, product, people and capital. Then there is an uncomfortable pause. Only once in 15 years, after posing that question to dozens of groups of experienced business-people, have I ever gotten a spontaneous reply that identifies the fifth component—organization.

Many business leaders still take organization too much for granted when they make plans to expand product lines or enter new markets.

It is not that these business leaders are unaware of the importance of creating and continuing to develop an effective organization. They all devote considerable time trying to find better ways to organize their companies. Even so, they take organization so much for granted that they don't fully consider how its direct power to shape their success in the market is equal to the power generated by their products, their people or their available capital.

Yet, as many an entrepreneur has learned, an expanding market and a popular product, even combined with dedicated staff, are not enough to ensure success without effective organization, as the following example shows.

WHO IS STEERING THE SHIP? Lyle Bowlin's Internet bookstore business, based in Cedar Falls, Iowa, became an overnight media darling in 1999. But within a year, the company had closed, the victim mainly of inadequate organizational development even as its sales grew.

Two glowing op-ed columns in *The New York Times* and a *Time* magazine profile had featured Bowlin's Web site: www.Positively-You.com. He had appeared on Good Morning America and Fox News. He had received an advance for collaborating on Mom&Pop.com, a book of advice for other start-ups seeking to go online.

Before the media flurry, Bowlin had made a small profit for four months by keeping his expenses down. There was little organization. He answered each e-mail personally, and his wife packed and delivered the books. Most customers were in town, so she dropped the books off by car.

With the media attention, Positively-You's monthly orders shot up from $2,000 to $50,000 a month. Books began to pile up in the Bowlins' living room. TV crews knocked at the door. Their friends joined them after work to pack and ship books. They taught their children how to address labels.

As the business grew, more friends and relatives helped out as volunteers and paid staffers. Yet, as *The Wall Street Journal* notes, "with all those helping hands, it was unclear who was steering the ship." When the media flurry passed on, sales declined while margins stayed tight. In November 1999, the investors agreed to fill orders for Christmas and then shut down the site.[1]

As this entrepreneur learned, a business must *develop* as it increases its sales. Specifically, it must acquire or enhance the capacity of its organization—the structure, systems, and network of accountability that the company uses to create and deliver its products to customers.

There was plenty of human energy in Cedar Falls. A market wanted the product. Capital was available for promising dot-com businesses. What was missing was an organization to link the other components together in a pattern of sustained productivity, profit and growth.

It seems so obvious that it's all too easy to forget.

TERADYNE ADAPTS ITS ORGANIZATION TO THE PROJECT. Many of the new approaches to markets and products discussed in the previous two chapters will require major changes in organizational design. Trying to implement new directions in what is sold, to whom and how requires far more than tinkering with organization structures and systems. It requires rethinking organization patterns *simultaneously* with shifting direction in markets or products.

Teradyne Corporation, a $1.8 billion Boston company that dominates its market for making automated testing equipment used by electronics and telecom companies, illustrates how innovative organizational structures can be used to release human energy. In 1998, Teradyne introduced a tester, called Integra, based on a new, lower-cost technology.

To bring Integra to market, Teradyne's founder and chairman, Alex d'Arbeloff, established a novel governance structure. The project's leader, Marc Levine, reported not to a boss but to an internal board of directors. The internal executives, including current Teradyne CEO George Chamillard, operated like a venture capitalist board. They set guidelines and stayed clear of everyday operations.

Once the product was launched, Integra became a regular division of Teradyne. Levine gets his budget through the same process as everyone else. He has customers to serve, targets to meet, improvements to make.

Chamillard told *Fortune's* Thomas Stewart, "We could have given the project to a division, but they would never have put their best people on it." Integra's strategy—to start out producing lower-cost product for the low end of the market—was fundamentally different from what the rest of the company was doing and would have conflicted with the strategy of any division in which it was placed. The strategy of reporting to an internal board also allowed Levine to take technological risks without worrying about existing customers. As Stewart notes, "As business increases in speed and knowledge intensity, structures have to adapt too."[2]

Organization Issue #2: Adapting to New Technology

A second challenge in organizational design—another old one with new urgency—is to keep up with the evolution of technology. For example, keeping up with major technological change often requires not just an organizational redesign but a whole new concept—or central organizing idea—of how a business affected by that change should operate.

Since the mid-19th century, people had been sending messages over wires in Morse code. Then, in 1901, Gugliemo Marconi successfully completed the first transatlantic wireless transmission. Pioneers like David Sarnoff, who was to lead RCA for 40 years, saw the entertainment potential of using the new medium as a "household utility" to send entertainment into homes. By the early 1920s, radio stations were growing like dot-coms, from 30 in 1922 to 556 in 1923.

All that was lacking was the right concept to turn the new medium into a money-maker. Then in August 1922, WEAF, a New York station owned by AT&T, aired a real estate ad, and advertiser-supported commercial radio was born.[3]

> **The challenge: to determine how technology will necessitate redesigning the structure and systems of companies to align with their industry's new business concepts.**

Thomas Edison's original business concept for electricity required customers to pay a flat fee to connect with the network, much like today's model for Internet access. But Edison soon realized that the dramatic difference in wealth and usage between his first customer—the J.P. Morgan Bank—and his subsequent small-business customers required a more flexible concept. So he invented a device to measure electricity use, charged accordingly and created the concept of a public utility business.[4]

GROPING FOR NEW BUSINESS CONCEPTS. Today, *Forbes* notes, much of the experimentation on the Net involves the same groping for new business concepts to accommodate the distinct characteristics of the new technology. Entrepreneurs experiment with revenue-making ideas such as subscriptions, advertisements, banners, links, licensing and auctions. Investors wait to see whether enough people buy. When the right concept emerges, companies, indeed whole industries, will be organized around it.[5]

RENEWING AN OLD SEARCH. Business everywhere, on the Net and off, is now engaged in a widespread search to find new business organizational concepts. This search is not new, however. As Peter Drucker observes: "For more than a century the study of organization has rested on one assumption: 'There is—or there must be—one right organization.' What is presented as the 'one right organization' has changed more than once. But the search for the one right organization has continued and continues today."[6]

The challenge here—not just for high-tech companies, but for all businesses—is to determine how information-age technology will necessitate redesigning the structure and systems of their individual companies to align with their industry's new business concepts.

Industries that propose to shift a major portion of their sales to the Internet, for example, will have to reorganize their sales forces. This change is already quite visible in companies in the financial services industry. Companies like Merrill Lynch and American Express Financial Advisors, for example, are reorganizing their sales distribution channels by separating "high-end" clients who still want—and are willing to pay for—personal relationships with sales reps from a more mass-market distribution channel that wants to buy at a cheaper price largely over the Net.

Organizational Issue #3: Designing for Uncentralized Thinking

Traditional organization structure was based on command-and-control authority—a top-down flow of information and decision-making modeled on the military. The information age makes that structure increasingly obsolete. Responsiveness to customers requires faster action, not layers of approval. The technology permits this change, but patterns of thinking still lag in many companies.

Information technology's power to move information at high speeds is, of course, one reason for the massive layoffs in major corporations in 1980s and 1990s. Middle managers whose primary purpose was relaying information up and down the hierarchy were suddenly gone, their function replaced by networked computers moving information faster and often more accurately than human beings.

A PREMIUM ON SELF-DISCIPLINE. If the traditional business organization resembles a military battalion, the information-driven organization more closely resembles a symphony orchestra.

"All instruments play the same score" in the orchestra, Peter Drucker notes, "but each plays a different part. They play together, but they rarely play in unison. There are more violins but the first violin is not the boss of the horns; indeed the first violin is not even the boss of the other violins. And the same orchestra can, within the short span of an evening, play five pieces of music, each completely different in style, its scoring, and its solo instruments."[7]

There is at least one important difference between an orchestra and a business, however. In the orchestra, the score is given in advance to both players and conductor. In business, Drucker adds, "the score is being written as it is being played." That puts a premium on self-discipline at every level of the business, as well as on clearly defined expectations and operating values for every job.

As was discussed in the two previous chapters, work is steadily becoming more mental, less physical. Information-age technology is accelerating this trend. As a result, an ever-increasing number of people will work as professional specialists—market researchers, editors or computer programmers. Organizational discipline among a group of professional specialists can no longer rely primarily on financial controls, which were the major form of discipline in the command-and-control business structure. Instead, following Drucker's orchestra analogy, organizations will evolve toward discipline that depends more on shared values, open communication, and clearly understood responsibilities. With these self-discipline tools in place, the "soloists" can play in unison and harmony.

For example, by the end of 2000, about 75 companies had already created "chief privacy officers," a new, high-profile position that didn't exist two years earlier. The number of these positions is expected to grow as large corporations seek to allay the fears of consumers about privacy issues. According to a study by the consulting firm Fiderus, about one-third of Americans still say that concerns about privacy prevent them from shopping online.[8]

Coordinating the new flow of information to and from these privacy watchdogs cannot easily be left to traditional command-and-control structures. For these positions to succeed, responses to customer concerns will have to be fast, while delegation of authority to fix problems will have to fly through and around the older hierarchical structure. That will require redesigning structures and responsibilities with new flows of information to cope with the new challenge of privacy.

TOWARD THE *UNCENTRALIZED* ORGANIZATION. All this rethinking about organizational concepts and structures may be leading us toward what some experts call the "self-organizing" or "uncentralized" organization.

In the early 1990s, the "self-organizing system" was a remote idea, discussed in fairly theoretical terms. By 2000, however, self-organization was "rapidly becoming a very hot idea," according to Bernard Wysocki Jr. in *The Wall Street Journal.*

The essence of the concept: Top-down planning has ceased to be the only way, or even the best way, to build something big and lasting. Notes Wysocki, "Unorganized assemblies of people can create everything from marketplaces to computer systems almost spontaneously, on the fly, from the bottom up."

To illustrate the concept, Wysocki compares the organizing principles of Microsoft's Windows platform and the Linux operating system. Microsoft employs an army of programmers who churn out proprietary code while on the company payroll. Linux is an evolving collaboration of thousands of software writers around the globe. "The brains behind Linux programming exist not within the walls of any company but inside the heads of people who amount to volunteers," says Wysocki.

The self-organizing system seems made for the Internet culture. As Wysocki says, the concept "doesn't respect traditional hierarchies. It brings in expertise from the edges of the networks." To proponents of self-organizing as a business model, these advantages can be profound and commercially powerful."[9]

DECENTRALIZATION: NOT A TRUE ALTERNATIVE. Internet technology has brought self-organizing to the forefront, but the management concepts behind self-organizing systems have been gaining ground for years. For most of the past century, says Harlan Cleveland, "the search has been on for alternatives to centralization." Cleveland says the obvious candidate—decentralization—is not a true alternative.

In one version or another, decentralization has been a popular management concept since GM's Alfred Sloan set up quasi-autonomous business units in the 1920s to produce and sell cars to different market segments under the brand names Chevrolet, Pontiac, Oldsmobile, Buick and Cadillac. The strategy was a brilliant success. Anyone who bought $25,000 of GM common stock in 1921 was a millionaire by 1929, when GM was earning the then-astronomical profits of $200 million a year.

But Cleveland believes that decentralization is an unsatisfactory alternative to centralization, because the former keeps control centralized even while subdividing and parceling out the work to be done.

Cleveland deftly mixes long reflection on leadership issues with decades of practical experience. He is author or co-author of a dozen books on executive leadership and international affairs. He has served as a UN relief executive, Assistant Secretary of State, U.S. Ambassador to NATO, president of the University of Hawaii and president of the World Academy of Art and Science.

NO MORE PYRAMIDS. The opposite of centralization, Cleveland insists, is not decentralization but *uncentralization*. As early as 1972, in his book *The Future Executive,* Cleveland foresaw that organizations that get things done in the future "will no longer be hierarchical pyramids with most of the real control at the top. They will be systems—interlaced webs of tension in which control is loose, power diffused, and centers of decision plural. 'Decision-making' will become an increasingly intricate process of multilateral brokerage both inside and outside the organization which thinks it has the responsibility for making, or at least announcing, the decision."[10]

In the same book, Cleveland identifies public universities as an early example of the shift toward multiple power centers within the same organization. While administrators had the big offices and high salaries, university centers of influence expanded to include professors, students, generous alumni, and even politicians and their constituents.[11] Looking back from today's perspective, the former university president notes wryly, "Only when a campus crisis blew up, did the administrators notice a sudden absence of volunteers to share in the university's governance."

In government, Cleveland says, public officials often must listen more to legislators and pressure groups than to their nominal administrative superiors. Even the military is not exempt. As early as 1970, in Vietnam, platoon leaders held "consent-building discussions about why it was important to take that next hill— or even to fight that war."

> **Organizations that get things done in the future "will no longer be hierarchical pyramids with most of the real control at the top."**

The Internet is the currently prominent—and perhaps the most dramatic example—yet of an uncentralized organization. No one is in charge, but everyone has mutually agreed to adhere to a well-defined set of technical standards and procedures. Yet, within that "uncentralized" universe, competition rages without relief or quarter.

No centralized controlling authority dictated our e-mail addresses the way the centralized Post Office dictated our zip codes or our phone company assigned our area code. Yet while choosing an individual address, we agreed voluntarily to accept a standard Internet format that enables a Microsoft Network subscriber to receive a message from an America Online subscriber. So far at least, the sense of individual freedom energizing the "uncentralized" Internet has proven stronger than two formal and usually centralized restrictions—censorship and taxation.

VISA AND ISO. Before the advent of the Internet, business was deeply involved in other uncentralized systems. Cleveland cites two easily recognized examples:

Visa operates a highly visible, uncentralized system. Owned by 22,000 financial institutions and accepted by 15 million merchants in more than 200 countries, Visa's "products" are used by three-quarters of a million people, who make 14 billion transactions a year worth $1.25 trillion—the world's largest single block of consumer purchasing power. The network has been growing by 20 to 50 percent a year for three decades.

What is especially interesting is that the banks that issue your Visa cards all fiercely compete with one another. Yet, they have all agreed on technical standards like the size and format of a card in order to expand the market for their individual services.

ISO, the international standard-setting organization, based in Geneva, Switzerland, has published some 9,300 international standards since starting operations in 1951. The technical work carried out by ISO's 30,000 technical volunteers is both complex and uncentralized. As the organization's Web site notes, 2,700 committees and working groups bring together "qualified representatives of industry, research institutes, government authorities, consumer bodies and international organizations from all over the world." The committees operate as equal partners in resolving problems of global standardization.

Three specific strengths underpin the ISO system, says Cleveland:

1. **The standards are voluntary but are enforced in the marketplace.** Try producing screws that aren't ISO standard. The word gets around fast, and customers will shun you.

2. **Approved standards are industrywide.** That means they provide the same solutions to satisfy suppliers and customers around the world.

3. **ISO develops standards by consensus.** Everyone does not have to agree for standards to be adopted, or the system would be ineffective. However, final publication requires approval by two-thirds of those actively involved and endorsement by three-quarters of the national standard-setting bodies that vote on the issue.[12]

FROM PERSONAL AUTHORITY TO STANDARDS AND VALUES. A paradox exists in uncentralized systems. "The key to a genuinely *uncentralized* system is mutually agreed [upon] standards [for] whatever is *central* to the system," says Cleveland, and thus cannot be left to individual choices or market outcomes."[13]

Movement toward more uncentralized decision-making depends on the continued shift of centers of power from personal authority, that is, power vested in an individual at the top of an organizational hierarchy, toward impersonal standards and values. People at the periphery must have guidance to make rapid and correct decisions. If the source of that guidance will be less dependent on personal authority, then it must become more dependent on something else.

That something is already evolving—more emphasis on clear standards and well-defined values that give front-line people the authority and confidence to take action without waiting for authorization from above.

No less a numbers man than Federal Reserve Chairman Alan Greenspan argues that today's economy promotes—and rewards—adherence to corporate values like trustworthiness. "Having a reputation for fair dealing is a profoundly practical virtue," according to Greenspan. He says that this is especially true today, when service-sector companies are replacing manufacturing firms as the main engines of growth. Building the right kind of reputation in the service sector, where human relationships are key, takes commitment not just to financial results, but to values like quality and customer service.[14]

Any business leader contemplating an organizational redesign should ask: Does our new design move us more toward uncentralization or is it an attempt to preserve an increasingly obsolete centralization?

Organizational Issue #4: Adjusting to the Effects of Economic Convergence

The driving ethos of the Cold War was economic and political separation. The driving ethos of post–Cold War globalization is economic integration—the convergence of markets, industries, and even relationships between individual companies. Each of these developments presents new challenges in organizing companies.

In the marketplace, convergence plays out among nations. The U.S., Canada and Mexico formed NAFTA. European economic unity moved forward with a common currency. Coordination among national central banks became a regular tool in isolating economic epidemics. Technology facilitated nonstop global movements of cash and securities, raising international economic coordination from desirable concept to necessity.

Corporations are instruments of society. When a seismic shift in political and economic direction occurs, corporations respond. Consciously or unconsciously, they mirror the evolution of society. International coordination and convergence became a major catalyst behind the current drive for greater integration among corporations of every size.

Corporate convergence cuts across industries and nations. In its present stage it includes common forms, such as:

- **National and cross-border mergers,**
- **Formal and informal alliances, and**
- **Closer collaboration between larger customer companies and their suppliers.**

NATIONAL AND CROSS-BORDER MERGER MANIA. Cross-border mergers and acquisition (M&A) activity grew by nearly 50% in 1999, according to the Organization for Economic Cooperation and Development (OECD). In all, the 29 industrialized countries that make up the OECD spent about $767 billion buying companies in other countries, up from $515 billion in 1998.

The Paris-based research and policy coordination group offered several reasons for the M&A boom:

- **Traditional operational reasons,** where the one company had assets or capabilities lacked by the other.
- **Changing national attitudes toward takeovers,** especially hostile ones. (Chapter Three, on globalization, showed how, as more countries welcomed the capital and expertise brought by multinational corporations, legal and other barriers to cross-border acquisitions lessened in many countries. In the 1980s, for example, there was outspoken, often bitter, opposition to foreign takeovers in the U.S., particularly by the Japanese. A best-selling book and popular motion picture, Michael Crichton's *Rising Sun*, caught the mood of the moment. A decade later, as confidence rose about America's overall competitiveness in the global market, major foreign takeovers caused barely a stir in the U.S.)

- **A booming stock market,** providing more currency to use in acquisitions.
- **The introduction of the Euro,** which reduced transaction costs and eliminated intra-European currency risks.

"Asia has started to catch up in the worldwide surge in M&A," the OECD *Financial Market Trends* bulletin noted. The biggest Asian acquirer remains Japan, followed by Singapore, Hong Kong and China. Companies from the U.S. spent $20 billion buying Asian firms in 1999, more than companies from any other country.

Industry-specific forces. Industry-specific forces also drive cross-border acquisitions: Retailers want to exploit the capacity of new technologies to manage cross-border supply chains and centralized purchasing, tying together companies in different countries far more easily. Pharmaceutical and chemical companies see the potential for expanded scale in research and development. The fragmented European financial service industry wants to consolidate.[15]

"A mixed bag." Popular as they are, mergers are a mixed bag when it comes to increasing shareholder value. To borrow Samuel Johnson's famous comment about second marriages, mergers are too often "a triumph of hope over experience." A report by consulting firm KPMG concluded that more than 80% of corporate mergers and acquisitions failed to enhance shareholder value."[16]

Cautionary statistics are unlikely to slow the pace. In 1999 alone, worldwide M&A activity rose by more than one-third, to more than $3.4 trillion.[17] The hot pace of cross-border mergers and acquisitions will continue unabated, because the underlying causes are just too strong to resist. Deregulation, growing global markets, the benefits of scale in integrating industries and rising stock prices will continue to provide an important rationale for consolidation.

As one analyst put it in describing how the pressure to improve top line growth will continue to drive the merger wave, "The most important goal is to be number one or number two in the marketplace, and internal growth won't get you there."[18] Although the analyst is probably correct, companies should approach any mergers or acquisitions strategy with a healthy dose of caution. The financial people and investment bankers always seem able to run numbers that make that proposed merger look like a no-brainer.

After champagne, a values conflict. The problems usually arise after the numbers are run, the papers are signed and the champagne glasses are empty. That's when strong value conflicts occur, or when customers become disenchanted with service delivery that no longer seems so prompt or personal as it did when the smaller unit ran the business. Or when smaller, more agile competitors leap in to take advantage of uncertain marketing direction. Or when talented professionals who said "no thanks" to the search consultants last week begin thinking, "What if my job is one of those rationalized cost savings they are bragging about in the merger or press release?" Or perhaps the thoughts run, "The senior executives took care of themselves handsomely in this merger, so maybe it's time for me to look out more for myself."

THE STRATEGIC ALLIANCE SOLUTION. Companies wary of mergers often turn to strategic alliances with customers, fellow suppliers and even competitors. This strategy has much to commend it from the point of view of converting corporate energy into profitability, growth and quality. Continuity of individual corporate management is preserved (direction). Commitments are less binding and involve less legal hassle (organization). Fewer jobs are threatened (people). The focus is usually precise— well-defined areas where collaboration will probably pay off for all partners (direction), and that often means finding ways to eliminate or reduce overlapping costs or serve customers better (organization).

For example, alliances among trucking, shipping and rail companies offer customers "seamless transportation," with no worry about how freight will transfer from one mode to the next en route to its final destination. The next step will aim for greater consolidation for e-commerce deliveries. Freight volume from electronic transactions keeps growing, encouraging wholesalers and retailers to look for alliances among shippers to streamline delivery systems and lower costs.

To be sure, alliances have drawbacks. If mergers are marriages, strategic alliances are agreements to live together without the "till death do us part" commitment. In business, as in love, that missing "link" may allow one partner to shirk the work necessary to make the relationship work or even to part company at will, leaving the other partner in the lurch.

> **If mergers are marriages, strategic alliances are agreements to live together without the "till death do us part" commitment.**

Interpersonal skills for alliances. For all their risks, alliances and partnerships are becoming a far more important part of work in the information age than even 10 years ago, says Harvard Professor Rosabeth Moss Kanter. This means, Kanter adds, that people throughout a company "need to take partners into account when they are developing their own strategies."

Kanter cites the example of airlines, many of which are now part of global networks sometimes linking eight or nine different companies. As a result, people in each airline share complex relationships with other partners, says Kanter. They must simultaneously be "diplomats for the partner, ambassadors for their company to the partner, and diplomats in terms of dealing with situations in which their own company's goals might be in conflict with those of a partner."[19]

Although few companies are yet offering diplomatic training on partnering skills, many are making alliances a key organizational strategy. Consulting company Booz, Allen & Hamilton estimated that between 1995 and 1998 some 32,000 corporate alliances had been formed around the world. Three-quarters of these alliances have been across borders. Booz Allen also estimates that strategic partnerships in 1998 accounted for 18 percent of the revenues of America's biggest companies.[20]

COLLABORATION BETWEEN CUSTOMERS AND SUPPLIERS. In addition to mergers and alliances, corporate convergence appears frequently today in a third guise—closer collaboration between large companies and their suppliers. Information technology linking operations of geographically separate organizations will raise the potential gains, and the stakes, for thousands of companies. Already, sophisticated electronic auction programs tell buyers just how much money the company is saving compared with the last time it bought the same product.

The disadvantage of openness will be the suppliers' loss of ability to hide costs caused by inefficiencies.

In the pre-Internet days, suppliers submitted sealed bids and buyers selected the best offer. In an Internet auction, competing suppliers see each other's bids online. By 2010, such networked databases will be a common feature everywhere in business.

Technology will change far more than just the purchasing phase of production. It is already changing the way customers and suppliers work together after a bid is accepted. For example, using Internet links, Honeywell's Avionics Division can keep track of production schedules at one of its major customers. Honeywell today has much more exact information about how many planes Cessna will make in the months ahead, how many of each model it will make and what their delivery dates will be.

Honeywell, in turn, is now setting up similar links with some of *its* 800 suppliers. When the system is fully operational, Honeywell will take the information about Cessna's production plans and convert it into parts numbers for its suppliers, who can then bid on the work.[21]

Suppliers enjoy decided advantages in the new collaboration. Inventory management, for example, can be more profitably managed when customer requirements and supplier's available raw materials can be more closely calibrated. The disadvantage of openness will be the suppliers' loss of ability to hide costs caused by inefficiencies. There will simply be less "give" in the relationship, and from the point of view of many suppliers, far more "take" on the part of large manufacturers, who will have a new weapon with which to push suppliers to sell to them at even slimmer profit margins.

Organizing the electronic marketplace. Information-age technology is also breeding a new type of electronically organized marketplace, in which, companies in the same industry are offering their products jointly to buyers on a common Web site (discussed in Chapter Five).

In addition to compressing costs through greater transparency, the Internet is changing two other important aspects of business in the U.S., according to *New York Times* reporter Lewis Uchitelle:

First, in a step back from convergence, customers are discounting long-term relationships in accepting bids from suppliers. They tend to give their business to the qualified bidder with the lowest price.

Second, the Internet makes worldwide bidding far more feasible, although recruiting of overseas suppliers remains a rather old-fashioned task for the moment. Half of the 500 employees of FreeMarket, a Web auction site, "spend their time not running electronic auctions, but searching for suppliers in trade association directories and trips abroad," Uchitelle reports.[22] As databases of suppliers grow in size, accuracy and depth, however, the existing trend toward worldwide bidding will certainly accelerate.

Long-term relationships under pressure. A disadvantage of this global search for lower bids is the rising level of acrimony it has created between some of America's most respected manufacturers and their long-time suppliers.

The tooling and machining industry is composed of small to mid-size businesses that make tools, dies and molds, and manufacture many of the parts that are the vital components of every manufactured product from furniture to autos and planes. As industry leader Matthew Coffey describes the present situation, "You may be doing millions of dollars of business with a particular customer, and all of a sudden you are told 'Move to Mexico to do this work or we're moving it to Mexico.'"

Coffey, president of the National Tooling & Machining Association (NTMA), says that such news "creates heartburn dilemma" among his members. Coffey says that some of the most respected names in American business today are using their "economic muscle" to ignore what "we came to think of as a system based on standards of conduct, trust and loyalty."

Adding further pressure is the tendency, widely observed since the end of 1999, for large manufacturers to ask for year-end rebates from their U.S. suppliers for work they had already completed and sometimes had even paid for. Quoting comedian W.C. Fields, Coffey describes the situation faced by his members as "an insurmountable opportunity."

The correct response to the challenges faced by small business, Coffey insists, is to use the Internet to go global, diversifying customers even as the multinationals are diversifying suppliers. "No matter whether you are a one-person, a hundred-person, a five-hundred person company, you now have access to the entire world," Coffey says. By promoting your business globally via the Internet, you empower yourself to reach new markets, "because not all the products in the world are made by big global companies." There are plenty of medium-size companies all over the world looking for suppliers.

The Internet also offers small businesses new opportunities to lower costs by forming online buying groups for their basic raw materials and supplies. The NTMA is currently investigating establishing such a buying group among its members for commonly used materials.[23]

For larger companies, however, expansion into the global marketplace creates other new organizational challenges, as the next section discusses.

Organizational Issue #5: Moving Toward a Global Perspective

Terms like *global* and *globalization* are sometimes used interchangeably with words such as *international, transnational* and *multinational*. When passengers fly from Boston to Toronto, they use an "international transportation service." A retail chain operating in both Britain and Ireland can claim to be a "transnational business." A bank with offices in several Asian countries can claim to be "multinational." None of these services, however, make the retail chain or the bank a global company.

A global company is one that does business in both the Eastern and Western hemispheres, but also in the Northern and Southern ones. Beyond this geographic difference, the global company is increasingly distinguished by how it is organized.

The still-powerful multinational corporation, which may well be remembered as the predecessor to the global company, was the dominant model for international business for most of the 20th century. The multinational corporation is organized around separate subsidiaries, each generally operating within a distinct national market.

CORPORATE COLONIALISM. The organization of the multinational corporation usually consists of a parent company, most commonly located in the developed world, and several subsidiaries, normally one for each national market where the parent wants to operate. "Though freed of coercion, this organization model resembled a new form of colonialism, corporate colonialism," says Panos Mourdoukoutas, professor of economics at Long Island University, New York.[24]

In his book *The Global Corporation: The Decolonization of International Business,* Mourdoukoutas argues that the resemblance to colonialism arises from how the multinational organizes and distributes power. Because of its equity control, the parent company has the power to appoint top management of the subsidiaries. It makes—or exercises veto power over—strategic decisions regarding pricing, marketing, distribution, product development, business alliances and expansion into new markets.

"And as was the case with traditional colonialism," Mourdoukoutas adds, subsidiaries were usually limited to producing and selling within their local market and with the parent company.[25]

COLLABORATION AMONG SUBSIDIARIES. In the global corporation, the traditional parent-subsidiary, one-to-one relationship is evolving into a networking model. Direct collaboration among regional subsidiaries of the same company is more common than previously, when subsidiaries were connected to each other mostly through parent headquarters. In going after business in China, Asian subsidiaries of global companies now often collaborate without involvement by the parent. Also, in the global model, subsidiaries have more freedom to participate in local or regional alliances with other firms.

One strength of the global company is a heightened ability to assemble talent pools from throughout the network of subsidiaries. GM relies on the expertise of its global workforce. Engineers from Mexico are assigned to Asia. Teams from Brazil and Germany participated in designing GM's new plants. We've already come a long way from the days when the heavy thinking was reserved for Detroit and the implementation was left for the subsidiaries.

DIMINISHING STRENGTHS. In the post–World War II era, multinationals enjoyed a competitive advantage because of their adaptable organization structure. They were designed to support both a central unity of purpose and local flexibility. Although there were many failures, the multinational structure served well as an effective instrument for overcoming trade barriers, dealing with local government regulations and marketing for individual tastes in local markets.

Now, external pressures discount the value of these strengths. For example, the multinational subsidiary was useful in getting around tariff barriers. How valuable is that in a world in which tariffs keep dropping anyway?

For awhile longer, however, we will be operating with both the global and multinational models in place. Until protectionism and regulation are eliminated across all industries and nations, "each of the two models can be applied in its own world market environments," says Mourdoukoutas.[26]

INDUSTRY-SPECIFIC STRATEGIES. In many cases, industry-specific strategies will determine whether a company stays with the multinational model or builds a global framework for its operations. Consumer companies, for example, will be slow to give up the benefits of the multinational model in an industry that must cater to strong local preferences in taste. McDonald's embraces a model it calls "multilocalism" for its 26,000 restaurants worldwide. That means selling mostly through franchisees catering to local tastes. In India, Maharaja Mac is a special item at most McDonald's restaurants, but it includes no beef. Mutton, lettuce, cheese, pepper and coriander serve as substitutes in a nation where the cow is a sacred symbol.

The big U.S. automakers illustrate how different organizing strategies for international operations are evolving at different paces even within the same industry. GM is setting up an integrated Asian production system using its vast parts-making capabilities. Ford is relying on alliances with local partners in select markets like India. DaimlerChrysler wants to manufacture in relatively few countries. For the moment, its primary emphasis is on exporting.

In many cases, industry-specific strategies will determine whether a company stays with the multinational model or builds a global framework for its operations.

"Regardless of the tactics followed by individual corporations, the waves of corporate alliances and restructuring in the international field are pointing in the same direction—the dismantling of hierarchical parent/subsidiary coordinating system," says Panos Mourdoukoutas.[27] The emerging structure clearly has the edge in today's increasingly integrated world markets. As commodities and resources flow more freely across national borders and local markets, strategies that deal with one country in isolation make less and less sense for more and more companies.

Summary and Conclusions

Humanity's greatest invention, the organization, continues to evolve. Globalization creates new models for international business. New technologies offer the potential for liberating and energizing people who have worked at the periphery of corporate power. New attitudes redefine what should drive a company and how a company should organize to respond to societal change.

Leaders can no longer take organization for granted until something goes wrong. The old business motto—"If it ain't broke, don't fix it"—was once widely applied to organizational tinkering. Then when something went wrong, managers suddenly took notice of organization. They cut staff, closed subsidiaries, simplified the organization, "got back to basics." It often worked, but the cost and waste were high.

This practice will no longer be good enough. What is required is nothing less than a continuous reevaluation of the principles and structure of organization. Begin by accepting Peter Drucker's wise advice: There is no perfect organization, no universal model that fits everyone. Organizations must be redesigned to meet the needs of the customers they serve, and thereby to maximize profitability. The key isn't either/or, big vs. small, mergers or alliances, but what makes sense. Consider every option. There is no magic formula for success.

> **The key to organization isn't either/or, big vs. small, mergers or alliances, but what makes sense. Consider every option. There is no magic formula for success.**

In anticipating how organizations will evolve, forget most of the end-of-century hype. True, there were some appealing, if half-baked, ideas, such as these: The organization of business as we have learned to know it in the past 150 years will cease to exist. Big companies will become little more than downsized brand names, temporary homes for scores of freelancers who will form virtual teams on wireless networks. Best of all, there will be no meetings—e-mail will make them obsolete.

Anyone who works in a big company or even a medium-size one knows that these visions of business life are still quite distant on the horizon, if they ever come to pass at all. In looking at Business 2010, assume the continuing presence and power of the corporation as the primary organizing form for work, because the corporation—not just a legal form, but an enduring concept holding together a network of structures and systems—is currently our most tested and effective instrument to convert human energy into performance in business.

Although business organizations will continue to be with us for some time, they are now evolving rapidly in at least three important ways in response to pressure from society, customers, competition and the public.

First, the expanding global market calls for a redesign of the way companies manage across borders. The multinational corporate model that has dominated international business in the past century is giving way to global organizations.

Second, since the Industrial Revolution, the organization of most businesses has been based on the premise of delineated markets, industries and technologies. Today, all three are converging, requiring a rethinking of corporate structure and organization.

Third, increasingly, the most valued assets today are knowledge and information rather than land, buildings, machinery and equipment. Skill in managing assets, no matter what their composition, remains a true test of organizational strength. However, a fundamental shift in how assets are valued is fostering a parallel shift from decentralized to uncentralized organizations more attuned to managing mental assets.

This shift means that as organizational power evolves from few centers to many, companies governed by numbers, hierarchy, and proprietary systems must learn to rely more on standards, values and open systems.

Capital:
An End to Limits?

KEY CHAPTER THEMES

- *Business development depends on three major material resources:*
  1. Physical assets such as plant, equipment and raw materials,
  2. The knowledge and information necessary to create products and serve markets, and
  3. Money to fund operations, finance expansion and ensure continuity.

- *Access to all three has shifted from a climate of shortage to one of far greater availability.*

- *The key to this shift is not the material resources themselves but a nonmaterial resource— human ingenuity.*

"If two percent of the population can grow all the food we eat, what if another two percent can manufacture all the refrigerators and other things we need?" —GEORGE BENNETT, CHAIRMAN, SYMMETRIX, INC.

"Everybody wants a play in the venture business." —GEOFFREY Y. YANG, PARTNER, INSTITUTIONAL VENTURE PARTNERS

T O EXIST AND GROW, A BUSINESS MUST HAVE A MARket, and it must provide that market with products and services that meet the needs and desires of customers. Leaders of the business must organize and continually upgrade the structures, systems and coordinating mechanisms that help manage the business internally and link it externally with customers, suppliers and business allies. Dramatic changes in these components have been the focus of the previous three chapters.

The fourth vital component in business can be summarized under the heading "capital"—all the nonhuman resources that companies use to maintain and grow their businesses. Here again, basic changes are radically shifting direction and priorities. To grow in alignment with its market, any business must have three, key nonhuman resources:

1. **Access to the physical plant, machinery, equipment and raw materials** necessary to make its product or produce its service.
2. **The right information**—a resource with the rare capacity to keep gaining value each time it is used.
3. **Capital** to fund operations, finance expansion and ensure continuity.

Human resources, which are so important a component that they are the key to all the others, are discussed on their own in the next chapter.

In considering the evolution of nonhuman resources, we immediately encounter the same kind of transformation we found in market, products and services, and organization. What used to seem so tangible is now far more ephemeral.

Major companies like Cisco produce huge wealth without commensurate investment in plant and equipment. In this newer model, one company provides the ideas, marketing, and access to capital and leaves the investment in physical assets to its suppliers. IBM goes into steep decline while loaded with physical assets only to be reborn on intangible services. The cost of opening a retail bank branch has really shrunk; you'll now find one inside the door of the supermarket, next to the soft-drink machine.

To realize the significance of the shrinking importance of material resources, it is important to understand first that this phenomenon is in no way new. Since humanity's earliest days, the relevance and productivity of material resources have depended on the quantity and availability of nonmaterial resources. It was the nonmaterial thinking power of early humans that turned the material resources of trees into canoes and bows. Throughout history, progress has always depended on the capacity of nonmaterial resources like scientific discoveries and technological innovations to turn basic minerals and materials into benefits for humanity.

Technology: Organized Thought

One of the most effective of our nonmaterial resources is organization. When Thomas Edison organized one of the world's first truly effective research laboratories, he accelerated our ability to find new capacities in the materials all around us. The same is true for Henry Ford's assembly line, the financing structures of J.P. Morgan and even the franchising genius of McDonald's Ray Kroc. Each brought a new energy and organization to an older process of converting commodities and raw materials to human use.

This human ability to visualize and think in an organized fashion has always been at the core of our capacity to increase the productivity of any basic resource—land, water, minerals or fuel, for example. Before we invented the mortgage system, farmers had to amass and invest the total cost of their farms. With mortgages, farmers can first borrow and then use the asset to raise funds for more advanced technology. The productivity of the land asset is enhanced by human ingenuity.

Technology is organized and replicable thinking. That's what enabled us to convert sand—the humblest of raw materials—first into bricks and glass, and then into fiber-optic cables and

Edison, Ford, Morgan, Kroc: Each brought a new energy and organization to an older process of converting commodities and raw materials to human use.

intelligent microprocessors. We took petroleum and converted it into lamp oil and then gasoline. Then we learned how to use the same material to make plastics, clothing and lifesaving pharmaceuticals. India's "Green Revolution" worked with the same land that farmers had tilled in the same way for thousands of years. The new technology increased grain production by 50% within five years, by 100% in 10 years and by 400% in 25 years.

Technology now permits us to implant some capacity to replicate human thinking into physical objects. A Swiss aluminum executive suggests the power of this marriage in a memorable short aphorism, "The smarter the metal, the less it weighs."[1]

For example, a hand-held personal assistant can "remember" your appointments and key phone numbers. Properly networked, computers can work out availabilities and conflicts and distribute a schedule for a meeting involving dozens of executives. In a more recent breakthrough, researchers at Brandeis University in Waltham, Mass., instructed a software program to come up with the best design for robots with simple, mobile parts. After days of "brainstorming," the computer program evaluated the viability of each potential design with a virtual "fitness test" and selected the most promising models for review by humans.[2]

There are at least three significant implications for business of the shift toward greater importance of nonmaterial resources like organization and thought, compared with physical assets like land, metals and materials:

1. The idea that there were finite "limits of growth" due to lack of resources, a popular concept a quarter-century, ago, seems more dated every year. The term, says Harlan Cleveland, "applies only to limits of physical development." Not so long ago economists held that the pace of development for a nation or region depended heavily on the ratio of population to physical resources such as land, oil or minerals. Too much population in relation to too few resources spelled either poverty or a "limit" to growth. Yet in an economic world increasingly dominated by a resource called information, says Cleveland, "the only limits, the really alarming limits, are the limits to imagination and creativity..."[3]

2. Exploiting the explosive potential of nonmaterial resources will require a higher level of organization than using basic material resources. The technology involved in cultivating hybrid wheat, traveling in space or engaging in electronic commerce requires far more stringent procedures and organization than growing regular wheat, driving a car or using regular mail service.

The Internet, for example, is a valuable nonmaterial resource that requires rigorous standards and discipline from users—in short, a higher level or organization. E-tailing, for example, must be supported by a national system of credit; complex technology for ordering, receiving and processing orders; and a linked system of delivery from remote sites. These systems, all relatively new in human experience, must work together seamlessly. Compare that level of complexity with the level of organization required for a family in a developing country to purchase supplies from a small rural shop less than a mile away.

3. Efficiency of operations—a constant war on wasted time, effort and cash—remains a vital element in conserving or multiplying resources, whether material or nonmaterial. Companies today are consciously expanding their use of outsourcing, not just in emergencies but as an ongoing strategy to concentrate their resources on higher-level and more profitable work. A similar motive encourages what some experts call corporate cannibalization—the systematic abandonment of a still-viable product or service in favor of a later innovation before a competitor can introduce that innovation. Companies today employ both strategies in an attempt to upgrade the return they get from their material and nonmaterial resources alike.

Nothing in this change means that material resources are somehow no longer important, only that their importance has lessened in relation to nonmaterial resources. The rest of this chapter looks at how the creative power of human thought has:
- **Changed** the availability of key commodities,
- **Redefined** the value of information as a source of growth and innovation, and
- **Opened** the way for new definitions and potentials in how we create and use money.

Material Resources: From Heavy to Light, From Shortage to Surplus

The transition from manufacturing to services reduces the need for material assets. There are costs associated with producing those intangibles so prized today, but the costs are different from the heavy, before-the-fact costs of an earlier era. No one has to invest in a factory to elevate and personalize customer service.

The Internet has accelerated this trend, but it is a long-term phenomenon. Federal Reserve Chairman Alan Greenspan once noted that through the second half of the 20th century, the U.S. tripled the real value of its output with no increase in the weight of the materials produced. Knowledge-based technology was the root cause of this shift. For example, we replaced basic metals with plastics and coal with diesel fuel.

The speed with which material assets lose value today is another indication of their lessening importance. Our current depreciation system is outdated, the U.S. Treasury conceded in a recent study. Internal Revenue Service tables listing useful lives of business assets have been in place for years and don't reflect the speed with which technology makes assets obsolete.

Commercial real estate illustrates the problem. The Treasury study suggests that a write-off over 20 to 30 years would more closely approximate today's useful life for a commercial building. That would be more realistic than the current 39-year depreciation schedule.

Computers are another common example. Today, most business computers are replaced faster than their official IRS useful life of five years.

Another candidate for reform: used assets, which the IRS treats as having useful lives that are the same as those for assets that are purchased new.[4]

Manufacturing's Revolution in a Box

Accelerating technology will drive this trend from heavy to light, from expensive to cheap, even faster in the years ahead. *Time* magazine called one such new technology "the revolution in a box." The process, called virtual engineered composite, or VEC, permits producers to scatter small manufacturing cells around the world to make products close to where they could be used. The expertise to run the system would reside at a central control center linked to the cells by the Internet. If this process proves to be effective, says *Time*, it could make large centralized factories obsolete.

To be sure, many hurdles remain in proving the technology's effectiveness in widespread applications and then convincing the bigger segments of the manufacturing industry, which are generally conservative. As *The New York Times* notes, "Computer-based technology generally seeps, rather than bursts into manufacturing." The segments most likely to be interested initially are manufacturers of boats and other marine products, like jet skis, as well as bathtubs and paneling for buildings, trucks, rail cars or specialty vehicles.[5]

The Law of Increasing Returns

Every Economics 101 student learned about the power of diminishing returns: Increased supply begets lower value. Until recently, the principle was so obvious it went unchallenged. Now economist W. Brian Arthur has popularized the concept of "increasing returns." Products used in networks—faxes, e-mail or cell phone services, for example—increase in value as the supply grows. That explains the seemingly insane strategy of giving away your basic product for nothing. Cell phone service took off when the phone companies practically gave the phones away, relying on customers' growing use of airtime to produce profit.

All this change doesn't repeal the ancient law of diminishing returns, but it does make it relevant only to a shrinking portion of our economic life. "Consider the magnitude of all this," says *The Wall Street Journal,* "Instead of causing prices to rise, economic growth is actually propelling them lower."[6]

Long-Term Pressure on Commodity Prices

Business still depends heavily on commodity materials like oil, lumber and plastic resins. Although prices periodically spike in many raw materials, the underlying cause is often short-term politics rather than long-term economics. In fact, long-term economics tends to promote the use of less expensive substitutes for commodities in short supply.

In manufacturing, new technologies make it possible to produce more products with fewer and newer resources. The growing global marketplace contributes to the steady downward pressure on the prices of manufactured products. We are approaching a time when a single major country could provide the entire world's demand for many specific products. The trend has resulted in global surpluses in categories such as steel, basic chemicals and computer memory chips.

Also, the rapid expansion of information technology makes everyone seem smarter and work faster. In a transparent marketplace, everyone quickly knows the price of critically important items, which pushes out intermediary costs and intensifies the downward pressure. As was discussed in earlier chapters, this change keeps pressure to reduce prices on almost everyone who works as an intermediary between buyers and sellers.

Prices convey information about scarcity; the information that long-term pricing trends convey is that primary commodities and commodity business products are more available than ever before. Despite sometimes fierce, temporary reverses in that pattern, this trend will probably continue in the years ahead.

Cheap Energy: Can It Last?

The marketplace presents one stubborn exception to this projected downward trend in commodity prices. As I write this chapter, there is great concern about dramatic increases in the price of one key commodity, oil, which recently reached a 10-year high in the price per barrel. A decade of rapid worldwide growth, fueled in part by energy-hungry electronic devices, raises the specter of ever-rising prices, perhaps even the prospect that rising energy costs could actually halt global economic expansion. How real is this threat?

Easily overlooked amid the present concerns are longer-term economic and intellectual initiatives that will likely improve the future outlook for energy supply and demand. For one thing, temporary shortages always spur investment and innovation. Rising prices encourage investment by petroleum producers. Investment, in turn, brightens the outlook for drilling companies and sends ripples of economic benefits—more jobs, rising wages and expanding tax bases—from West Virginia to California.

EXPANSION OF OIL PRODUCTION. Capital spending in the oil and gas exploration and production industry was projected to rise by about 15% in 2000 and probably by a similar amount in 2001. Even an expected softening in oil and gas prices in 2001 will not be enough to slow this rate of investment.

Meanwhile, new technology is helping the oil industry tap reserves at depths that were unheard of just 25 years ago. In that era, offshore drilling rarely penetrated more than 300 feet below the ocean floor. Now, offshore drilling of exploratory wells has reached more than 7,500 feet. On land, wells of 30,000 feet are possible.[7]

Three-dimensional seismic analysis is another important technological tool for the oil and gas industry. Using this tool, scientists can more accurately determine a particular site's feasibility for drilling oil or gas. Historically, in some areas, only one in 10 wells drilled actually resulted in the discovery of oil and gas reserves. Seismic analysis technology has increased the success rate to 50%.

Easily overlooked amid the present concerns are longer-term economic and intellectual initiatives that will probably improve the future outlook for energy supply and demand.

Energy price increases have also accelerated the search for new oil and gas fields by our northern neighbor. Canada already is the top exporter of natural gas to the U.S., second only to Saudi Arabia as our major supplier of oil. Atlantic Canada, the region from Nova Scotia to Labrador, could prove to be "the next-generation North Sea or Prudhoe Bay," according to *The New York Times*.[8]

Exxon Mobil now estimates the potential of Eastern Canada's conventional offshore reserves at 40 billion barrels, in addition to the estimated 34 billion barrels in Western Canada. "When you see an iceberg, you only see 10 percent," says Brian Tobin, premier of Newfoundland and Labrador. "Well, our oil and gas industry is an iceberg waiting to reveal itself."[9]

To be sure, environmental activists and their government allies remain worried by the potential environmental impact of the search for new oil and gas sources. However, the industry argues that new exploration and production techniques are more environmentally sensitive than ever. The American Petroleum Institute, for example, says that drilling sites on Alaska's North Slope are almost 90% smaller than they were in the 1970s when drilling began there.[10]

THE ELECTRIC REVOLUTION. Electric power is another energy source set for a period of tumultuous price upheavals, which *The Economist* predicts will be "as dramatic as the revolution that hit the world's telecommunications industry in the 1980s." Driving this change is a cleaner, more localized technology, popularly called micropower, which generates electricity by small-scale fuel cells and gas turbines.

Micropower offers substantial advantages over old-fashioned, centralized power stations in terms of efficiency, reliability, environmental friendliness and, increasingly, price, adds *The Economist*. Micropower lets decentralized local users declare independence from large electric grids. That's an appealing feature for many poor countries that foresee the opportunity to develop their energy production and distribution without having to build giant and costly power stations. Another advantage is that micropower users can sell their surplus energy back to the grid.

Despite the benefits, micropower must compete in an environment of policies and regulations that were put in place to support the centralized model. As a result, the revolution must still overcome three substantial barriers:

1. **Discriminatory taxation,** which favors other energy sources;
2. **Lack of uniform technical standards,** such as procedures for users to hook into grids; and
3. **Regulatory confusion** over, for example, interstate trading of electricity.

In short, micropower must reach a higher level of organization before it can live up to the potential envisioned by its enthusiasts. If these barriers can be overcome, says *The Economist,* in a few decades "the notion of a micropower unit in every home and office may even have come to fruition."[11]

THE OLD WORKHORSES. In the meantime, traditional sources of power haven't yet gone the way of the dinosaur, despite some appearances to the contrary. For example, no major, new generating plants have been built in California since the 1980s. A 1996 law even forced power companies to obtain regulator approval before performing major repairs or "refits" on existing plants. But as trouble loomed in 2000, the California state legislature passed fast-track measures to reduce regulatory barriers to building new plants.

Nuclear power remains another possible source of energy relief. Here again, the barriers are high, but the potential payoff is high, too. The basic energy fact is that the splitting of the nucleus of an atom of uranium produces 10 million times the energy produced by the combustion of an atom of carbon from coal. Still, public concerns about safety remain a formidable barrier.

"The expansion of nuclear power depends substantially on politics, and this politics has come out differently in different countries," says John McCarthy, a Stanford University computer science professor who writes about the sustainability of human progress. "Very likely," McCarthy continues, "after some time the countries whose policies turn out badly will copy the countries whose policies turn out well." [12]

A Worldwatch Institute paper reports that wind power has become a $2 billion global business and is growing at 25% a year.

ALTERNATIVE POWER SOLUTIONS. The search for innovative energy solutions goes well beyond traditional sources and methods, and in countries where energy prices are generally higher than they are in the U.S., there is more incentive to develop new solutions. A Worldwatch Institute paper reports that wind power has become a $2 billion global business and is growing at 25% a year. India, China and a dozen European countries have installed thousands of wind turbines that generate electricity at a cost comparable to new, coal-fired power plants. In the 1990s Germany alone created 10,000 new jobs in its wind power industry.

Solar power, adds Worldwatch, is the second-fastest-growing energy source today. Some 400,000 homes, many in remote areas not reached by power lines, were already using solar power by 1997. [13]

Even after decades of talking about alternative power sources, however, relatively little progress has been made. As author and Manhattan Institute fellow Peter Huber writes: "Wind, solar and other 'alternative' energies sound great in theory, but they rarely make much economic or environmental sense in practice. They require a lot of expensive, unreliable hardware. And they generally use more land to deliver less energy."

CHAPTER EIGHT BUSINESS 2010

Although the success of any specific new source of power remains problematical, the momentum behind the search will certainly accelerate, even in the U.S., in the years ahead. Huber and fellow energy consultant Mark P. Mills estimate that the use of home and office computers, phone lines, printers, fax machines and other peripheral devices accounted for 13% of America's energy use in 1999. Further, they project that Internet-related energy usage will likely rise to 35% or more of a rising energy usage by the end of the decade.[14]

All alternatives to our present power system are now in various stages of readiness. All of them face substantial barriers. However, it seems safe to expect that despite periodic price spikes and setbacks, the long-term, technology-driven trend from shortage and high prices to greater abundance and lower prices will continue even in energy.

Water, Water Everywhere, but a Higher Cost per Drink

Ironically, a vital commodity that seems certain to rise in price in the short term is one we take so much for granted that we don't consider it a commodity at all. The next decade will see prices for water used by business and residents creep up by about 6% a year. That's enough to bring about major transformation in how Americans use, price and regulate water.

Water is already a big global enterprise. According to Azurix Corp., a spin-off of energy giant Enron, annual revenues from the business of water total about $300 billion a year. That includes the costs for collecting, treating, sorting and supplying drinking water, and for collecting, treating and disposing of wastewater and by-products.[15]

Conservation actually reduced U.S. water use by 10% between 1980 and 1995. However, if nothing changes by 2020, projected daily water use will be up by 9 billion gallons a day, a 2.5% increase over the figure for 2000. Reasons include population shifts from colder climes to Sunbelt states and from

194

cities to suburbs. In both cases, the move means extra water for pampered lawns and gardens. There will also be growing demand for increased irrigation of crops. Expansion of water-intensive industries such as pulp and paper, chemicals and pharmaceuticals, food processing and semiconductors also will raise demand for water.

More than rising demand, however, shrinking water supplies will change the economics of water. Environmental concerns are slowing construction of new dams, and some old dams are being demolished to restore the natural flow of streams and rivers. Either way, we are diminishing a traditional route to increasing water supplies.

The staggering cost of updating aging water infrastructure is sure to encourage more privatization of water, especially when communities add in the cost of meeting tougher government regulations.

Aging water infrastructure also will take a toll. U.S. water authorities need to come up with $325 billion between 2000 and 2020 to update and replace water pipes, storage systems, purification and wastewater treatment plants, according to the American Water Works Association. That staggering figure is sure to encourage more privatization of water, especially when communities add in the cost of meeting tougher government regulations like the Clean Water Act and the Safe Drinking Water Act.

Privatization, an organization structure that is generally more efficient that public ownership, is already having an impact. Asset sales and total privatization of water utilities are already common in smaller towns, many of which simply want to get out of the business. American Water Works Co., based in Voorhees, N.J., says it acquired one municipal water company for just one dollar.

Cities still resist sale of assets, turning instead to another organizational innovation—long-term operating contracts. Federal tax legislation passed in 1997 now permits public water utilities to enter into 20-year operating contracts without affecting the tax-exempt status of their water bonds. The previous law limited such deals to five years.

Consumers and businesses will benefit from privatization.

Costs will likely rise, but they will probably rise less and more slowly under private companies, which are able to employ larger economies of scale. Whether publicly or privately owned, water companies are sure to apply new technical solutions to conservation and new purification and filtration systems.

Wastewater from some industrial or household activities—so-called gray water—has tremendous potential as a new source of nonpotable water.

For example, the recycling of water will grow. Local governments will encourage—and in some cases require—the reuse of wastewater from some industrial or household activities. This so-called gray water has tremendous potential as a new source of nonpotable water. Desalination is another technology offering great potential. Already about 100 Florida cities use desalination to reclaim ground water that has become too salty for use, or to desalinate seawater. Also, municipal water authorities are starting to use carbon, long used for home water filters, to improve purification.

From today's perspective, a major water shortage certainly lies ahead. However, as water issues rise more to the forefront of public consciousness, look for additional technical and organizational innovations. There are plenty of efficiencies to pursue.

Information: A Resource That Keeps Growing

The word *scarcity* can hardly appear in the same sentence with the resource called *information*. The cost of information declines every day, as its availability increases. The incredible growth of data bases and analysis on the Internet has changed the resource rules of the game irrevocably.

"As far as we can see in the future, information will be playing the lead role in world history that physical labor, stone, bronze, land, minerals, metal and energy once played," says Harlan Cleveland. That change means that people who grew up appreciating the importance of certain limited resources must now think in new ways.

Profound and exciting differences exist between information and the dominant resources that preceded it. The biggest change of all, says Cleveland, is that information consists of symbols, not things, making it far more accessible than any of the world's dominant resources before. Cleveland defines at least six implications for the future as information rises to a leading position among the world's resources. Each of these changes distinguishes information from all other physical resources:

■ **"Information is not necessarily depletive:** it *expands as it's used.*

■ **It is easily *transportable,*** at close to the speed of light.

■ **Information *leaks* so easily** that it is much harder to hide and to hoard than tangible resources.

■ **The spread of knowledge *empowers the many,*** simply by eroding the influence that once empowered the few who were 'in the know.'

■ **Information *cannot be owned*** (though its delivery service can), so the phrase 'intellectual property' is an oxymoron.

■ **And giving or selling information is not an exchange transaction,** it's a *sharing* transaction."[16]

Accurate gauges to the dollars-and-cents impact of this change are hard to come by. However, in one illuminating analysis, Credit Suisse First Boston calculated reductions in working capital, property, plant and equipment as a proxy for the substitution of knowledge for physical assets. The study covered only a small subset of the economy—industrial members of the Standard & Poor's 500-Stock Index. Yet the study estimated that those companies alone created $245 billion in wealth in the 1990s just by converting "atoms to bits."[17]

Another example of converting physical resources into more profitable knowledge-based assets comes from one of our most mature industries—the railroad. Florida East Coast Railroad entered the information age business by collecting rent from giant telecommunications companies that wanted to bury cable beside its tracks. Then, in 1998, the company decided to jump into the market directly by selling transmission capacities to telephone companies, wireless services and Internet service providers. The company's fiber-optic cables now run alongside train cars piled high with crushed stone, building materials and vehicles.[18]

An Expanding Universe of Information

Enthusiasts earlier described the resource of World Wide Web as a giant brain, linking companies and individuals though available information. That analogy now may be too conservative. It may be more appropriate to compare the Web not to one brain but to a rapidly expanding universe, more unfathomable than we at first imagined.

BrightPlanet, a Sioux Falls, S.D. start-up, published a paper in late 2000 estimating that the Web was already 500 times larger than the maps of it provided by popular search engines. Using its new software, BrightPlanet estimated that 550 billion documents were stored on the Web. Combined, Internet search engines now index only about 1 billion pages, mostly home sites that house huge data bases. Many of the additional documents identified by BrightPlanet are in those databases. Even the 1 billion indexed pages represents a quantum leap from the figure estimated as recently as 1994, when Lycos, one the first Web search engines, had an index of only 54,000 pages.[19]

New Ways to Count in the Information Age

The shift from physical to nonmaterial resources requires new ways of measuring productivity as well as business risk. Increasingly, this requirement exposes the inadequacy of our 500-year-old system of accounting.

Many businesses have already responded by shifting from traditional cost accounting to activity-based costing. First adopted in manufacturing, the new system is now spreading to service firms and even some nonprofits like universities. Traditional cost accounting, popularized 70 years ago by General Motors, was based on the premise that you could figure out the actual cost of a product by adding the costs of all the individual operations required to produce it. Activity-based costing starts with a different and more comprehensive assumption: that every business is one integrated process, beginning when materials and supplies arrive and continuing even after the product or service is delivered.

Activity-based costing shows why traditional cost accounting hasn't worked for service companies, says Peter F. Drucker. "Service companies cannot start with the cost of individual operations.... They must start with the assumption that there is only *one* cost: that of the total system. And it is a fixed cost over any given time period." For example, banks using the new system must ask, Which activity is at the center of costs and results? There is really only one answer: The customer. That means, says Drucker, that the *yield* per customer—both the volume of services a customer uses and the mix of those services—determines costs and profitability, and therefore competitiveness.

Over the next decade, the dominance of knowledge-based service companies—and the service component of traditional companies—will continue to increase in our economy. That will keep the pressure on for better and better techniques to measure service productivity, and will create what Drucker calls real "result control." He predicts that "for most knowledge-based and service work, we should, within ten years, have developed reliable tools to measure and manage costs and to relate those costs to results."[20]

A Macro-Level Accounting Challenge

The task of accurately measuring the true value of economic costs in the age of information becomes a challenge at the national level as well. "As sources of wealth migrate from natural resources and capital toward information and skilled people, traditional economic yardsticks look as old-fashioned as a slide rule," says *Fortune*.

Take an everyday example—the cost of lighting. Yale professor William Nordhaus compared the price of lumins (a standard unit of measurement of light) over time. In 1750 B.C., Nordhaus estimates, the average Babylonian, relying on oil lamps fueled by sesame oil, would have had to work 350,000 hours to buy as many lumens as the average American could buy with one hour's work in 1992.

Nordhaus's analysis takes into account improvements in quality and efficiency by focusing on the price of the service delivered to the customer. For example, that new computer you just bought delivers to you a far higher quality of speed and convenience than the one you bought 5 or 10 years ago, probably for more money. Nordhaus makes the point that official statistics can't possibly adjust quickly enough to the new and better to accurately reflect the impact of major innovations.

Why is getting a better handle on accurate measures important? *Fortune* cites several reasons. Alan Greenspan and the Federal Reserve make key decisions based on these figures, which may be inaccurate. So do investors. "If the information is not good, decisions will be flawed," adds *Fortune*. And any flaw in the system could be getting worse because of the acceleration in product and service innovation and the shift to knowledge-based value.[21]

Risk Management in the Information Age

Another new way of counting focuses on calculating risk. We know how to evaluate and manage risk in a world dominated by physical assets. You figure out the cost of replacing the building, equipment or foreign exchange and insure it against reasonable risk of whole or partial loss. For those kinds of risk we have in place simple, well-organized and proven systems.

Now turn to a world dominated by intellectual assets and human capital. Whatever systems now exist are hardly simple or well organized, and certainly not yet proven. The emerging problem centers on a host of new risks that don't take an objective form at all, says risk management expert Donald Lessard, deputy dean of the Sloan School at MIT.

"Think of the difference between the e-world and the physical world," Lessard says. "Today if you were to value a shopping center, you'd go out and count the visitors. Before, you'd look at the buildings." Today's intangible risks include hard-to-anticipate threats like a sudden attack on your reputation, brand or business model; loss of key skilled people; or theft of the process you use to create new products.[22]

Expanding options is one key to managing new kinds of risk today. For example, to protect your cash flow from the loss of a people-based asset, consider expanding use of teams to diversify the ownership of vital knowledge. Or to lower the risk of a big capital expenditure to enter a new market, consider the organizational options such as creating alliances, even with a competitor.

Developing options has been one key to Microsoft's success in a highly volatile market, according to Eric D. Beinhocker, a principal in the Washington, D.C., office of the large consulting firm McKinsey & Co. Beinhocker remembers wandering the floor of Comdex, the computer industry's big trade show, in the pivotal year of 1988. Writing in the Sloan Management Review, Beinhocker recalls the scene and the reactions on the Comdex floor:

> Amid the uncertainty, there was something very curious about the Microsoft booth....While most booths concentrated on a single blockbuster technology, Microsoft's resembled a Middle Eastern bazaar. In one corner, the company was previewing the second version of its much-criticized Windows system, which had as yet gained little market share. In another, it touted its latest release of DOS. Elsewhere, it was displaying OS/2, which it had developed with IBM. In addition, Microsoft was demonstrating major new releases of Word, Excel and other applications that ran on Apple's Macintosh; indeed, they were the most popular programs for it. Finally, in a distant corner, Microsoft displayed SCO Unix, a PC-compatible version of the operating system, developed by a firm that had a marketing agreement with Microsoft.

Microsoft's strategy—or apparent lack of it—was criticized at the show and in the press. With 20-20 hindsight, we know the outcome of this story, but it was in no way obvious then that the Windows operating system would win. That being in the case, Microsoft "followed the only robust strategy: betting on every horse," Beinhocker says.[23]

Managing risk by exploring and developing a variety of options has always been an attractive strategy for imaginative businesspeople. Look in the next decade for this intuitive approach to become a far more formalized technique, with its own methodology and applications. Risk will never disappear in a competitive economy, but it is sure to be managed far more analytically and with far greater rigor in a world where piling up physical assets not longer ensures survival.

Money: New Ways to Spread It Around

There are many ways to look at money, but most practical people focus on utility rather than mystique. "Money is like manure," said the Elizabethan philosopher-statesman Francis Bacon, "of very little use except it be spread." Jerry Weaver, a highly successful entrepreneur in Gadsden, Ala., makes the same point more elegantly: "Money is just another commodity." Weaver should know—over four decades he parlayed the capital represented by a couple of small metal-working machines into a businesses with annual revenues of more $250 million employing about 1,800 people.

Money is primarily a social system and convention. For legitimacy, it relies on trust—confidence in government, laws, political and economic institutions, and law and order. We often feel dominated and limited by the instrument we have created for our own use and satisfaction. Jerry Weaver's definition is far closer to the truth. Accelerating technology and innovation in organizational efficiency can enhance the productivity of any asset. In this, money is no different from any other commodity.

Creative Vehicles to Spread It Around

Never before have we had so many creative business vehicles and techniques to spread money around so quickly. At the same time, the growth and volatility of the international financial markets and the growing impact of new forms of money have raised new risks, propelling us into unknown territory.

Although the risks at any time are specific—to a country, a commodity, a currency, or a defined investment vehicle—the overall outlook is for continued long-term expansion of sources of money.

The expanded availability of money arises in part because our definition of stored value has changed. Over the centuries, many physical objects substituted for money—pigs, beads, and shells, for example. By the 19th century, everyone in the then-developed world had settled on a definition of what money was—it was gold. More precisely, it was national currencies like dollars and pounds backed by one near-universal standard—the price of gold.

The dollar's supremacy arises not from its record as a store of value but from the role of the U.S. as the world's largest economy, home base of the leading capital markets.

Now there are dozens of national currencies, none of them backed by gold or any other specific valuable. This potentially chaotic situation works reasonably well in practice because of an informal hierarchy of currencies, with the U.S. dollar still number one. The dollar's supremacy arises not from its record as a store of value but from the role of the U.S. as the world's largest economy, home base of the leading capital markets.

Expectations Determine Value

The dollar's supremacy illustrates another key aspect of money. The real determinants of money's value at any time are human expectations, attitudes and values. When these expand—as they have in the U.S.—the value of money linked to those expectations, attitudes and values will rise as well. When for any reason they decline, the value of money decreases.

Like any form of organization, the money system can become better organized and more productive. Early purchasers of vehicles had to pay cash, substituting one asset for another. Then credit made it possible to purchase that commercial vehicle on the prospect of future earnings. Now businesses can lease a truck, gaining the economic value of the asset without ever owning it. Each of these simple developments made the cash used to pay for the economic value of the vehicle more productive.

Many of the trends discussed in this book are fueling changes in our worldwide money system today. Technology in a global marketplace vastly enhances our system for money transactions, both improving the coordination of financial activities and increasing the speed of transactions.

Whereas predicting short-term fluctuations in stock prices is a proven folly, it is clear that the long-term global expansion of sources of capital has barely begun to gather momentum.

As units of currency fly through cyberspace, each becomes infinitely more productive than the system when gold coins passed from hand to hand. Using information technology, manufacturers or retailers can conduct more transactions per day using the same capital base, thereby increasing the productivity of their money. Such changes have the equivalent effect of creating new money by expanding the money supply, because money is less likely to be tied up in fewer, slower and less productive transactions.

Bringing more stable and reliable structures to international currency is a key challenge for the next decade. Business needs a vibrant and stable equity culture to keep growing, because investors need a dependable structure on which to calculate future risks. Investors are searching for opportunity through equity shares as never before. In 1999, the Australian Stock Exchange announced that 54% of the country's adult population owned stock in companies; the figure in Canada was 52%. In the U.S., in 1999, just under half of all adults owned stock, directly or through vehicles such as mutual funds.

A Momentous Milestone

Global capital markets passed a momentous milestone at the end of 1999. Morgan Stanley Capital International, which publishes a variety of indices for clients in the investment management community, estimated that at that time the market value of stocks traded on the world's largest 48 markets hit $31.7 trillion, for the first time surpassing the value of the world's total output of goods and services ($30.1 trillion in 1999, according to the International Monetary Fund).

Whereas predicting short-term fluctuations in stock prices is a proven folly, it is clear that the long-term global expansion of sources of capital has barely begun to gather momentum.

This change illustrates still another key aspect of money: its capacity to mobilize and increase the productive use of under-utilized resources. Debt or credit enables people who have amassed surplus wealth to lend it to others through a variety of investment and borrowing vehicles.

In the 19th century, the U.S. financed construction of its transcontinental railways system through foreign debt. In more recent times, China borrowed $130 billion of surplus savings, much of it from Western nations. The Chinese used those savings to generate millions of jobs, thereby harnessing under-utilized human resources. The people in those jobs created infrastructure, products and services that exist today because the surplus savings were invested.

Two decades ago former Citibank chairman Walter Wriston summarized this process in the phrase, "Debt is a developer." With the benefit of hindsight, we know that not all the foreign debt amassed 20 years ago produced effective development. Yet the essential truth remains, with perhaps one caveat added: "Wisely invested, debt is a developer."

New Forms of Money

Beyond the issues raised by the global markets, the growing variety of new forms of money raises new challenges and opportunities for business.

Digital currency still remains a long shot to replace cash anytime soon, even though many merchants would welcome it. Credit cards, today's primary medium of exchange on the Internet, take a healthy bite from the merchant's profits.

When it comes to money, people are conservative and slow to change. We have been hearing about the coming "cashless society" since credit cards gained wide popularity in the 1970s. We still aren't anywhere near there, perhaps because of cash's one great advantage over checks, credit cards and most current forms of e-cash—the old-fashioned stuff is still anonymous.

It's a safe bet that governments would be distressed by the creation of any truly anonymous form of e-cash because of the new forms of money laundering and tax evasion that would probably emerge in the wake of such a change.

COMPANY CURRENCIES. Some of the best-known U.S. brand names are, in effect, creating their own currency. Frequent Flyer Services, a consulting firm, estimates there are now more than 3 trillion unused air miles in frequent flyer programs. Because airlines sell miles for between one and three cents, that asset is worth between $30 billion and $90 billion to individual consumers and companies.

The 38 million members of American Airlines frequent flyer program can now acquire and spend their miles through purchases on AOL, the world's largest online service. Other airlines will probably follow this initiative, unlocking buying power in the billions.[24]

A SECOND ROUND FOR E-CASH. For e-commerce to keep exploding, we must eventually develop workable alternatives to just using credit cards. Aside from the desire for anonymity, many potential buyers—particularly those outside the U.S.—don't have access to plastic money. Also, there is a growing need for a new currency to facilitate online trading between individuals. Despite these needs, most experts believe credit cards will remain the most popular medium of exchange in e-commerce for some time.[25]

Innovation: The Newest King of Resources

For most of human history, land was the undisputed king of resources. From the fiefdoms of the Middle Ages to the plantations of early America, land was the source of wealth and power, rigorously defended and passed from generation to generation. As we moved into the industrial era, capital slowly emerged as rival for the crown. Instead of landowners who produced wealth from the soil, the new wealth creators were capitalists, an elite group of individuals who could materialize this rare commodity and apply it profitably. Their skill was part dazzling art form, part financial wizardry, and perhaps above all, a commitment to hard work and risk.

No more. Today, most of us are at least part-time capitalists, even those of us whose risk and hard work consist mostly of reading our mutual fund statements each quarter. The rapidly growing equity funds and global markets take our savings and invest them in companies of which we have never even heard.

In the late 1990s, entrepreneurs with a good idea did not have to go on bent knees to a banker, but instead waited for the venture capitalists to call them. Good ideas no longer chase capital; the reverse was true.

What changed after the shakeout in technology stocks was the direction rather than the flow of capital.

To be sure, things slowed down considerably after the decline of dot-com share prices in late 2001. It was no longer enough to add ".com" to the name of a traditional business concept while creating a sketchy plan for big success. Investors, once burned, were twice shy. Still, sources of venture capital remained for good ideas, including ideas backed by sports stars, Hollywood directors, wealthy executives and corporations.

Other corporate "angels" are retiring baby boomers or owners of successful dot.coms. They are usually interested in investing at least $50,000 but not more than $3 million. There are plenty of companies that will, for a fee, match angels and entrepreneurs, including ACE-Net, Seedstage.com and OffRoad Capital.[26]

What changed after the shakeout in technology stocks was the *direction* rather than the *flow* of capital—away from hot e-tailing start-ups toward computer software and infrastructure companies that produce things to make the Internet faster and easier to use. Venture capital firms keep bringing in the cash, and the entrepreneurial energy in the economy is not likely to let up soon.

The dollar volume of venture capital investments in 2000 was expected to double from the total of $58.4 billion in 1999.

Industry analysts say that dot-com companies' reversal of fortune hasn't deterred venture capitalists or kept them away from Internet investments; it has steered them into other niches of the Internet sector. To the extent that any other industry is on the radar screens of venture capitalists, it is health care, where investments are increasing.[27]

Who Wants to Be an Entrepreneur?

One venture capital firm provides entrepreneurial hopefuls with a one-minute opportunity to make their case. Draper Atlantic, a Reston, Va., affiliate of Draper, Fisher, Juvetson (which is headquartered in Redwood City, Cal.) conducts its casting call once a month at sessions named Fastpitch. Draper's aim is to sign up the next big Net winners before they even put a plan to paper.

Capital is now so plentiful that it flows even to the poorest entrepreneurs in our society and elsewhere through efforts such as microenterprise programs.

Would-be entrepreneurs begin by applying at the Web site of netpreneur.org, a nonprofit organization with a mission to jump-start entrepreneurs. Netpreneur selects 18 candidates for each monthly session. In pairs, candidates each make 60-second presentations. The other 16 candidates select one winner from each pair. Each of the nine winners gets to make a three-minute presentation at a meeting of Draper executives and guest judges. That group picks one winner, who gets an hour's consulting time plus the opportunity to make a formal presentation to Draper Atlantic later. Winners represent a wide variety of ideas in areas, including: Internet and intranet applications and services, optoelectronics and fiber-optics, e-commerce, networking and telephony software applications.[28]

More Help for Low-Income Entrepreneurs

The Small Business Administration (SBA) is expanding its loan program for entrepreneurs in low- and moderate-income areas—borrowers who often get passed over by banks and other lenders. In partnership with the National Community Reinvestment Coalition, a nonprofit trade association committed to revitalizing distressed communities by ensuring fair and equal access to credit, capital and banking services and products in these communities, the SBA is taking its Community Express loan program nationwide, with up to 500 lenders in 20 locations.

Participating banks can make loans to lower-income borrowers with less risk because the loans are partially guaranteed by the SBA (80% for loans up to $100,000). The banks like the program because they know that companies that get good start-up support will likely come back for additional banking services later on.[29]

Capital for the 'Poorest of the Poor'

Capital is now so plentiful that it flows even to the poorest entrepreneurs in our society and elsewhere. Microenterprise programs run by community development corporations, nonprofits and government agencies aim to bootstrap people out of poverty through entrepreneurship.

In the U.S., that translates into making market-rate loans starting as low as $500 to people who couldn't qualify through the regular channels. There's no need to bring in three years' tax returns, and lenders will accept personal property like cars for collateral. "We evaluate their initiative, their knowledge of their business, the desire and capacity to repay," says Terri Ludwig, CEO of Accion New York, part of the nation's largest microlender, Accion International in Boston.[30]

The effort has has been underway for some time in the international development community. In 1999, Trickle Up, a 20-year-old, New York–based nonprofit, raised $2.4 million to lift "the poorest of the poor" around the world. Trickle Up helped launch nearly 9,000 business in 37 countries. Women led 65% of the businesses; refugees or other displaced people rebuilding their lives accounted for 22%. Trickle Up works through local partners and makes outright grants of $100 to would-be entrepreneurs internationally and grants of $700 to those in the U.S.[31]

Summary and Conclusions

The instruments of our remarkable economic growth—science and technology, capital and global infrastructure—are so compelling that they are often mistaken for the source of the growth. In assessing the potential for future growth, we have in the past tended to focus on the availability of a few key material resources—raw materials, production capacity and money. Although these are obviously important, they are less important in a world in which information and human ingenuity have become the dominant resources.

The importance of these two resources is not new. What is new is our greater awareness of them and the acceleration of our capacity to employ them. The net impact of this change is to convert what once were scarce resources into readily available tools for human development.

Over the next decades, we will be getting used to the idea of abundance where once we focused on scarcity.

What is still too scarce today is our acceptance of this change. Those who came to maturity in a climate dominated by economic scarcity have trouble emotionally accepting the change. Young people, in the jargon of the day, "get it," while their elders keep waiting for the "inevitable" economic collapse.

There is a parallel in one of the great feats of the 20th century—placing a man on the moon in 1969. We have had a long hiatus in enthusiasm for space travel in the decades since. Scientists speculate that that people born in the decades before 1960s actually had difficulty emotionally accepting that such an accomplishment was really possible. As we move further into the 21st century, human mentality will tip to a new balance. Once a majority of the population have always lived with the possibility of space travel, the excitement and potential will return.

Intellectual acceptance alone is not usually enough to spark a true revision in global thought patterns. It took nearly a century after the discovery of America before a later generation of Europeans began serious colonization efforts to exploit the new opportunity. And, of course, nearly 400 years after Copernicus published *On the Revolutions of the Heavenly Spheres*, we still talk confidently about how the sun rises in the East.

Over the next decades, we will be getting used to the idea of abundance where once we focused on scarcity. To be sure, the distribution of resources is far from balanced, or even equitable, and periodic global shortages will undoubtedly occur. However, both these phenomena are less a case of true shortages than temporary capacity failures rooted in political conflict and inadequate structures and systems for managing diverse interests and priorities.

In the 1990s, the International Commission on Peace and Food prepared a report for the United Nations on the availability of resources for human development. The report acknowledged the many problems of poverty, hunger and disease facing the world. However, the 25 commissioners, from 15 countries, concluded that the central issue was not scarcity of material resources but a scarcity of *imagination*.

> For millennia, we have tended to overlook or, at best, grossly underestimate the greatest of all resources and the true source of all discoveries, inventions, creativity and productive power found in nature— the resource that has made minerals into ships that sail the skies, fashioned grains of sand into tiny electronic brains, released the energy of the sun from the atom, modified the genetic code of plants to increase their vigour and productivity—the ultimate resource, the human being.[32]

The next chapter in this section discusses how changes in that ultimate resource will affect businesses in the next decade.

People: No Truce in the War for Talent

KEY CHAPTER THEMES

- *Human assets: The determinant of economic value*

- *From a surplus to a shortage of people*

- *Recruitment of the best—but the best for what?*

- *Four key recruiting strategies*

- *New rules for retaining your best employees*

- *Checklist for creating a great place to work*

*"The relationship we have with our people,
and the culture of our company are our
most sustainable competitive advantages."*
—HAROLD SCHULTZ, CHAIRMAN OF STARBUCKS CORP.

*"Companies are about to engage in a war
for executive talent that will remain a defining
characteristic of their competitive landscape
for decades to come. Yet most are ill prepared,
and even the best are vulnerable."*
—MCKINSEY CO. REPORT 2000

U NTIL RECENTLY CORPORATE ASSETS WERE MEASURED by adding up the value of land, buildings, equipment, cash, brand recognition and goodwill. Today, the most valuable assets of a business— the energy, creativity and mental agility of its people—outweigh the value of all its other assets combined.

The five components of a business (market, products and services, organization, capital and people) have been around for as long as there have been business organizations. Keeping them in reasonable balance has always been a priority. In every era, however, one component commands the greatest respect and attention.

In the 20 years after World War II, production was the prime driver. So much market demand had built up through 15 years of depression and war that the motto for the new era could well have been, "If you make it, they will come." Engineering and production managers were in great demand.

The late 1960s and early 1970s initiated the era of market-driven rather than product-driven organizations. Rising efficiencies in production had created product surpluses. Competition increased at home and abroad, boosting the premium on those companies that knew how best to appeal to customers' changing demands. Recruiting fever focused on people who knew how to define and woo a market.

In the late 1970s and 1980s, finance—and the finance executive—stepped to the fore. To be sure, the other components continued to evolve. In production, the emphasis shifted to better quality and lower cost. Marketing introduced a host of sophisticated analytical techniques to better identify markets and buying patterns. In organization, the focus shifted toward decentralization and moving decision-making close to the customer. Overall, however, the greatest emphasis was on finance. Tougher times put a premium on the ability to cut costs, downsize, consolidate or eliminate losing operations and manage the balance sheet.

Since the mid 1990s we have been in a new era. The focus in this era is—and will remain—on people. How to attract, retain and motivate skilled people now represents the critical competitive edge. This new focus coincides with unexpected shortages of talented people. As a result, the people component—and the human resources executive—has risen to a leading position in almost every company.

This situation is a major and still not fully appreciated shift. Until recently, managers viewed human resources as a cost, not an asset. Traditionally, you rose in the business ranks by being skilled at "making it, selling it or counting it." Although those are still well-tested paths, we have now added one more trail to the top—by being accomplished at recruiting and retaining skilled people to make it, sell it or count it. That expanded definition certainly includes full-time human resources executives, but it also refers to everyone in business with a responsibility for the performance of others.

This change in emphasis arises from the conjunction of three strong business currents, each of which is rising in intensity:

1. **The shortage** of skilled people,
2. **The shift** from physical to mental work, and

3. **An accelerating transition** in the location and exercise of decision-making power.

From a Surplus to a Shortage of People

Remember back to the early 1990s, when economic pundits predicted rising levels of unemployment and even "the end of work"? Their logic seemed impeccable. The rise of industrial automation and the decline in post–Cold War defense spending meant that we were heading for a period of sustained job loss.

In retrospect, the economists should have taken more account of the burst of self-confidence that was likely to follow the unexpected end of the Cold War. They should also have looked at the long-term impact of technology on jobs. Finally, they should have considered the rate at which knowledge was becoming the prime business asset. True, we had less need for physical labor, but our need for mental work was increasing exponentially.

Longer-term trends also refuted short-term logic. Consider these two examples:

In the 1890s economic doomsayers also misread the signs. They predicted that technology would replace people and result in far fewer jobs. But during the century that ensued—one of rapid technological advancement in the most technologically advanced nation in the world—the number of people employed in the U.S. rose 400%, from 29 million to more than 134 million workers, and the proportion of the population employed reached an all-time high.

After World War II, many businesspeople expected a downtown like the sharp, nasty recessions that had followed previous conflicts, as the economy retooled for peacetime expansion. Moreover, many business leaders of the mid and late 1940s were survivors of the Great Depression, barely more than a decade in the past. One of that group, Montgomery Ward's president, Sewell Avery, had shrewdly steered his company through the depressed 1930s by keeping a tight rein on cash flow. Expecting a postwar depression that never came, Avery sat on a mound of cash in the '40s and early 1950s. Meanwhile, his competitor, Sears CEO General Robert Wood, read the new demographics right and rapidly expanded his company into new suburban markets. Montgomery Ward, which closed its doors in early 2001, never regained its lost momentum.

Labor Bureau forecasts indicate that the country will add another 13 million jobs by 2005 and that the employment rate will rise even higher. By now, we all know what the implications are. Human resources professionals, already struggling with the tightest market for talent in 40 years, foresee no end to the shortage of gifted people.

A Threat to the Economy?

Have we reached the point at which a lack of workers could actually stall U.S. economic progress in the years ahead? That's not a serious threat so long as labor shortages show up in areas and specialties in which lower-skilled workers can get training for more skilled jobs. When that happens, it is healthy for the economy as a whole.

Alan Krueger, an economist at Princeton University, identifies the opportunity like this: "There is still a sufficiently large pool of lower-skilled workers who are available to join the labor force. And as the demand for these workers picks up, you will see more occupational upgrading—more people who go from McDonald's to higher-paying jobs, and companies provide the training."[1]

Women and immigrants represent two other large and still underutilized sources of workers. Nearly half of the women working in the U.S. today do so only part-time. Opportunities available in the U.S. economy have already prompted nearly a million women a year since 1994 to switch from part-time to full-time work.

"The immigrants in question are not so much the uncounted people already here illegally, but [people] who move across the border when jobs become available," says *New York Times* reporter Louis Uchitelle. The flow of people across the border has kept supply and demand in balance at the lower end. Skilled women expanding their hours of work have led to less pressure in the middle.[2]

Roots of the Talent Wars

To understand today's talent wars, look first at demographic and economic statistics. In the last three decades of the 20th century, the nation's economy doubled, while the birthrate fell by 24%. In April 2000, the U.S. unemployment rate dipped below 4% for the first time in 30 years.

Meanwhile, the graying of America is creating the hourglass-shaped workforce discussed in Chapter Two. Assuming that companies stop pushing graybeards out the door (as is already happening), working Americans aged 55 to 64 will increase by 56% between 2000 and 2010 and will represent nearly 14% of the workforce by 2008, up from 9.6% in 1998. A second assumption is that the kind of proactive policies described later in this chapter succeed in keeping millions of older, more experienced workers in place (still an open question).

Meanwhile, for the first time in 25 years, the youth labor force—of 16- to 24-year-olds—will grow faster than the overall labor force.

These two ends of the hourglass squarely focus attention on the biggest shortage today, and tomorrow: the shortage of highly skilled, technology-savvy people in the middle.

Creation of a Cyber Corps

To see what's happening, look at the U.S. federal government, a megaenterprise that keeps detailed personnel data. Between 2000 and 2005, some 30% of the government's 1.6 million full-time employees will be eligible to retire. An additional 20% could seek early retirement. Of the Air Force's civilian staff of 165,000 employees, for example, 45% will be eligible for retirement or an "early out" by 2005.[3]

Like industry, the government is exploring a range of recruiting initiatives, from two-year internships aimed at attracting talented youngsters to signing bonuses for jobs requiring in-demand skills. The U.S. Army had to nearly double its signing bonus to $20,000 for certain recruits to try to meet its 2000 recruiting target of 80,000 people. President Clinton, at a speech at the National Academy of Sciences, proposed a $25-million program to bolster the government's ranks of computer experts in the years ahead. The program, similar to the military's Reserve Officers Training Corps, would pay the costs for two years of college or graduate school for 300 students a year. In return, the students would agree to work for the government on computer security for one to two years.[4]

Expansion of the Knowledge-based Workforce

Understanding the root causes of today's shortage of key people requires more than counting heads in demographic cohorts. It is also important to assess the knowledge and skill inside those heads. Jobs in our economy have been steadily shifting from physical to mental work. Moreover, the emphasis on products and services that add intangible benefits requires a still higher proportion of mental work, and information technology keeps raising the value of knowledge as a competitive resource.

All these trends combine to make people who know how to gather, analyze and use information an especially valued competitive asset. That cadre of professionals whom Peter Drucker 40 years ago identified as "knowledge workers" are most in demand—and will remain so. The Information Technology Association of America expected that half of 1.6 million new jobs in 2000–01 involving computer, Internet and telecommunications expertise would go unfilled.[5]

The greatest competition of all—even greater than that for skilled technologists in the middle ranks—focuses on senior executive talent. Already, stock prices rise and fall with the addition or loss of key executives. For example, after Citigroup's James Dimon resigned in late 1998, the company's stock price fell almost three points in two days, and it was subsequently downgraded by analysts in two Wall Street investment firms.[6]

Competition for senior talent has gotten so fierce that when the CEO of Relativity Technologies, a start-up in Cary, N.C., approached two leading executive search firms to find a president, he received an extraordinary answer. To find the right candidate, both firms wanted a sizable equity position in addition to a six-figure cash fee.[7]

Power to the Periphery

Adding still further to the shortage, changes in organization design raise the premium on people with greater knowledge and skill *at every level of a company*. The driving force behind this evolution is society's changing attitude toward where and how decisions should be made.

The same trend appears not only in business but in every aspect of organized life. Decision-making is migrating from the national to state and local governments, from one political or national center to many, as well as from corporate headquarters to operating divisions and local branch offices. Parents have a greater say about education. Patients demand partnership with doctors on health care issues. Worshipers want more say in church decisions. The pace varies from sector to sector, but the pattern is always recognizable—away from centers of authority to the periphery in organizations of every size, configuration and type.

Underlying these contemporary trends is a longer-term shift in society's expectations for who should make decisions and how. To project the effect of this trend on people in your organization and your industry, first take a look at the longer-term evolution of organizational decision-making.

Organizations evolved as mechanisms for individuals and groups to accomplish work. Early in human development, survival and defense absorbed most of society's energy. The power to act centered on the *personal authority* of a strong leader—the monarch, the general, the feudal lord or the largest landowner.

Over generations, human activities increased in scope and complexity. Leaders learned to extend their authority in new ways. Administrative systems, still highly centralized, employed a more impersonal authority—based on edicts, rules and procedures—to handle the widening scope of the leader's influence.

More efficient administrative and operating systems enabled human activity to expand into commerce, exploration and manufacturing. Physical distance between the leader and those being governed stretched longer. Leaders needed still more efficient methods to handle a wider spectrum of activities. Personal authority, even when channeled through administrative systems, lost effectiveness as distance and complexity increased.

Newer, more open organizational models require people who are capable of thinking and deciding for themselves.

New power-sharing models evolved. Leaders discovered that delegating specific activities to representative interests commanded greater energy and resources, producing more favorable results. The monarch shared responsibility for national defense with feudal lords. Merchants took charge of acquiring or producing goods and luxuries. Bankers operating in strategic locations assembled the resources to finance wars and major projects. The leader still ruled, but power flowed to other, more representative centers of influence as well.

Over centuries, the evolution toward decentralization gathered momentum. The shift from personal leader to a system governed by representative interests is still far from completed. However, as was discussed in more detail in Chapter Seven, many areas of life and business are already evolving into a still later stage, toward "uncentralization": a system whereby decision-making authority rests not so much with representative groups as with competent individuals at many levels. Excitement about the "empowering" potential of the Internet reflects the latest expansion of this long trend.

Newer, more open organizational models require people who are capable of thinking and deciding for themselves, not just faithfully executing the will of one leader or exclusively representing the interests of a group. Even the best people require guidance—a situation that puts a greater premium on *impersonal power,* that is, the values and standards that can serve as a framework for decisions at the periphery.

Widespread requirements for educated, proactive people

at every level of the organization drive many of the changes reshaping corporate human resources today. The questions in human resources have not changed: How do we recruit, retain, motivate and develop the people we need now and in the future? But accelerating decentralization of authority, as well the shift from personal to impersonal authority, creates a new context to those questions.

Expanded political and social freedom gives individual workers a greater desire and capacity to think, decide and act on their own. Higher levels of education elevate the capabilities of people to solve problems and exercise authority. Availability and access to information enhance the decision-making potential of people everywhere, not just at the center.

The expansion of consumer-driven markets places far greater pressure on organizations for fast, flexible responses to customer demands. Increasingly, those responses must come from front-line people with the authority to act. Public concern for health and environmental safety has forced authority and responsibility down to the level of those workers actually capable of monitoring and controlling local activities.

All these pressures push organizations toward greater decentralization of authority. Innovative approaches have demonstrated again and again that delegating more authority to properly trained and motivated workers can dramatically enhance product quality. Access of workers to financial information and their involvement in financial decisions have demonstrated equally dramatic enhancements in profitability. Streamlining organizations by elimination of layers and steps has steadily cut time and cost in decision-making.

Formal organizations have learned that success comes from evolving into less formal social institutions that are increasingly driven by voluntary acceptance. Authority grows out of shared values, knowledge and skills rather than by force of external authority. The "dressing down" fad at work is a trivial but immediately visual representation of these important changes.

All these changes are reshaping the two most basic human resources issues: recruitment and retention of the right people. The rest of this chapter deals with changing responses to these issues.

Recruiting the Best People— But Best for What?

As noted earlier, the current shortage of people is not just a temporary phenomenon. Technology puts a premium on a whole new level of technical skills. The rapid expansion of knowledge work accelerates the shift from physical to mental work in both the growing service sector and in most segments of manufacturing. Demographic upheavals produce shortages of critically important cohort groups in the coming "hourglass" employee market. These changes require companies to think anew about how they recruit, retain and develop their people.

Ask senior executives what kind of people they're looking for and the answer will invariably be, "We want 'A' people— only the best." Too few companies think about the underlying issue—the best at what?

The first step is to think through the kind of culture for which you are recruiting. In their book *Finding & Keeping Great Employees*, consultants Jim Harris and Joan Brannick identify four primary types of core cultures:

1. **Customer service.** The focus is on customer solutions (examples: Nordstrom, Home Depot, Northwestern Mutual Insurance).
2. **Innovation.** The aim is to be first in new markets and with new products, not always with flawless execution. At Cisco Systems, they like to say, "Being first is not elegant."
3. **Operational excellence.** The imperative here is minimizing costs while maximizing productivity and efficiency. General Electric's Workout and Six Sigma efforts are major tools in achieving these corporate goals.
4. **A culture of spirit.** These companies pay a lot of attention to unleashing people's energy, creativity and enthusiasm. ServiceMaster Corp. focuses on the spiritual side of people doing even the lowest-level task.[8]

Most successful companies combine elements of all these cultures, but the first issue in recruitment is to identify what type of culture dominates in your company. Then you must recruit talented employees able to align themselves with your particular priorities.[9] Once your priorities are clear, you can select appropriate recruiting strategies and techniques.

Four Key Recruiting Strategies

With today's severe shortage of talented people, companies are turning to a mix of the following four, broad recruiting strategies: (1) going deeper into nontraditional labor pools, (2) diversifying and upgrading recruiting techniques, (3) tapping into the growing pool of talented temporary workers and (4) shifting work to where the workers are.

1. Going Deeper Into Nontraditional Labor Pools

Until recently, women employed in manufacturing were typically relegated to lower-level machine work or assembly jobs. Between 1990 and 1999, however, the proportion of executive administrative jobs held by women in the manufacturing sector rose from 26% to 33%.

The future looks even brighter, manufacturing consultant Patricia E. Moody told *Fortune*. That's because of the continuing trend in manufacturing away from physical labor, requiring less education, toward jobs putting a greater premium on education, such as computer scientists, engineers and design professionals. The substantial expansion of the number of women in colleges suggests a growing pool of nontraditional talent for manufacturers.

"A woman with the right credentials can make incredible inroads," Moody says.[10] The flip side is that less-educated, traditional blue-collar workers will continue to be squeezed out. Many will end up working at the lower-paying end of the service sector, in fast-food restaurants, for example.

In the service sector, many companies with a long history of hiring women are now redoubling efforts to promote women. Marriott International, Inc., has hired women almost from its beginning as a small restaurant chain in Washington, D.C., in 1927. "We have had small 'd' diversity for some time," says Brendan M. Keegan, Marriott's executive vice president of human resources.

Since the late 1990s, Marriott has emphasized promoting women to more senior positions. At the prompting of its board, Marriott initiated the effort to double the number of women managers within three years. The effort began with a two-day conference attended by its top 100 women. The event has since evolved into an annual Worldwide Leadership Conference. Before the first meeting, Marriott surveyed women throughout the company to determine the major issues. "Opportunity was *the* issue," says Keegan.

Marriott identified management of diversity as one of the company's key competencies.

Marriott has long been a company known for its effective systems. As a Marriott executive once told me: "We are the most systems-oriented company in the universe." The feeling among the senior women was that the promotion system lacked fairness. "The idea was the system favored whom you knew," said Keegan, and women did not do as well in that climate, because they were not previously well represented in the top ranks of Marriott executives.

After the meeting, Marriott set out not only to reform the system but also to give women more opportunities to come to the attention of senior managers. The company formed a Women's Council to focus on opportunity issues. The Council highlighted for senior managers problems that women identified as blocking their advancement.

As a result, the company added more flexibility to its scheduling, acknowledging that, as the primary caregivers in most families, women had special challenges dealing with the demands of a round-the-clock, year-round business. The company added rigor to its assessment and compensation systems, paying more attention to managers' management of diversity in their units, which it identified as a key, core competency for its managers. It began posting more job openings, up to the level of those that reported directly to the chairman. It introduced a two-day program on executive development techniques for women. It retained a consulting group to provide individualized coaching for its top 100 women executives.

Perhaps most important of all, Marriott identified management of diversity as one of the *company's* key competencies. Keegan calls this "the single greatest incentive," because good performance on all key competencies is a major criterion for promotion.

These changes required a whole new mindset. "It's like a marketing project," says Keegan. "You have to segment the labor force by psychographics—who likes to work mornings and who in the evenings?"

Without this kind of flexibility, says Keegan, "our industry does not get a crack at the best and brightest people." So far, the effort has been credited with the appointment of four women to general manager and two senior women to vice president. Keegan says the company now plans to use this model to speed managerial development of minorities—African Americans, Asians, Hispanics.

The impetus behind all of Marriott's diversity efforts is unquestionably the great shortage of talented people, Keegan says. "It's not because it's a nice thing to do. It's not because of the government. It's because of the labor market we have today and the customer markets we have today. We have no choice except to seek talent where it is today."

Looking ahead, Keegan says, companies "will be dealing more and more with the big 'D'—the real diversity, diversity of thought." The next frontier, he believes, is mastering "how to manage people who want to work in a diverse environment, want to contribute, want to be rewarded for that." This kind of diversity of thought promotes creativity and has "huge implications" for business. "It means we have to develop leaders who are comfortable in that environment, who know how to exploit it, leverage it, and not be threatened by it."

FRANCHISING OPPORTUNITY. Minorities may well represent the future of franchising. Retail franchises have saturated suburban locations. Also, the pool of 1980s and 1990s downsized-managers-turned-franchisees has dried up in the heat of a strong economy. Minority entrepreneurs not only represent an untapped source of talent; they also serve as entrées to urban minority neighborhoods now targeted by retailers.

"From fast-food restaurants, hotel chains to tax preparers, janitorial companies and vitamin hawkers, franchisers increasingly are marketing their businesses through minority publications and trade fairs," says the *Los Angeles Times*. Coming up with the equity to purchase a franchise is a problem for many would-be minority franchise owners. Some franchisers have created special programs to enable more minority recruits to come up with the necessary equity, while others are working with community development organizations to start stores in urban zones that offer state and federal tax breaks.[11]

EXPANDING OPPORTUNITIES FOR PEOPLE WITH DISABILITIES. People with disabilities are increasingly a mainstream source of workers for industry. Goodwill Industries International is one of the world's largest nonprofit providers of employment and training services for people with disabilities including development disorders, physical disabilities, psychiatric illness and other disadvantaging conditions, including welfare dependency, illiteracy, criminal history and homelessness. In 1999, Goodwill placed 66,136 people in competitive employment in such fields as customer-service call centers, banking and health care. The 1999 total represented a 13.5% increase over the 58,265 people placed by the organization in 1998.

EXPLORING A MATURING TALENT POOL. The demographic squeeze has prompted companies to take another look at older job candidates. DAK Associates of Conshohocken, Pa., a recruiting firm that specializes in recruiting managers for financial services companies, reports that companies are going deeper into the over-50 pool of talent. Daniel A. Kreuter, president and founder of DAK, says that the proportion of people in the 50+ age group that his firm places has soared from just 5% a decade ago to 20% today.[12]

Monsanto Company brings back retirees as temps or part-timers to fill gaps and save money. In one year, the company's Retiree Resource Corp. saved Monsanto some $600,000, primarily in overhead from agency fees.[13] This trend will accelerate in the years ahead. In a 1999 survey of 586 large employers,

Watson, Wyatt Worldwide, a New York consulting firm special-
izing in human resources and risk management, found that
16% now offer "phased retirement," while 28% say that they
may set up such programs within the next three years.[14]

GIVING EX-CONVICTS A SECOND CHANCE. "A tight labor market is
accomplishing what years of pleas and programs from penal
experts and social sciences have failed to do," *The Wall Street
Journal* reports. "It is persuading America's employers to hire
ex-convicts." The pool of ex-convicts is growing substantially
because of the record number of felony convictions in the late
1980s. About 2.5 million felons were on probation or parole in
1998, up from 1.5 million a decade ago.[15]

Accelerating this trend, the Federal Bureau of Prisons
(FBP) sponsors programs that are designed to find jobs for former inmates. Some 3,000 inmates and more than a thousand
employers have participated in 70 FBP job fairs since 1997.[16]

As these examples illustrate, employers are willing to adapt
to—or even embrace—the necessity of going after talent in
new places. As one talent pool after another is tapped, the challenge will require even greater creativity.

2. Diversifying and Upgrading Recruiting Practices

Winning the talent wars requires changes in specific recruiting
tools and techniques as well as in broad search strategies.
Robert Barner, vice president of organizational development
and learning for Choice Hotels International, says that new or
revised techniques are redefining the field of finding and
selecting executives. For example:

WEB-BASED CONNECTION. The success of new Internet career
sites, such as Monster.com, has brought more traditional
search firms looking for executives as six-figure salary levels
into online recruiting. As the online job market has expanded, more companies have found it convenient to widen their
searches by placing their help wanted ads on the Web, where
more job seekers or even mildly interested browsers
will see them.

CONTINUAL HIRING. The McKinsey Company study "The War for Talent" reported that 31% of human resources directors at leading companies recruit continuously rather than simply fill openings.

CULTURAL COMPATIBILITY. Employers today are more aware of the importance of cultural fit in executive selection. This focus has encouraged the use of diagnostic tools to assess a candidate's leadership style in relation to the company culture.

WHOLESALE ACQUISITION OF TALENT. From 1994 to 1997, Cisco purchased 19 new companies, primarily to acquire expertise. As Cisco CEO John Chambers says, in high-tech acquisitions you are really only acquiring people. "That's why so many [acquisitions] fail."[17]

TALENT WARS ON CAMPUS. There's a seventh strategy that complements Barner's six: People shortages combined with the rising expectations of a new generation puts a premium on spotting and recruiting the best talent early at colleges and universities.

"Goldman Sachs, McKinsey and others have gotten used to the assumption that they can simply pick from the cream of American business school graduates every year," says *The Economist*. "Now these firms are having to pull out all the stops to persuade any MBAs to choose them."

Of the Harvard Business School Class of 1999, only 39% went to investment banks or consulting firms, compared with more than half in 1994. The intensity of this competition favors fast action. According to Dean Paul Danos of the Tuck School of Business (Dartmouth), a record 85% of the Class of 2000 had already accepted a job offer by January, "and the rest were holding out for something better." Their average starting salary exceeded $130,000.[18]

Some leading companies have widened their search to schools where they never recruited before. "The top firms are coming up empty more often at the top schools," says Stuart I. Greenbaum, dean of the Olin School at Washington University in St. Louis. "It's opened a whole new tier of opportunities for our students."

The number of on-campus recruiters increased by 15% in one year at the Kelley School of Business at Indiana University. A.T. Kearney, a global management consulting firm, now recruits at the Cox School of Business at Southern Methodist University. Anderson Consulting, Goldman Sachs, and Morgan Stanley Dean Witter have also expanded the pool of colleges from which they recruit.[19]

In addition to MBAs, liberal arts graduates with computer skills are in demand. A coalition of Virginia colleges created Tek.xam, which tests liberal arts grads on their knowledge of computers, word processing, and spreadsheet and presentation software applications. The five-hour exam also tests students' ability to find and evaluate information on the Internet and their awareness of legal and ethical problems in information technology. The exam spread quickly to other states. Educators said that although the test may encourage liberal arts colleges to add more computer courses, many students who have acquired computer skills through regular high school and college work would do well on the exam.[20]

People shortages combined with the rising expectations of a new generation puts a premium on spotting and recruiting the best talent early.

The need for early action to recruit the best has even cascaded to the undergraduate level. Companies are finding that they must become more involved with college freshmen and sophomores. Today, when you go after seniors in college, "you've waited way too long, because seniors already have job offers" says Judith Mancuso of Pittsburgh's Carnegie Mellon University.[21]

Going after students even earlier, Marriott International sponsors the Marriott Hospitality Public Charter High School in downtown Washington, D.C. The capital's new convention center, expected to open in 2003, will create 10,000 new hospitality jobs. Marriott and other supporters say the aim of the school is to give students sufficient academic and on-the-job training to go to college or directly into the industry after college.[22]

Private career colleges, another recruiting source, are getting more attention. More than 3,600 accredited private career schools in the U.S. have a total of 1.1 million full-time students, of whom 36% are minorities and more than 70% are self-supporting. Most such schools have only a single location, but many are part of a chain of campuses. ITT Technical Institute, for example, has more than 60 locations in 27 states and offers degree programs to more than 27,000 students.[23]

3. Taking Advantage of the Temp Boom

Another source of help comes from outsourcing whole projects or from delegating individual pieces of work to the growing group of available freelancers. *New York Times* reporter Abby Ellin calls this group "Generation 1099," because their income is reported to the IRS via Form 1099 rather than a W-2.[24]

Particularly noteworthy is the growing number of temporary workers in or near the executive suite.

About 1 in 10 American workers, or 12.5 million people, are now employed as independent contractors or on some sort of temporary contract. The fastest-growing part of California's economy is the temp business. It has added as many jobs as the software and electronic equipment industries combined.[25]

Helping to fuel this boom, companies like Freeagent.com and Aquent offer independent contractors the group buying power for such benefits as health and retirement plans. This trend is popular because it supports both an expanded aspiration for individual freedom and a potential for corporate competitive advantage through cost flexibility. For these reasons, it will only accelerate in the future.

Particularly noteworthy is the growing number of temporary workers in or near the executive suite. In 1996, John Tatum, a CPA and attorney, formed Tatum CFO Partners in Atlanta with seven other "downsized" CFOs. "I realized that we had supercharged CFOs and all this intellectual capital that we could transfer to other companies," says Tatum.[26] The firm has now grown to 258 partners in 22 cities, working in all kinds of companies, from venture-backed start-ups to multinational companies. In all, America's 5.6 million executive temps make up 7% of the U.S. temporary workforce, and their wages totaled $2.8 billion in 1998, up 800% since 1991.[27]

4. Taking the Jobs to the People

When you can't get people where you are, go to where they are. Gateway founder Ted Waitt reluctantly decided that if he wanted to attract the world's best executives, he couldn't keep his headquarters near his boyhood home in North Sioux City, S.D. He moved the personal computer maker's headquarters to talent-friendly San Diego.[28]

Tax breaks and cheap labor used to be top attractions for luring new businesses to new locations, but no more. "Nothing else...not location, incentives or costs...comes close to the need for qualified workers," says Rob DeRocker of Development Counsellors International, an economic development marketing firm. Finding skilled workers is a special problem for high-tech industries—the industries most coveted by communities.

Just about every state now is expanding facilities for worker training geared just to meet the demands of business. Georgia's Quick Start program provides training services for more than 2,600 businesses. The Maricopa Community College system in Phoenix prepares semiconductor industry workers and auto repair people. In St. Louis, the International Institute places immigrants, primarily from eastern Europe, with manufacturing companies in the area.[29]

Regions with low unemployment now must offer amenities and benefits to keep high-profile workers from moving on. The Research Triangle Park in Raleigh-Durham provides workers with onsite day care, counseling, family days and "bring your child to work" days. Although companies elsewhere offer similar benefits, they don't usually do so on a communitywide scale.[30]

The intensity of the search for people sometimes encourages companies in people-short areas to cooperate rather than raid others for talent. "If someone stays in town, you may get him back," says John C. Haller, one of the founders of MapInfo, a software company in Troy, N.Y. "If he goes to California, he's gone forever." Haller himself illustrates an example of how this unusual cooperation works. When Haller was feeling restless after 10 years with MapInfo, chairman Michael D. Marvin arranged for him to teach classes at the nearby Rensselaer Polytechnic Institute and to consult with a small local start-up dot-com. Six months later, Haller returned to MapInfo as chief technology officer. Three years later, Haller and Steve Lombardi, another MapInfo employee, started another Internet company with MapInfo's money. "I had just gotten a great job offer in California," says Lombardi, "and they knew it would take an Internet project to keep me here."[31]

Importing Talent

Still another popular solution involves importing talent from other countries. Demand for "H1b" visas reached the annual 115,000 limit in just the first six months of 2000. These visas were established in 1990 to permit foreigners with college degrees or higher to work for a renewable, three-year term for U.S. employers who petitioned on their behalf.[32]

One of the fastest-growing visa categories is the "NAFTA TN" visa, which offers an unlimited number of temporary visas for professional workers from Canada and Mexico. Janet Pelletier, Canadian regional sales manager for Brass Ring, Inc., reports a "dramatic increase" in the number of U.S. high-tech companies attending job fairs in Ottawa.[33]

Moving Call Centers to India

Of course, in a global economy, opportunities for moving work to other countries continue to expand. Ireland is one of the world's fastest-growing economies, partly because of the 20,000 jobs created by companies establishing telemarketing operations there.

The call-center business is taking off in India. Leased-line prices have fallen dramatically. The Indian government has removed government restrictions, replacing them in many cases with incentives for non-Indian firms to establish call centers and other information technology–enabled businesses. The technological infrastructure needed for a 21st-century, global telecommunications business is being put in place. Salaries for English-speaking college graduates are about one-tenth of the salaries of similar workers in the developed world.

Large Western companies, such as airlines and insurance

companies, also are candidates for establishing "back-office" centers in India to handle paperwork. The time-zone difference means that work sent via the Internet when the Western companies close business at the end of the day can be completed and returned to the sender by the time they open the next morning.

Medical transcription is another service business taking off in India. The industry is relatively easy to set up, because it is not so dependent on excellent telecom links as are, for example, back-office centers.

To Retain Your Most Valuable Assets, Build a Great Place to Work

Savvy employers learned one important lesson from the recruiting scramble just described: The most cost-effective way to have good employees is to build an environment that keeps the good ones you already have.

Wal-Mart recently revamped its human resources philosophy from "getting, keeping, and growing employees" to "keeping, growing, and getting" them. The shift isn't just semantics, says Coleman Peterson, senior vice president of Wal-Mart's People Division. It indicates an increased emphasis on retaining and developing the talent Wal-Mart already has, rather than the "hire, hire, hire" strategy Peterson says categorized the company in the past.

Revised Wal-Mart priorities include assigning a mentor to new employees during their first 90 days and assessing their progress at 30-, 60-, and 90-day intervals. Efforts like this have helped Wal-Mart reduce attrition rates by 25%.[34]

Such focus pays off in dollars and cents. Experienced human resources executives estimate that the cost to replace an employee can be as much as 150% of the departing person's salary. That's likely to reflect just the direct costs. The indirect loss—the intellectual wealth inside a valued employee's head—can be many times that.

"If a $2,000 desktop computer disappears from an employee's desk, I guarantee there'll be an investigation, a whole to-do," says Maury Hanigan, founder of Hanigan Consulting Group, in New York City. "But if a $100,000 executive with all kinds of client relationships gets poached by a competitor, there's no investigation."[35]

The Shredded Social Contract

The old social contract between employers and employees has long since been shredded. Bosses who are still upset by its passing should remember that, a decade ago, it wasn't employees who started the tough talk about the need to compete by being "lean and mean."

Even when it wasn't explicitly spelled out, employees got the message. "You are responsible for your own career. You have a job with us as long as it is mutually profitable. In the meantime, manage your career by developing yourself." In many cases, the job-hopping youngsters of today are the sons and daughters of people who, in the 1980s, anticipated a gold watch and got a pink slip instead.

Motivators and 'Demotivators'

The key elements in any retention program have been known for decades. More than a generation ago, management expert Frederick Hertzberg categorized them as "hygiene" factors and "motivators."

The hygiene factors are the basic elements in a job package: pay, benefits, security and physical work conditions. Hertzberg's point was that when employers didn't get these issues right, employees were demotivated, but getting them right didn't actually motivate anybody to better performance. Doubt that? How long were you motivated by your last pay increase after you received it?

The true motivators, Hertzberg contended, kicked in once the basics were satisfactory. These included higher values like involvement and participation in decision-making, opportunities to grow through training and development, and individualized attention from a caring supervisor.

Today, the key elements of a basic employment package—security, pay, benefits and adequate working conditions—are still in place. However, employers were caught off guard when the expectations for each element changed dramatically—usually in a way that favors employees.

Once Downsized, Twice Wary

Even in a booming economy, job security is still an issue. Employers today feel, with some justification, that all the insecurity is now on their side. Yet, in the midst of one of the most robust job markets in history, many American workers and managers still worry about their job security—and with reason. True, we have been creating more than a hundred thousand new jobs a month. Yet, as *The Economist* notes, "it is also true that in 1998 and 1999 some 300,000 people have been filing first claims for unemployment each week, indicating that many must endure the stressful experience of losing their job before finding another one."[36]

Employees who fell victim to the dot-com shake-out in the summer of 2000 began looking for two things from prospective employers—a stable salary and good prospects for corporate longevity.

Even for those bright, young dot-com employees, the security represented by a salary and a brand-name company, rather than the allure of options, quickly became an important issue—once they had been downsized. Recruiters and executives report that employees who fell victim to the dot-com shake-out in the summer of 2000 began looking for two things from prospective employers—a stable salary and good prospects for corporate longevity.[37]

No one in the private sector today expects a guarantee of a job for life. However, any revised definition of security now means a clear understanding of the rules of engagement, and that suggests a need for far more openness about the company's strategies, prospects and competitive position. Given the technological evolution discussed earlier, the necessary communication vehicles are readily put in place.

No More One-Size-Fits-All Pay Plans

In pay, perhaps the biggest change is the move away from "one size fits all" pay plans to more targeted efforts aimed specifically at high-impact employees.

Peter Cappelli, a Wharton School professor of management, says the focus from here on will shift "from broad retention programs to highly targeted efforts aimed at particular employees or groups of employees." Writing in the *Harvard Business Review*, Cappelli says that once you have established targeted retention programs, you can use a number of mechanisms to encourage the right people to stay. However, pay-based incentives will no longer protect your most sought after people, Cappelli insists. Recruiters routinely buy out golden handcuffs with signing bonuses that Cappelli calls "golden hellos."

Companies should consider creating special "hot skills" premiums for employees whose expertise is crucial and in short supply.

Instead, Cappelli suggests that companies should consider creating special "hot skills" premiums for employees whose expertise is crucial and in short supply. The premiums can cease when the skills become readily available or an employer decides that the skills are no longer so important to its business.

Another technique involves distributing any signing bonus over time. For senior executives, this can be a matter of years, but the principle can also apply to retaining lower-level employees. Burger King, Cappelli notes, offers workers a signing bonus, but withholds payment until they've been on the job for three months. "Three months may not seem like a long time, but in the fast-food industry, where annual turnover averages 300%, it's an eternity."[38]

Rainmakers—those rare people who can find and sell new high-volume customers, rather than coax more business from existing customers—present management with difficult pay decisions. "Let's get something straight from the outset," says consultant and author Allan Weiss. "People who acquire business are much more valuable than people who deliver business, simply because the skills of the former are in far scarcer supply than the latter."

"It's tough to make rain, Weiss adds, "it's easy to buy umbrellas." The best kind of pay plan for a rainmaker, Weiss says, is a competitive base accompanied by an uncapped incentive connected to the volume of new business, not repeat business.[39]

Weiss's focus on special treatment for rainmakers may seem to contradict some of the emphasis earlier in this book and elsewhere on the importance of outstanding customer service. Aren't the people who keep customers happy as valuable as the people who bring them in? The most superficial analysis will uncover that every business absolutely needs customer acquisition, no matter how effective its customer service. Achieving lifetime customers is an excellent philosophy for any business, but it cannot be an absolute standard. Every business, no matter how excellent its service, loses a fair number of customers every year. Customers die. They retire. They get acquired by competitors who are committed to a different supplier. One way or another, they disappear. Without new customers to replace them, the business declines. No matter how a company chooses to approach this challenge, Weiss is correct: Rainmakers are tougher to get, "grow" and keep than are people who deliver the product or service, and the compensation package should reflect that fact.

> **Companies eager to hold on to their top producers are far less likely today to worry about creating disparities among workers with the same title.**

Companies eager to hold on to their top producers are far less likely today to worry about creating disparities among workers with the same title. "We're making sure a larger percentage of our pay goes to the very best performers," says Rick Martino, IBM's vice president for talent.[40]

Jim Howard, managing partner of Smith and Howard, an Atlanta CPA firm, came up with a novel approach to personalizing compensation. He asks each of the 40 professionals in his company to write him a one-page letter each year describing the comp plan that would most motivate them to help the firm reach its goals. Individual plans may include a bonus, extra vacation time or even upgraded equipment like a new personal computer. "My experience shows me that people know what will motivate them and more often than not, they come up with a fair salary."[41]

Discrepancies in Pay Between the Old and the New Economies

Whatever the plan, executive compensation at the most senior levels continues to spiral upward in response to the talent shortage. The leaders of new technology companies earned an average of $27 million in 1999, including salary and the estimated value of their stock options, according to *The New York Times*.[42]

Even after the subsequent shake-out in technology stocks and the steady merging of the old and new economies are considered, something fundamental has changed. And even after a decade of huge pay increases, the average compensation for chief executives shot up an additional 23% to $11.9 million in 1999. "Valuing stock options in the most widely used way," says *New York Times* reporter David Leonhardt, "a chief executive now makes more in a single day than the typical American worker does in a year."[43]

The Old-New Economy split is apparent throughout the economy, not just at the top. Dismal Sciences, an economic consulting firm in West Chester, Pa., tracked the wage progress of 129 common occupations between 1991 and 1999. Of these, 24, including teachers, salespeople and aircraft pilots, saw their wages decline after adjusting for inflation. "The new economy and old economy are written all over these numbers," says Mark Zandi, chief economist at Dismal Sciences. "The new economy is driving strong wage increases, and for the folks in the old economy, their wages are being constrained."[44]

To be sure, demographics patterns will likely change the earnings outlook for some of these professions in the years ahead. As the first wave of baby boomers, born between 1946 and 1964, leaves the workforce, many sectors will have to work hard to find replacements, undoubtedly improving salaries in, for example, education. Many education employees—teachers, school administrators, janitors—work for state and local education systems that have defined-benefit pension plans, which provide the most benefits to those workers who retire as soon as they are eligible, often after 30 years.

Continuing to expand discrepancies is hardly healthy for the long-term development of either companies or society. In the short term, however, the situation suggests a continuing pressure from employees, especially from talented senior and middle-level managers, for a bigger piece of the pie. At the lower levels, managers can expect pressure from unions and politicians to lift the minimum wage, which is now so low in relation to the marketplace that at the start of 2000 it set pay for less than 10% of the U.S., workforce.

The Benefits Boom

Nowhere are the rules changing faster than in employee benefits. People who have benefits in one job are reluctant to wait to get them in the next. To stay competitive, employers are reducing or eliminating probationary periods for benefits like savings plans, vacation time, profit sharing and sometimes even medical insurance. Although hard figures are scarce, the trend appears to be spreading fastest in 401(k) retirement plans.[45]

The benefits frontier now includes perks and ideas undreamed of just a few years ago:

LONG-TERM CARE INSURANCE. This is a benefit that more companies hope to use in their retention efforts. According to a survey conducted by RewardsPlus of America Corp., an optional benefits company in Baltimore, Md., about 70% of the 86 private and publicly held companies polled said that they would be interested in finding a way to offer their employees this type of insurance as an optional benefit. Again, the key factor is the graying of the American workforce.[46] "Companies have always been motivated by economic self-interest," says RewardsPlus CEO Ken Barksdale. "Today, it so happens that recruitment and retention are enormous corporate priorities. Companies have realized some of the short-sightedness of the age of downsizing and are trying to strike a better balance."

WORK-FAMILY PROGRAMS. Once, only the salary elite at office towers and the suburban campuses of big cities enjoyed this benefit. Now, reports *The Wall Street Journal,* you find these programs in the most unexpected places. For example, at Harley-Davidson's York, Pa., plant, 75% of the workers are men; yet these men pushed for, and are the heaviest users of, the nearby child care center, where Harley offers discounted slots. Adds *The Journal,* "Up next at Harley: a private room for nursing mothers."[47]

HEALTH CARE PLANS. The Internet is sparking a new look at ways to improve one of business's most costly benefits, health care plans. As outlined in a Booz-Allen & Hamilton report, under such a plan, employers would allocate funds to each employee on a risk-adjusted basis. The employee would then purchase health insurance from a wide set of health care options that had been preapproved by the employer. Once again, the plan emphasizes managing the employer's costs while giving workers more individual choice, rather than one-size-fits-all solutions.[48]

CUSTOMIZATION OF BENEFITS. Harvard professor Peter Cappelli believes that such employee choice will accelerate into even greater customization of both existing and new benefits. "Each employee would be able to allocate a set amount of money to 'purchase' options in such areas as career development and balance of work and personal life. The amount available would depend on the importance of the employee to the company."[49]

NICE-TO-HAVE PERKS. "Free lunch (though not to the employer) is one of the many perks that more and more employers are starting to offer their staff," *The Economist* reports. "Texas Instruments' concierge team will repair an employee's pick-up truck. Sun Microsystems provides an in-house laundry... Netscape has its own dentist; Intuit offers in-chair massage."[50]

CHILD CARE AND ELDER CARE. Projecting the demographics ahead, companies can expect rising demand for expansion of child care and elder care benefits. By 2020, there will be 27.7 persons age 65 or older for every 100 working-age adults, a 28.5%

increase in just over two decades. And as Generation Xers start their families, the birthrate from 2000 to 2012 could reach 4.3 million annually, equaling the number of births in 1957, the peak year of baby boom births.[51]

The New Mantra: Flexibility

New definitions for satisfactory working conditions are evolving rapidly, once again to accommodate valuable employees. In the past, work design meant laying out processes strictly to improve productivity and profitability. Now, work-design processes often emphasize customizing work flows to match the needs of scarce workers. The new mantra is flexibility, flexibility, flexibility.

At IBM, the company that once prohibited blue shirts and floral ties, managers can work part-time—and from home—so that they can better juggle the demands of their children and their jobs.[52]

When people in the payroll department at Merck & Co.'s Whitehouse Station, N.J., headquarters complained about habitual overtime, the company realized that it had to computerize more of the work. It was also clear that the 9-to-5 workday didn't match the cyclical pile-up of work. Automation and new schedules helped shrink departmental overtime by 50% and permitted a doubling of the number of people with flexible work arrangements.

"At the end of the workday," *Business Week* reports, "workers care more about having control over when, where, and how they work than anything else. Flex time, telecommuting and part-time work arrangements are employee favorites."[53]

In a survey by consultants Challenger, Gray & Christmas, 43% of human resources executives said that an increasingly mobile, telecommuting workforce would be the biggest workplace trend in the 21st century. Some companies are already reporting that productivity rates for telecommuters are 20% to 25% higher than for employees who work solely in the office. Longer, more productive working hours appear to be the key. At AT&T, for example, where 29% of managers telecommute at least once a week (up from 8% in 1994), the company found that, on average, telecommuters put in five more hours a week when working at home rather than at the office.[54]

With the number of people working 60 or more hours a week hitting its highest point in two decades, more companies are permitting—even encouraging—executives to "take a break." At Intel, all full-time employees get eight weeks off, paid, every seven years. "Microsoft Achievement Awards" provide eight weeks of paid vacation to consistently high performers with at least seven years' tenure.[55]

Higher Workplace Values

Even upgrading the basics of the old work contract—security, pay, benefits and work conditions—will no longer be enough to ensure long-term loyalty of top performers. Once the basics are covered, high performers look to satisfy other needs, most important, opportunities to keep up with change and to grow on the job.

CORPORATE UNIVERSITIES. Companies now spend about $56 billion a year on formal training, according to the American Society for Training and Development in Alexandria, Va.[56] Companies increasingly are offering learning opportunities through their corporate universities. Such education facilities give companies a clear competitive advantage in recruiting and retaining the best and brightest employees, says Jeanne C. Meister, president of the New York consulting firm Corporate University Xchange, Inc.

Another advantage in a world where knowledge expands exponentially, Meister says, is that "corporate universities provide learning on demand—they 'happen' or take place anywhere, thanks to distance-learning technology and the use of satellite campuses."[57]

This learning-on-demand capacity of the Internet will revolutionize training over the next decade. As high-speed, dedicated Internet connections spread throughout industry, the slow nature of today's Internet training will speed up. The price per student will drop, while expanded accessibility will open training possibilities that are only glimpsed now.

As a harbinger of the next phase, Peter Drucker, America's leading management philosopher, has already developed 30 hours of Internet-based, interactive educational material with entrepreneur Alexander Brigham. In the program, Drucker expounds his principles, followed by multiple-choice questions. After viewers click on their answers, Drucker responds in his Viennese accent with comments like "Excellent" or "Very good" or "Sorry, you are wrong." E-mails periodically remind users of the goals they set for themselves during the course.[58]

COACHING. In alignment with the trend toward individualization of benefits, more companies are now offering personal coaching for senior employees. *Forbes* reports that General Electric, Sony, and Johnson & Johnson use coaches. In 2000, Ernst & Young will have spent $2 million on them. At Hewlett-Packard, a few people in human resources spend a lot of time finding coaches for hundreds of employees. "So many companies have mushroomed from start-ups to huge overnight successes," one coach told *Forbes*. "You've got all these 30-year-old vice presidents with no management experience."

Coaches use a variety of techniques. Typically, they start by offering clients a confidential evaluation based on personality tests. They also use "360-degree" feedback instruments that allow bosses, peers and "direct reports" to anonymously assess the individual's performance. Coaches may follow their clients around for the day, observing their behavior in a variety of management situations. After assessing clients, coaches advise them on how to improve their performance. The cost can be high, in some cases, as much as $10,000 for one person. However, the demand is likely to continue, given the even higher cost of losing a promising executive who needs only some fine-tuning to move to the next level of performance.[59]

RETRAINING. The task of educating employees and boosting their performance goes far beyond executives, however. "A whopping 75% of today's workforce needs retraining just to keep pace," *The Kiplinger Letter* reports. Fortunately, more training assets are available every day. Revamped federal programs permit states to mold training to match the needs of

---

BOX 9-1 Is Yours a Great Place to Work?

Yours is a great place to work when your employees answer yes to these 12 Gallup questions.*

1. Do I know what is expected of me at work?
2. Do I have the equipment and material I need to do my work right?
3. At work, do I have the opportunity to do what I do best every day?
4. In the last 7 days, have I received recognition or praise for good work?
5. Does my supervisor or someone at work seem to care about me as a person?
6. Is there someone at work who encourages my development?
7. At work, do my opinions seem to count?
8. Does the mission/purpose of my company make me feel my work is important?
9. Are my co-workers committed to doing quality work?
10. Do I have a best friend at work?
11. In the last 6 months, have I talked to someone about my progress?
12. This last year, have I had opportunities at work to learn and grow?

*Copyright 1993-2001 by The Gallup Organization. The Q12 items are owned by The Gallup Organization and cannot be used without Gallup's written consent.

---

local businesses. Area workforce-investment boards, staffed by business owners, give business more say in how such funds are spent.

Many community colleges have formed a partnership with ACT, an education services firm, to open centers for testing and training in more than 100 communities.[60] The first center opened in Cedar Rapids, Iowa, in July 2000. Training at the centers will include state-of-the-art courseware in such topics as adult literacy, computer basics, information technology and English as a second language. Since most of the courses will be Web-based, people will be able to take courses via computer, either at work or at home. This kind of grass-roots effort will accelerate a boom in training.[61]

Individualized Services for Key Employees

Every level of the retention effort reflects the movement toward treating key employees like customers who require individualized services, resulting in personalized pay and benefits packages, working conditions matched to individual needs, and specially tailored training, development and coaching. Even with expansive company-sponsored efforts, however, retention rates can falter whenever one other key step is missing: clear evidence of personal attention to individual employee concerns.

In today's world, everyone—up to the CEO—needs that kind of personalized communication. Cisco CEO John Chambers lists his birthday breakfasts as probably "the most valuable sessions I do with employees. Once a month anybody who has a birthday in that month can come and participate in a quiz session with Chambers for about an hour and a half, and anything is fair game." Chambers deliberately excludes directors and vice presidents from the breakfasts so that people who usually don't get a chance to communicate with him get one. "And every single time, I learn two or three things that either I need to do differently, or things that I thought were working one way and weren't."[62]

Even closer to the front lines, immediate supervisors create the climate that can ultimately make or break any corporate retention effort.

Even closer to the front lines, immediate supervisors create the climate that can ultimately make or break any corporate retention effort. Validating this idea is a Gallup Organization study that shows most workers rate having a caring boss even higher than money or fringe benefits. In a study covering 700 companies with 2 million employees, Gallup found that the length of time employees stay at a company and the extent to which they are productive are determined by their relationship with their immediate supervisors. "People join companies and leave managers," says Marcus Buckingham, a senior managing consultant at Gallup and the primary analyst for the study.[63]

That raises another question: What are the characteristics of a good supervisor? For 20 years, The Gallup Organization has been gathering data on what makes a great place to work, in the opinion of employees. After extensive study, Gallup has isolated the 12 characteristics of a strong workplace as seen through the eyes of the most successful and productive employees. (See the box on page 246.)

If your employees can answer yes to each of the 12 Gallup questions in the box, you have a strong workplace, a workplace where the best people are far more likely to want to work and stay. A yes to virtually every question depends on the actions of immediate supervisors, supported by a competitive and focused effort to retain valuable employees.

Summary and Conclusions

People are now the critical resource for every manager in every company. For the next decade at least, the shortage of skills will only intensify, putting a premium on recruiting, retaining and developing the kind of people who can build competitive advantage. That's the new priority in a world where knowledge and skills are more valuable that hard assets.

While the intensity of this effort raises the profile of human resources professionals, all managers will be judged from now on by their capacity to energize and deploy the human assets for which they are accountable.

How resourceful is the manager in spotting, recruiting and keeping talent? How creative is the manager in designing work flows that simultaneously increase productivity while releasing the employee energy through attention to individual needs? Who will emerge most successfully from the management challenges posed by increased telecommuting, flexible pay plans and individualized benefits? Who will be most successful in finding and developing talent in nontraditional pools?

The 1980s were a decade when skilled managers advanced by reducing waste and maximizing the use of their available physical assets. The competition since the mid 1990s has focused on reducing wasted human energy and maximizing employee brain-power at every level of the company.

Priorities for Success

ART ONE IDENTIFIED FIVE FORCES RESHAPING OUR world. Part Two described how those forces influence the five components of your business: market, technology (products and services), organization, capital and people.

Part Three summarizes the major implications arising from the issues raised in Parts One and Two, and outlines specific strategies that companies use to profit from the changes around us.

As business follows society into the next phase of development, there will be a heightened emphasis on values—those vital, sometimes elusive, operational qualities such as customer service, development of people and speed of response. As societal values change, so companies must choose which values to introduce or elevate in response. This part identifies specific values that can help any company stay in tune with societal change.

Part Three concludes with five priorities for any company to deal with the issues raised in this book. With each priority, I have included a list of specific questions to help focus your management team on the overriding question, What should we do first?

Companies that address the issues in this chapter in a thoughtful and proactive way will be the best prepared for the challenges and opportunities of *Business 2010*.

Riding the River of Opportunity: Aligning Your Company With Accelerating Change

KEY CHAPTER THEMES

- *Establishing a framework for decisions*

- *Understanding evolving societal values*

- *Considering the implications for business*

- *Tracking the values evolution in government*

- *Positioning your company for Business 2010*

"For most CEOs, the three things to worry about are (1) Do they really understand all the shifts? (2) Are their strategies sufficiently creative and innovative to respond to those shifts? (3) Are they going to succeed, given the high risk they're taking? Every one of those things is a big deal."
—GRADY MEANS, GLOBAL LEADER OF PRICEWATERHOUSECOOPER'S STRATEGY CONSULTING PRACTICE

"This historical change is not just technologically driven. Culture, religion, family structure, social institutions, values—all are in the process of changing each other through complex feedback with one another." —ALVIN TOFFLER, AUTHOR OF *FUTURE SHOCK* AND *CREATING A NEW CIVILIZATION*

N O ONE, NO MATTER HOW SMART, CAN, WITH complete assurance, predict the future for 10 minutes, let alone 10 years. What we can understand, however, is that we are on a journey to the future—a journey with historical precedents and a sense of direction.

Freedom, for example, has been a rising force in the world for centuries. That force has been constrained or sometimes even reversed for decades. However, any objective reading of our past suggests that we are heading toward even more expansive definitions of human liberty. Combine the power of that force with supporting forces like the growth of mass education, globalization and an explosion in communication technology, and a bet on expanding freedom seems even more of a sure thing.

The exciting potential of the business world of 2010 arises from the acceleration of all the currents that promote human aspiration and choice. Our headlong rush into the future won't be without problems, nor will all companies, industries and individuals prosper. Some, indeed, will fail.

A Continuum Between Yesterday and Tomorrow

The best opportunity for any business to succeed consists of first carefully observing the world and then aligning the organization with the evolving direction. One premise of this book is that there is a continuum between yesterday and tomorrow. Not everyone agrees. There are thoughtful people who believe that we have crossed some invisible breaking point in history, after which the future will be radically different from the past.

The idea here is that, yes, the future *will* be radically different because significant forces *long in motion* are accelerating to a new level. The jet engine and the space shuttle were not created independent of the airplane; they accelerated the technology of flying through the air to new levels of achievement. We have accelerated the process of human development, adding whole new dimensions, but we have not invented it anew.

For sustained business success, bet on accelerated evolution. Align your business with the direction of long-unfolding trends and count on rapid acceleration. That's the one sure bet in this climate of extraordinary opportunity and turbulence.

Abandon 'Either/Or'

After careful observation, the second step in aligning your organization or yourself correctly is to abandon "either/or" thinking. Take freedom as it applies to companies, for example. The issue is never freedom *or* discipline. Just as all companies require freedom to prosper and grow, so do they require a solid base of discipline. That is as true today as it was 100 years ago. What has changed is our definition of discipline.

As many start-ups have discovered, the freedom to respond to customers when and how each employee chooses leads to chaos and increased costs. At the same time, tightly strapping employees into inflexible procedures runs counter to their potential, as well as to every requirement of business today. Front-line people are better educated. With effective training, most workers are capable of making appropriate decisions independently. Customers want quicker responses. Technology can instantly transfer information to decision-makers anywhere in the company. Human resources consists less and less of "hands" and more and more of brains.

Substitute 'Above' or 'Below' the Line

How is a company to get the right balance between discipline and freedom? Instead of either/or thinking, try substituting another equation—one that places any values conflict, such as freedom vs. discipline, "above the line" or "below the line."

Think of discipline as a below-the-line requirement. Here everything must be clear—responsibilities, quality standards, accounting rules, adherence to external regulations, policies, procedures, and all the mechanics of creating and delivering effective products and services to a market. Above the line, everything should be governed by freedom. Here lies the opportunity for individual contribution and imagination in serving customers.

Of course, the proportion of freedom above the line will vary with the industry and the company's position in the industry. I once carried out a consulting assignment at a nuclear power company. Everyone involved, definitely including me, favored rigid and extensive below-the-line controls. That said, most mature companies err on the side of relying too heavily on below-the-line structure and controls. Equally, in their urge to break the mold of past practices, many exuberant start-ups too long postpone the hard work of establishing the right structures, systems and procedures to move the company to the next level of performance.

Think of companies with enviable reputations for exceptional customer service—Marriott, Northwestern Mutual, Disney and Ritz-Carlton, for example. They all display a finely nuanced mix of above-the-line freedom and below-the-line discipline.

In 1928, Bill Marriott Sr. opened the first of his small Hot Shoppes in Washington, D.C. By the early 1930s, when there were five restaurants, Bill and his wife were essentially the whole organization, as he ran from site to site to ensure quality and consistency. When he made plans to open a sixth restaurant, he went to an experienced business lawyer to close the deal. The lawyer advised him against expanding, because he believed it was impossible for one man to control the business. "You can't control the rootbeer in 8 or 10 different shops," the lawyer told the young entrepreneur. "You can't control all these people who make your sandwiches and be sure they are all up to your standards. The bigger you get, the less control you have."[1]

Marriott did not accept the lawyer's verdict. Instead, he encouraged his company's growth by simultaneously combining rigorous centralization of authority, to ensure quality, with decentralization of authority, to encourage entrepreneurship and individual initiative. To keep the business growing, Marriott had to introduce structure and systems. He established a central commissary to purchase food and to prepare standard items for distribution to his small Hot Shoppe chain. Bill Marriott Jr. carried the same systemization to a far higher level as the company entered the hotel business.

Now, as was described in the previous chapter, Marriott is adapting below-the-line discipline and systemization to promote greater freedom of opportunity among its women employees. In modifying work-rule discipline, the company acknowledged employees' need for greater freedom, represented by flexibility of schedules even in a field requiring strict attendance discipline.

At Ritz-Carlton Hotels, employees are first trained in the "gold standards," which set out the company's service credo and its basic discipline for premium service. Then, in the words of one senior executive, employees are empowered "to move heaven and earth" to satisfy customers.

Disney World displays a similar mix of discipline and exacting—and well-enforced—standards for safety, which are not open to individual choice. Yet beyond such nonnegotiable, below-the-line discipline standards, Disney encourages its "cast members" to do whatever is necessary to make guests happy.

Northwestern Mutual's standards for issuing an insurance policy are among the most rigorous in the industry. Once you have a policy, however, employees treat you differentially, as the company strives to live up to its 100-plus-year commitment to be "the policyowner's company."

Thinking above *and* below the line, rather than either/or, changes perspective in healthy ways. Either/or is finite. Above/below is endlessly expansive. In either/or, to add an ounce of discipline, you subtract an ounce of freedom. This is the thought pattern of many leaders of troubled organizations, and nations. However, no organization or nation has a finite amount of either discipline or freedom. Both can be endlessly expanded in the interest of growth and development.

Business leaders who are aligned with societal change consciously or unconsciously seek to expand freedom of choice—among customers, employees and other stakeholders—at the same time that they seek to strengthen discipline by creating standards and values and diminishing the role of personal authority.

As was discussed in Chapter Eight, the evolution toward "uncentralized" organizations creates new pressures—and opportunities—to redefine the relationship between freedom and discipline in companies. The key to what Harlan Cleveland sometimes calls "the nobody-in-charge society" is a set of mutually agreed on values and standards, coupled with far greater freedom for people at the periphery to make rapid, individual decisions in alignment with those standards and values.

A Continuing Evolution of Societal and Business Values

Reasonable people can argue about the degree, direction and desirability of the changes we see today, but virtually everyone agrees that the changes are profound and that their pace is accelerating.

The turmoil about education curricula is one reflection of the pace of change. Not so long ago, a person graduated from high school or college with most of the skills required for a life-time of work. Now, that educational edge is gone in five to seven years. With that backdrop, it's understandable that we are arguing about what constitutes a basic education today.

A Fundamental Shift in Values

Shaping all this change is a fundamental shift in human values. Although we commonly apply the word *values* to ethical and cultural principles, there are many kinds of values. They may be physical (cleanliness, punctuality), organizational (communication, coordination), psychological (courage, generosity), mental (objectivity, sincerity), or spiritual (harmony, love, self-giving).

Whether linked to body, mind or spirit, values are central organizing principles or ideas that govern and determine human behavior. In a very real sense, values are our invisible organizers. Business values like customer service, quality, and respect for people give direction to our thought processes, sentiments, emotional energies, preferences and actions. In business and in life, we express values in everything we do or say. The conscious or subconscious values of any society or organization crucially determine how that society or business sees its strengths and envisions future possibilities.[2]

In a company, family or nation, values are the essence of knowledge gained from past experience. We extract a basic wisdom of life by distilling knowledge from its local circumstances and specific context. We then form that basic wisdom into conscious or unconscious values that shape our thoughts, decision-making, and actions from then on.

In some companies, values are communicated by a credo or values statement. In other companies, values are so strong that the employees internalize them.

The oldest conscious business value I have encountered in North America is that of safety at the DuPont Co. (formally known as E.I. du Pont de Nemours & Co., Inc.). The formal name, like the value, can be traced to company founder Eleutherè I. du Pont. The young émigré from revolutionary France came to America in 1790 after abandoning his property and privileges of aristocratic birth. However, he brought with him two valuable assets—technology and a new idea. The technology enabled him to produce the best gunpowder in the New World.

His idea, briefly, is the company's long-standing philosophy to produce only products that can be made, used, handled and disposed of safely. That's a lofty idea today in the age of environmentalism. It was an incredible idea 200 years ago, when a plentiful supply of laborers could be hired for a few cents a day to work in gunpowder plants that then had the tendency to blow up in what was considered a normal business risk. At the DuPont gunpowder plant on the Brandywine River outside Wilmington, Del., specially constructed shelters protected workers during dangerous steps in the gunpowder process.

In some companies, values are communicated by a credo or values statement. In other companies, values are so strong that the employees internalize them.

Like all effective values, DuPont's safety effort has steadily expanded in alignment with society's changing expectations and with the company's changing goals. Today, DuPont is evolving into a "science company focused on sustainable growth." During this transition, the company continues to work hard on its traditional safety efforts, although its performance is already the best in the chemical industry and ahead by a factor of eight or nine when compared with the all-industry average. Beyond this effort, however, DuPont has vastly expanded its definition of environmental safety to include "injuries and illnesses to our employees and contractors; incidents such as fires, explosions, accidental releases to the environment, and transportation accidents; global waste and emissions; and the use of depletable raw material and energy."

By 2010, for example, the company wants to get 10% of its total energy needs from renewable energy sources such as wind power, and to realize 25% of its revenues from nondepletable resources such as agricultural feedstock, up from 8% in 1999.

Chairman and CEO Charles O. Holliday, like other DuPont leaders before him, carries another title as well: "Chief Safety, Health and Environmental Officer." In his annual letter to shareholders, he reports first on the company's safety and environmental progress and challenges, and then on the financial results.

Values such as safety, hard work, responsibility, integrity, tolerance, and respect for one another are more than noble ideals. They are pragmatic principles, proven useful enough to be transmitted over generations as tools for future advancement. Our willingness to struggle in every generation to live up to them, and redefine them when necessary, demonstrates our inherent belief in their utility.

We tend to overlook the central role of values in the development of both societies and organizations, partly because they are intangible and partly because they become more internalized—and hence more invisible—over time.

A values shift underpins many of the changes we are living through. Businesses seeking to align themselves with these value changes must view them as a continuum. The rest of this section focuses on five specific societal value shifts of particular relevance to U.S. business.

1. From War Toward Peace

Watch the evening news and you will think we have moved scarcely an inch in the direction of peace. Stretch the time frame, and the picture changes for the better.

"Contrary to public perception, we're seeing a declining number of conflicts," David Malone, president of the International Peace Academy told *The Wall Street Journal*, in March, 2000.[3] The IPA is an independent, nonpartisan, international organization that advises the UN and others on peacekeeping and conflict resolution. "Wars between states have declined sharply," Malone added, "any many civil wars have been addressed very effectively."

To be sure, eras of peace have been declared before, only to end in massive bloodshed. In 1968, near the end of writing their massive 11-volume history of civilization, historians Will and Ariel Durant noted that in the previous 3,421 years of recorded history, they could find only 268 years without a significant war.[4] Any historian considering the years since would produce hardly any improvement in this ratio.

Yet today there is definitely a higher commitment—and better tools—to avoid at least macro-level conflict. Part of this change stems from an understanding of the power of nuclear weapons to destroy life and accumulated wealth. Part of stems from a wider global perspective. Recently, more attention has been focused on local and tribal conflict. A growing number of countries, including Canada and the nations of the European Union, now place a new discipline known as "conflict prevention" at the core of their diplomatic and foreign aid efforts.

A values shift underpins many of the changes we are living through. The rest of this section focuses on five specific societal value shifts of particular relevance to U.S. business.

Sweden's Uppsala University peace department keeps a widely cited list of regional conflicts. From 1992 to 1998, the university reports, conflicts declined in all five of the world's major regions from a total of 55 to 36. Preliminary figures from 1999 show a slight rise from 1998, but the numbers are still way down from the early 1990s.[5]

Since the end of the Cold War in 1989, world expenditures on armaments have declined from an all-time high of $1.3 trillion to the current level of about $850 billion, a drop of more than 40%. Some countries, notably China, India and Japan, are expected to increase overall military expenditures over the next 10 years. In 2000, both U.S. presidential candidates promised an increase in military spending, reflecting national support for a stronger military. However, in an absence of a major war, spending levels are unlikely to increase to anywhere near the levels of the early 1990s.

IMPLICATIONS FOR BUSINESS. Military spending boosts sales for specific companies and industries. However, the overall decline in military expenditure has been a boon to the commercial economy, especially in the U.S. Investment capital flowed out of government debt into public markets. This infusion of capital helped upgrade infrastructure, modernize plants and machinery, finance private research and development, restructure industries, and create new companies and technologies.

This massive shift in resources provided a significant part

of the capital to increase the productivity and living standards in the U.S. and around the world. One related result was the longest sustained economic expansion in the U.S. history and a dramatic transition from government deficits to surpluses. A world that turns increasingly to peaceful solutions offers expanding possibilities for business development, especially in the global market.

2. From Industrial to Technological Civilization
In less than 10 years, advances in telecommunications, computerization and new software developments have changed the way people communicate and conduct trade.

For the first time, says futurist Alvin Toffler, "we are creating a technological civilization that is not industrial....What we are living through is the rapid emergence and spread of a whole new way of life, and a totally new way of creating wealth."[6]

The Internet is the single greatest accelerator—and symbol—of the change. Like-minded individuals are forming their own networks in this new social climate around common interests in business, consumer and environmental issues; politics; sports; hobbies; and even sexual variations.

In an older model, knowledge, information, power and decision-making were located at the top of society and its organizations. Information flowed up from the bottom, but decisions came down from the top. Now the rapidly emerging model permits organizations or informal networks to collect, share and use information across multiple locations. Faith in technological innovation has become a value of society.

A longer-term shift from tangible products to intangible services also shapes the character of this new "technological civilization." Rising affluence shifts buying priorities from hard goods to services like education, securities, health care and tourism.

Services offer a wide field of opportunity for technology-based innovation. However, as was discussed earlier, such non-material resources as organization and technology are lifting even manufacturing and agriculture to new levels of productivity and performance.

IMPLICATIONS FOR BUSINESS. Private-sector companies are leading the way into the networked society. They are the first to exploit new technological resources for marketing, sharing information, and managing new business opportunities, projects, procurement, supply chains and customer service.

The automobile sector illustrates the potential of the new technologies to reduce costs and lift revenues for a traditional industry. Revenues from direct sales to consumers will rise, squeezing independent dealers. By 2010, traditional dealers will make only an estimated 55% of sales, down from 95% now.

Another technological innovation—one that will integrate advanced electronics into cars and trucks—is expected to be a $12-billion business by 2010, with 20% growth a year. High-tech devices embedded in rearview mirrors and other parts of cars will use satellite communications to turn on lights at home, send voice mail and faxes, provide traffic information and pay tolls automatically.

Electronic buying exchanges are expanding operating efficiencies for the industry. Covisint, an Internet purchasing exchange, brings together hundreds of suppliers competing for work from Ford, DaimlerChrysler and GM. Similar forms of joint e-purchasing will help auto companies reduce costs by pooling purchases of electricity and office supplies, among other items.[7]

Each corporate innovation helps define and redefine how the expanded resources can and should be used. Businesses will bear the brunt of the emerging arguments about the role of privacy in a networked society. As businesses test the frontiers, they will ignite the sparks in society that eventually will result in definition of the issue through legislation, court decisions and regulations that, in turn, will define business's freedom of action.

3. From a National Toward a Global Perspective

As recently as 50 years ago, Americans were widely derided in educated European circles for having a hopelessly provincial mentality. America refused to join the League of Nations after World War I. The isolationism of the 1930s, politically expressed as "America First," was a major force before the

U.S. entered World War II. Faith in a "Fortress America," separated by two oceans from foreign contamination, was long-standing and widespread.

Cultivated Americans looked to Europe for art, literature and style, as they had for at least two centuries. "Good Americans, when they die, go to Paris," said the 19th-century author and physician Oliver Wendell Holmes (Sr.).

Suspicion of foreign motives and foreigners was deeply ingrained in the American character—an ironic trait, inasmuch as most Americans had either been immigrants themselves or could identify near ancestors who came from other nations.

Early in our history, President Monroe announced that the U.S. would oppose any foreign intervention in the Western Hemisphere (the Monroe Doctrine). In the first decade of the 20th century, Theodore Roosevelt was the first president to publicly advocate the idea of America as a world power. Franklin Roosevelt, Harry Truman and Dwight Eisenhower, three later American presidents who helped translate Teddy Roosevelt's vision into reality, were all born in the 19th century, when Europe was the center of the world in every aspect of life.

THE WORLD VIEWED IN A DIFFERENT LIGHT. When John Kennedy, the first president born in the 20th century, took office in 1961, he and most of the young men around him had been junior officers in World War II. They took it for granted that the U.S. was a superpower, a global—if not *the* global—trendsetter with authority and responsibilities to match. Their ascension to power ratified a shift in American perspective that had been building for decades.

Those "New Frontiersmen" saw the world in a different light. They looked beyond Europe, exuding confidence in the destiny of America to lead not only the West but the world. They pictured the third world, not Europe, as the main theater of combat with Communism. Whereas previous generations of young Americans traveled overseas to learn, the new administration created the Peace Corps so that young Americans could go abroad to teach. The same leaders embroiled the U.S. in a disastrous struggle with Communist nationalism in Southeast Asia.

Forty years later and forty years wiser, we still debate the nature of America's role in the world, but we no longer debate that we have one. And, whether we're hooked on high-end wines, stereo equipment and luxury automobiles, or low-end apparel, kitchen appliances and ethnic foods, American consumers relish being part of a global market in products and ideas. No group seems more open to the lure of globalization than America's youngsters. Japan's "Pokémon: The First Movie" took in more than $32 million at the box office during its first weekend. In September 2000, the Harry Potter books from Britain held the four top spots on *The New York Times* list of best-selling children's books.

AN APPETITE FOR FOREIGN GOODS AND SERVICES. This appetite for foreign goods and services each year helps run up our trade deficit to levels that at one time were considered stratospheric. U.S. imports of goods and services exceeded exports by $271.3 billion in 1999, up more than $100 billion over the 1998 total. The deficit was the biggest since the Commerce Department began compiling numbers in 1992. Moreover, oil prices sent monthly deficits climbing to new highs in the summer of 2000.

Many economists remain sanguine, however, insisting that as long as the U.S. remains the world's strongest economy, American consumers will inevitably outspend their global counterparts. Many also argue that the large trade deficit helps keep U.S. inflation in check by providing U.S. consumers with an array of inexpensive imports.

America's "well-to-do are buying luxury goods from France, Italy and Belgium; the less flush are buying bargain-basement goods from China and the Far East," notes Bill Cheney, chief economist with John Hancock Financial Services Inc., in Boston. "Either way that's bad for the trade balances, but you won't hear any consumer complaints."[8]

At a time when we import more than any other nation, we also lead the world in export sales. We sell everything from soybeans to soda pop, from metal presses to Madonna releases. We lead the world in sales of computers, software, pharmaceuticals, aircraft, scientific instruments, medical devices, compact discs, agricultural products and much more. Like American consumers, businesses are reaching for new opportunities in the global market.

Even so, we still export a smaller share of our output than other developed nations—about 12% of our gross domestic product (GDP), compared with roughly 25% for Germany and Canada. The domestic market is so big that for decades many companies did not bother to look beyond U.S. borders for customers. In fact, 20 years ago, exports accounted for a mere 7.5% of GDP. That situation is now rapidly changing, as the significance of world markets becomes more apparent. Over the next decade the export share of our GDP will climb to 15%, representing a doubling of the percentage in 20 years.

A GROWING GLOBAL INFRASTRUCTURE. As the global perspective has grown in the U.S., we have helped sponsor a variety of political, economic, educational and other types of international organizations. Over the past half century we helped create and fund the United Nations, the International Monetary Fund (IMF), the World Bank, the Inter-American Development Bank, NATO (North Atlantic Treaty Organization), UNESCO (United Nations Educational, Scientific, and Cultural Organization), International Labor Organization (ILO), World Health Organization (WHO), and many others. The development of regional trade alliances like the North American Free Trade Agreement (NAFTA) is another sign that we are committed to strengthening an infrastructure for even greater global and regional cooperation and trade flows.

Support in the business community for these new organizations is far from universal. Many of the old complaints remain, some of them certainly reasonable, about the attitudes of foreigners in dealing with us and about the way international organizations spend U.S. taxpayers' money. However, the significant development is that these international organizations exist at all—and that they enjoy a measure of U.S. support that would have seemed incredible to most Americans as late as 1939. This shift in values seems likely only to gain momentum in the next decade.

IMPLICATIONS FOR BUSINESS. Start with globalization as a generator of U.S. economic activity. Each $1 billion in exports translates into 13,000 new jobs. About 12 million U.S. jobs, close to 10% of our overall employment, directly support exports today, a total that's sure to grow in the next decade. That figure counts only *direct* jobs. Each dollar of exports generates related economic activity in sales and purchases in related industries, such as processing and transportation.

Conversely, imports can mean job losses, as in the 1980s, when imports penetrated industries such as textiles, footwear, steel and autos. Some economists estimate that, in the early 1980s alone, the U.S. lost more than 2 million manufacturing jobs to foreign competition.

While gains and losses within industries are uneven, expanding international trade increases the total number of jobs in a country as a whole.

While gains and losses within industries are uneven, expanding international trade increases the total number of jobs in a country as a whole. Freedom of competition forces each country to exploit its competitive advantages, putting resources to their most efficient use. In 1997–99, for example, the U.S. added an estimated 1.7 million jobs thanks to reduction of trade barriers in North America (through NAFTA), and other parts of the world (through WTO and bilateral pacts with Pacific nations).[9]

Global opportunities. Beyond its impact in the U.S., globalization accelerates the growth of countries elsewhere, particularly developing countries, creating still more opportunities for sale of U.S. goods and services. The area of fastest growth will be Asia. The populations of three countries in the region— China, India and Indonesia—represent more than 60% of the world's people.

One statistic illustrates the changing patterns of world trade. In 1975, developing countries accounted for less than 7% of global trade in manufactured items. Today, that percentage has nearly tripled—and the growth will continue as these countries realign their economies toward more manufacturing and higher value-added services. Rising domestic market demand plus expansion of individual and economic freedom will likely spur higher rates of economic growth in these countries, where significant middle-class populations have already begun to emerge.

According to recent projections, Asia will account for 40% of all airliner sales in 10 to 15 years. Over the next decade, 50% of the world's investment in power generation will go to Asia. Even assuming that some Asian countries manage to leapfrog in technology to the new micropower systems discussed in Chapter Seven, the investment will still be huge. By 2010, total auto sales in Asia are expected to exceed sales in the U.S., with a significant potential remaining because the starting base is relatively low. An expansion of this scope is sure to increase concerns about pollution. However, as noted in Chapter Three, the World Bank has found that developing countries are facing up to the need to reduce environmental hazards, including pollution, at a much earlier stage of their development than was the case in the Western, developed countries.

> **Achievement of what nations or societies aspire to begets aspiration for still more. Expanding education and freedom will reinforce a climate of rising expectations.**

Aspiration begets aspiration. Achievement of what nations or societies aspire to begets aspiration for still more. As education and freedom expand throughout the developing world, they will reinforce a climate of rising expectations. By bringing the world to isolated villages, technology will speed the process.

Threatened industries, individuals and governments the world over will resist the tide, making it flow unevenly at best and reversing it in specific situations at worst, The outlook for Global Business 2010, however, is positive. Agile companies will find more innovative ways to search for opportunities in unfamiliar markets, develop niches protected from fierce global competitors, form alliances to add strength, produce world-class products even in domestic markets, and, perhaps most important of all, create environments that attract and retain talented people.

As Dave Rasmussen, the CEO of two Grand Rapids, Mich., companies that make tools, dies and molds for a variety of major corporations, told me: "In the 1980s, we complained about foreign competition. In the 1990s, we got excited about global opportunities. Now we understand we were always talking about the same thing."

4. From Centralized Authority Toward Freedom

In the 20th century, the U.S. became the leading modern society—"the first 20th-century country," in the words of Boston University historian David Fromkin. We achieved this status, Fromkin says, "in part by becoming the leader of the industrial revolution that began in England, and in part by becoming the leader of the political revolution that also began in Britain" with the Magna Carta. This "Great Charter," issued and reissued between 1215 and 1225, limited the rights of the English king.[10]

The American rebels of 1776 and the framers of the U.S. Constitution were clearly acting within the tradition of limiting the power of a central authority—king or government. However, it was not until Andrew Jackson became president in 1829 that the idea of truly popular democracy effectively entered the mainstream of our politics.

Jackson, says historian Paul Johnson, "was the first major figure in American politics to believe passionately and wholly in the popular will...." As governor of Florida, Jackson ruled that mere residence was enough to give an adult white male the vote. In 1822, he proposed that every free man in a nation or state should have the vote, arguing that the more people who could vote the better, since, if Washington was rotten, that gave them the remedy.[11]

While uneven in its speed of progress, this line of political thought is easily traceable for the next 180 years of our history—from the emancipation of slaves in the 1860s to the extension of voting rights to women and the direct election of Congress in the early 1900s; to Woodrow Wilson's proposal for nations' "self-determination" in international relations; to Franklin Roosevelt's campaigns to mobilize the power of government for the "forgotten man," who also happened to vote; to the Civil Rights movement of the 1960s; and to the efforts in our own time to limit the political clout of elites through campaign finance reform.

REFLECTIONS THROUGHOUT AMERICAN LIFE. This democratization of our politics is mirrored in every aspect of American life. What was once closed, except to the elite, continues to open wider for all. As this value has expanded, we have created or expanded institutions to support it.

Mutual funds make us all Wall Street capitalists. We produce more millionaires in a year than we used to in decades. College degrees, once a trademark of the elite, are a widely available passport to higher levels of society. Social Security, pensions and 401(k)s guarantee a basic retirement from work for millions. What was once "insider knowledge" is readily available on TV or the Internet. Mortgages make owning property, once an entitlement of the gentry, open to the masses.

Budget holiday packages create travel and get-away opportunities for workers. Talk radio and Internet sites give the people on the street the type of sounding board once enjoyed only by media moguls. Next time you sit in a wall-to-wall auto traffic jam, remember that until early in the 20th century a carriage was a luxury of the rich. True, gentlemen and farmers owned horses, but farm horses were seldom available for nonessential work.

The social impacts of these changes are easy to see all around us. Immigrants used to be pressured to conform socially to American (i.e., Anglo) norms. Today they are free to enjoy the benefits of American citizenship while retaining their own cultural identity. Television, radio and CDs bring "high" culture to anyone who wants it. Skillful mass production techniques make it more difficult to distinguish expensive clothes and accessories from cheaper knockoffs. Almost anyone who really cares to can be neatly dressed. Many don't care to—expressing their individuality by dressing down.

Not all of these expansions of freedom lead to desirable results for society or for individuals. But all of them represent irrefutable and accelerating trends that business must recognize and incorporate into its internal operations and external outlook.

IMPLICATIONS FOR BUSINESS. Bosses over age 40 have already noticed that probably no one under 30—and almost no one under 40—calls them sir or ma'am anymore. That would have been the norm not very long ago. If you are under 40 yourself, you won't care, and you might not even have noticed the change. You can still gain respect for your knowledge, expertise, age (in some organizations) and character, but deference to your role as boss is a rapidly diminishing asset.

A more serious implication is the continuing requirement for organizational restructuring. Every institution of society—business, government, education, labor—will evolve differently from here on as it tries to align itself with changed societal expectations and values.

Within businesses, restructuring translates into redistributing power and authority to where decisions are made. Power at the center will continue to be dispersed nationally and globally. Physical symbols often represent the magnitude of this psychological change.

> **Within businesses, restructuring translates into redistributing power and authority to where decisions are made. Power at the center will continue to be dispersed nationally and globally.**

Wilmington, Del., once epitomized the company town—headquarters of the mighty DuPont Co. The country's largest chemical company shook residents recently when it announced that it was selling three of its four headquarters buildings—about 10% of the city's office space.

As discussed earlier, DuPont is evolving from a chemical company to "a science company focused on sustainable growth." While keeping—and expanding—its traditional values, the company is now increasing its focus on products and services that promote the exploration of space, the improvement of agricultural productivity, the protection of lives, the saving of energy, and the comfort and appearance of clothing. Also, the company increasingly looks for growth in the global market. In keeping with trends in globalization and "uncentralization" discussed earlier, DuPont's building sale signals that the company no longer considers heavy centralized real estate investments, like large headquarters staffs, to be the best use of its corporate assets.

The move also illustrates how the shift from manufacturing to services has affected one city's workforce. DuPont's big building sale climaxed a decade during which the company sold off real estate and cut its Wilmington workforce. In the same era, MBNA, a giant credit card company, put up five buildings and hired thousands of workers in the Wilmington area.

A successful transformation into a new business era is not the first for the city. In 1904, when three du Pont cousins decided to build a large headquarters in Wilmington rather than relocate to New York or Philadelphia, the city was adjusting to the waning of two of its earlier mainstay industries—shipbuilding and the manufacture of railroad cars.[12]

5. From Conquering to Sustaining the Environment

For two centuries we focused on uncovering and applying nature's secrets to improve human health, comfort and enjoyment. Although this is still our quest, we have more recently added an expansive, new dimension. In barely four decades, we have revised centuries-old thought patterns about the importance of protecting and sustaining the natural environment around us.

In 1962, when Rachael Carson published the landmark environmentalist book *The Silent Spring*, she brought to public attention concerns that until then had been confined to specialists. In just a few years, a conservation movement that had focused almost exclusively on keeping the wilderness wild evolved into a global environmental cause.

Imagine predicting in the mid 1960s that millions of Americans by century's end would be regularly recycling their garbage. Or that major companies would have full-time environmental safety officers. Or that some consumers would base buying decisions on a company's environmental record. Or that environmental safety would dictate expensive aspects of the production, packaging and delivery of hundreds of products. "No way," would have been the likely reply.

It was only 30 years ago that some of our major rivers were on fire from industrial waste. Schools in Los Angeles were canceling gym classes because it was unsafe for children to play outside. The change is dramatic. Our air and water are both vastly improved. One evidence of our altered perspective is how often environmental hazards or events lead the evening television news shows. Thirty years ago, the same story would have merited two inches on page 26 of the evening paper, if that.

Environmental issues now regularly unite generations or rival political parties. When the leaders of the 1994 Republican congressional "Revolution" talked of modestly rolling back some existing environmental legislation, they were surprised to find opposition among newly elected Republican "Young Turks." The leaders quickly curtailed the effort.

While some environmental causes remain far from the mainstream, the consensus today is wide and deep. And, increasingly, the environmental movement is crossing borders.

In part, this shift in values is a product of our greater affluence. Hungry people don't worry much about pollution. Rising living standards give us the luxury to be concerned. The change is also attributable to education—in the classroom and by the media. Listen to a group of tenth- or eleventh-graders talk about technology. In their analysis of benefits and risks, they sound like the radical environmentalists of the 1970s. Any reputable high school science course will include modules on preserving the environment.

The openness and freedom of expression of our society also accelerated the pace and depth of the values shift toward environmentalism. In contrast, when the Iron Curtain lifted in the 1990s, it quickly became clear that a closed society with unaccountable leaders had felt little responsibility for the cleanliness of its soil, air or water.

While some environmental causes remain far from the mainstream, the consensus today is wide and deep. And, increasingly, the environmental movement is crossing borders, propelled by the same globalization, technological innovation and expanding education that has energized global business.

Until recently, environmental issues were isolated national concerns. Pollution stirred unease in one country, acid rain in another, and the loss of nonrenewable resources in a third.

Now the stage is widening. Better measuring tools are giving us more exact readings of environmental changes around the world. Every year that we do this, we add more information to our baseline measuring progress or deterioration.

"The stage appears to be set for a transformation in outlook similar to that which took place in economics in the 1930s," says historian David Fromkin. According to the dominant economic theory before the Great Depression, full employment would come about automatically in a completely free economy. The consensus, built up over generations, was that the government should not attempt to manage the economy. In fact, major economic disruptions, called panics prior to the 1930s, were viewed as uncontrollable by human intervention—in effect a force of nature.

Then with millions out of work in the Great Depression, people lost patience with that "invisible hand" explanation, however valid the theory. In time, governments took up full employment as a national goal. Similarly, adds Fromkin, a healthy overall global environment "may have to be a consciously set goal requiring, at some point in the future, some kind of overall governing body." Whatever the mechanism—the free market or government regulation—the key turning point will occur when human society as a whole assumes responsibility for the health of the planet.[13]

IMPLICATIONS FOR BUSINESS. In the early years of environmentalism, business adapted slowly and reluctantly to mandated changes. There were dire predictions of loss of efficiency and productivity because mounting environmental costs in the U.S. were not borne by foreign competitors.

Yet, so far at least, anecdotal evidence points in the opposite direction. In an era when companies have been steadily adopting better and more comprehensive environmental safeguards, the productivity and competitiveness of American companies soared to new heights. Meanwhile, other Western nations enacted legislation that was as tough as U.S. law, if not tougher. Although cause and effect are difficult to link scientifically, it's hard to argue that cleaning up our environment has damaged our economy.

Now, business will feel the impact of a new generation that accepts environmental safety and cleanliness as a given. The young people now entering business learned their science from the first wave of teachers fully influenced by the environmental movement. Every year from here on will bring more of such young adults into business. When business leaders try to explain the cost-benefit ratios of environmental safety, they can expect looks that say, "You just don't get it."

Many companies and industries already *do* get it, of course. In the auto industry, for example, companies are planning 100% recyclable cars and non-polluting engines. Other companies have learned the power of advertising their environmental safety efforts. And, everyone by now has learned the importance of avoiding the kind of environmental catastrophes that lead the evening news.

Even as companies have steadily adopted better and more comprehensive environmental safeguards, the productivity and competitiveness of American companies soared to new heights.

Meanwhile, the Environmental Protection Agency (EPA) is taking a fresh look at ways to resolve environmental problems. The emphasis now is on greater cooperative partnerships, and on simpler and more flexible processes for making rules. For example, EPA has been pilot-testing a new approach to broaden public participation in decisions about the use of older agricultural pesticides. The aim of the program is to make decisions more transparent to the agricultural community, whose members are most directly affected by EPA findings. The EPA is also concentrating on what it calls "equal environmental protection"—an effort to ensure that no group of people or geographic location bears a disproportionate exposure to pollutants.

6. A Values Shift for Government

It's not only big businesses like DuPont that must reinvent themselves. That urgent task confronts government as well. Business has a huge stake in this these values shifts, which mirror the forces that are propelling changes in companies and industries.

Business often views government as an uneasy ally at best or an adversary at worst. Yet how well and how quickly government can adapt to global and technological forces of change will have a major impact on business for decades. Government as a reactionary force has an unfortunate potential to slow business progress and retard its competitiveness. A responsive government, however, can help provide a predictable and stable infrastructure for greater corporate efficiency and international competitiveness.

Even before the collapse of the Soviet Union, the consensus supporting Big Government was beginning to shred.

To do that, government, like business, requires a 21st-century vision. Our current model of an activist and highly centralized federal government came of age under President Woodrow Wilson in the years before and during World War I. The young Democrats who served as Wilson's deputies, including Franklin Roosevelt who served as Wilson's secretary of the Navy, came back to Washington in 1933 during the worst economic crisis in our history. To combat the crisis, they created a host of "New Deal" programs modeled on Wilsonian ideals, requiring a stronger federal government for implementation.

In the late 1930s and early 1940s, as the New Deal evolved into a wartime economy, the need for a strong federal government became more widely accepted. The 50-year Cold War with its threat of nuclear annihilation further reinforced centralized federal authority. However, even before the collapse of the Soviet Union, the consensus supporting Big Government was beginning to shred. In the years since, many of government's strongest advocates have acknowledged the need for major reform.

RISING PRESSURES FOR REDESIGN. The next decade is likely to see changes in government roughly comparable to the revolution that has shaken business since the 1980s. So far, most of the improvements achieved under the banner of Reinventing Government are the type of operational efficiencies carried out in business in the late 1980s and early 1990s. Although there has been considerable downsizing, much of it in the military, there has been too little of what industry calls "rightsizing"—the reduction of a workforce to an optimum size on the basis of a reevaluation of the basic purpose and functions of the organization.

To be sure, there is a far greater focus on "the customer" in most government agencies. Missions, however, are still largely intact. Of course, government agencies have broad missions to serve large societal needs, but critics of large government charge, with justification, that, over time, agencies tend to develop what the nonprofit sector calls "mission creep." There is always one more worthy need to be served by an agency, at least in the mind of an ambitious agency chief.

The coming retirements among government employees discussed in Chapters Two and Eight will also create more pressure for more comprehensive redesigns of work flows. As citizens enjoy the speed, flexibility and personalization of responses from private-sector networks, expectations for government responsiveness are sure to rise, creating still more pressure for change.

Government, because of the scope of its activities, will never match the efficiency and speed of the private sector. Unlike business, government cannot choose its customers. Moreover, in social services particularly, government has to serve people who are least likely to welcome innovation in how their services are packaged, paid for or delivered—the poor, uneducated, elderly or infirm.

Also, government inherits by default many assignments that are simply not susceptible to cost-benefit analysis and short-term results. It was, after all, government-funded research that produced the Internet.

E-GOVERNMENT: COMING NEXT. Even within these limitations, however, there is vast scope for improving and speeding government services. Within the next five years, says *The Economist,* the Internet "will transform not only the way in which most public services are delivered, but also the fundamental relationship between government and citizen. After e-commerce and e-business, the next Internet revolution is e-government."[14]

Some American companies are already saving about 20% a year by putting their purchasing on the Web. If government could achieve just half that rate, it would save U.S. taxpayers $55 billion a year.

Then there is the potential for more direct access to information and services, a welcome alternative to standing in long lines at government offices. In Arizona, for example, most drivers can now go online and renew their licenses 24 hours a day, seven days a week. Transactions average two minutes each. Setting up the site, which is free to users, did not cost the state a cent. It was built and is maintained and hosted by IBM, which is paid about $4 for each vehicle registration, currently saving the state about $1.7 million a year.[15]

Government will certainly multiply this kind of operating and service efficiency by the thousands in the next decade, adding value and convenience for both businesses and individual citizens. Yet, reducing costs and adding services are only the beginning of the real challenge of "reinventing government." Like business, government must now reexamine its central purpose in an age of globalization, increasing individual freedom and instant communication.

A CONTRACT WITH AMERICA.COM. Former House Speaker Newt Gingrich was one of the more tech-friendly lawmakers in his days in power. He was a driving force behind putting congressional information online, and was a leader in blocking legislation restricting the emerging Internet industry. In the years since resigning as Speaker in 1998, Gingrich has spent considerable time in California, visiting and learning from start-ups and venture capitalists.

Government, he now believes, "has got to find a way to behave with the agility of tech companies." Without a rapid overhaul, the government risks irrelevance, because "the language of politics and government is increasingly isolated from the language of everyday life."

Some of the visionary ideas Gingrich now advocates are: a free computer for every four-year-old, an open Internet bidding process for weapons systems, online voting using a thumb print or eye identification, free online access for everyone and a medical smart card for everyone.[16]

Smart cards, which sandwich a microchip between slices of plastic, have been used in Europe for a variety of functions since mid 1970s. In the emerging Medicard model, local doctors, hospitals, ambulance companies, and pharmacies record customers' medical information on an individual's card. Embedded in the patient's card would be information about every diagnosis, operation and prescription, as well as insurance data, allergy information and emergency contacts. The aim would be to improve integrated care without building a centralized patient-tracking system.

GOVERNMENT AS REGULATOR. Other even more basic government roles await resolution, starting with the government's role as a regulator. Early in the 20th century, a series of landmark decisions shaped the relationship between the emerging industrialized economy and the government. One big issue was whether the government should ensure universal access to two new marvels—the telephone and electricity. Decisions then led to government-regulated, electric-utility monopolies and to development of the giant Ma Bell, a private telephone company that guaranteed access to service like a public utility until its breakup in 1984.

In 1911, the Supreme Court dissolved the Standard Oil Trust, clearly establishing the government's role in regulating monopoly power. Fear of economic size was something that had been building in America for more than 20 years. By 1882, Standard already controlled 80% of the nation's refining business, rising to more than 90% by 1900.

The Sherman Anti-Trust Act passed in 1890 at first did little to slow the concentration of economic power not only in oil but also in industries like tobacco and steel. Then, in a landmark decision two decades later, the court ordered the breakup of Standard Oil into 34 companies, among them companies that became Exxon, Amoco, Mobile and Chevron. With that decision, the Sherman act—as well as government's role as a "monopoly buster"—came of age. Three years later—in 1914—Congress passed legislation creating the Federal Trade Commission (FTC) to enforce a variety of antitrust and consumer protection laws.

Mirroring today's arguments about the Microsoft case, economists still argue whether Standard Oil's buying out of competitors and price cutting actually helped or hindered the growth of the industry and availability of cheap fuel. Even as the decision came down, Standard was being challenged by new sources of oil from Texas and the Mideast. Ironically, the biggest winner from the case was John D. Rockefeller, who had put together the Standard Oil Trust in 1882. As an original shareholder in the companies that formed Standard Oil, he found himself after the court's decision with a diversified portfolio of companies. Many of these newly liberated firms later successfully went to public markets seeking investment funds for future growth and enriching their original shareholders in the process.

The huge and violent antiglobalization demonstrations at the World Trade Organization 2000 meeting in Seattle signal what is to come in the next decade.

Today's era of technological innovation has created a whole new set of related issues. With the Microsoft case, the government signaled that it will resist any perceived stranglehold on the basic resource of the Information Age Economy—digitized information. Taxing Internet commerce is still a contentious issue, dividing state and national governments. So far, the U.S. government has taken a hands-off stance on taxing Internet transactions to help promote the new technology. The name Congress gave the 1998 Internet Tax Freedom Act betrays what state and local tax collectors are up against. Despite what many consumers believe, online retail sales are not, in fact, free of local and state taxes. However, in two decisions the Supreme Court has ruled that e-tailers have no legal obligation to collect taxes due on purchases ordered from another state.

The revolution in biology creates still other key issues. With the announcement of the world's first cloned animal in 1997, President Clinton almost immediately banned research into cloning humans and convened an ethics panel to study the issue.

The new technologies have spawned a whole range of

emerging privacy issues. How will government respond as the Internet makes your employment, insurance and financial records, among other records, ever more accessible to others? The Clinton White House in its first executive order of the year 2000 prohibited federal agencies from using genetic information in hiring or promotion decisions. Extending that limitation to the private sector is sure to stir controversy.[17] Insurance companies, for example, now have a right to demand physical exams for potential policyholders. Will that right be extended to genetic information that could indicate a disease risk that is not now apparent?

IMPLICATIONS FOR BUSINESS. As globalization accelerates, many new issues are beyond the power of national governments. Few global structures yet exist to deal with such issues as the international digital divide between rich and poor nations, a lack of international securities regulation and ground rules for concentration of corporate power.

Business may prefer that governments respond with benign neglect to such issues, but that is unlikely. The huge and violent antiglobalization demonstrations at the World Trade Organization 2000 meeting in Seattle signal what is to come in the next decade. The demonstrators, mostly in their 20s and 30s, are just as aware as business leaders are that many key decisions are no longer in the hands of national governments.

American business sees the migration of power from national governments as a huge unleashing of opportunity. To the mostly youthful dissenters, who are far more sophisticated and pragmatic than their Marxist predecessors, the impotence of national governments accelerates global inequities. In addition to demonstrating, they participate in hundreds of organizations that lobby for legislation like taxes on international capital flows and restraints on corporate giants whose activities result in job losses.

For now, equality remains a largely discredited notion in the U.S. Communism, humanity's brutal attempt at equality, degenerated into state totalitarianism. Socialism led to another dead-end. Yet equality lingers as an ideal even in the capitalistic West. Since the New Deal in the 1930s, the U.S. has emphasized meeting the minimum needs of all its citizens.

The support for state intervention to assist the disadvantaged is even stronger in Europe and Japan, and it is growing worldwide. At heart, opponents of globalization argue that globalization bestows its benefits unequally on rich and poor.

The coming debates on equality will be hampered by lack of commonly accepted measurements. Whereas many critics focus on numbers showing a spreading gap between high and low in our society and globally, others direct attention to how rapidly the floor has risen for everyone. In a new book, University of Chicago economic historian Robert W. Fogel says that increasing inequality is mostly a myth. Fogel, a Nobel Prize winner in 1993, argues in *The Fourth Great Awakening and the Future of Egalitarianism* that poorer people have actually been the biggest winners in the economic expansion in the West in the past century.

The coming debates on equality will be hampered by lack of commonly accepted measurements.

What differentiates Fogel's analysis from other analysis is his focus on the relationship between hours worked in the past and today to buy the basics of life. In 1880, Fogel says, covering a typical household's annual food bills cost 1,405 hours of labor, about half a year's wages, not counting unpaid time in the kitchen. The comparable figure today is 260 hours, and that price buys a much greater variety of food and convenience, including lots of restaurant meals. As a result, all Americans work many fewer hours to sustain a lifestyle that would have amazed our ancestors.[18]

The debate is important to business because if the ideal of equality gains a stronger philosophical base, it may fill a void created by the collapse of Communism. As *The Economist* put it on the tenth anniversary of the breaching of the Berlin Wall, "Among the new converts to democracy and market economics, as among the long-term believers, there is a marked absence of ideas and idealism."[19]

The magazine's point is well taken. Unless advocates of free markets develop and express a compelling, widely accepted philosophy to support the power of democratic capitalism to improve the lives of the poor, they will eventually end up defending materialism against the next, more dynamic vision of equality.

The free-market–capitalistic system at this moment stands almost universally acclaimed as the greatest wealth producer in human history, but its success in distributing wealth is controversial. Equality has not disappeared as a human aspiration; the issue is how equality will be defined in the years ahead.

Consistent with its values of expanding opportunities, business should energetically support efforts to widen *equality of opportunity*—greater access to health care, education and the basic infrastructure for development, for example. The alternative is that those hostile to the free-market system will turn the debate toward efforts to create *equality of outcome*, a concept frequently discredited by history, and just as frequently revived by those dissatisfied by the status quo.

Positioning Your Company: Five Priorities

This book offers a broad look at the forces and related trends most likely to influence the future of business— what strategic planners sometimes call an "environmental scan." For individual company executives, the next challenge is to identify which forces and trends are likely to have the greatest impact on their operations in the years ahead. Then the task is to align or realign the company with the direction in which society is moving.

The rest of this section focuses on five priorities for strategic direction in any company. All these priorities, deeply influenced by the five forces discussed at the start of the book, are important for all businesses. However, each planning team needs to rank these priorities as its situation demands. The discussion of each priority includes a few sample questions that will assist any team in addressing the question, What should we do first?

Pursuing any of these priorities involves far more than just "setting an objective" and "creating an action plan"—the usual steps in strategic planning. If that were all there were to it, thousands of companies would have long since achieved their ambitious change programs.

Rather, pursuing any of these priorities requires more than setting a target and following it with a by-the-numbers approach. Implementing the priorities will touch the very heart of any company—its values and the balance among its five, basic components—and will require the company to expand the capacity of one or more of the components in significant ways.

Lifting performance in any component requires implementing the values most immediately linked to that component. Discussion of each of the priorities will identify values likely to have the fastest impact.

To ensure success, think more widely about the priority itself. Ask, What components must we strengthen? What new or existing values can we elevate in accordance with our priorities?

Priority #1: Anticipate Market Needs

The purpose of business is to serve a societal need. Society's evolution is therefore a critical determinant in who wins and loses the business battle. In any review of historical business successes, there are always stories of companies that intuitively or consciously caught the next evolutionary wave:

- **Henry Ford** saw that the rising affluence of working Americans would open a stunning business opportunity to sell cars to the masses.

- **Charles E. Merrill** understood early that products for the elite could be sold profitably to the rising middle class. In his case, that meant making Merrill Lynch the world's largest retailer of securities by "taking Wall Street to Main Street."

- **Fifty years ago,** hardly any retailer asked "cash or credit card?" Then Diner's Club, building on the one-store credit systems popularized by retailers for preferred customers, created a card that could be used at many stores and restaurants.

- **Closer to our own time,** pioneers like Steve Jobs and Bill Gates saw the potential of selling information technology that could realize the rallying cry of 1960s activists—"power to the people."

The opportunities today are greater than ever. The mass market grows steadily in the U.S. and exponentially in the other parts of the world. Beyond the rising desire for more and better products, the demand for intangibles—better service, information, speed and convenience—is rapidly expanding.

Anticipating evolution always pays the biggest returns. However, this strategy carries the biggest risk. Those who wish to exploit the power of this priority with less risk can ensure that their company stays closely aligned with—but not necessarily ahead of—evolving change.

Being better to get bigger is a common enough strategy, but being better as a primary goal isn't a normal business idea at all.

ASK "HOW CAN WE SERVE?" Northwestern Mutual has a longstanding history of close alignment with its chosen market. To Northwestern, providing high-quality service to customers has always been more important than becoming a big company. The company has grown steadily and profitably by using its credo, drafted in 1888, as a guide to strategic direction. The credo, carved in stone in the lobby of the company's Milwaukee, Wis., headquarters, specifically directs Northwestern to avoid aiming to be the biggest but to be first "the policyowner's company."

Being better to get bigger is a common enough strategy, but being better as a primary goal isn't a normal business idea at all. It actually transforms normal business practice into the highest levels of a value called service. This is the key to long-time alignment with any market—don't begin by asking, What can we sell? Ask first, How can we serve?

With little fanfare, Northwestern Mutual is expanding its services in line with the changing needs of its policyowners. Demographic change has shifted traditional insurance patterns away from 25- to 40-years olds, toward the 45-to-60 age bracket, possibly because people today are less concerned about premature death. The older age cohort is interested—

and can afford—a wider array of financial services rather than just insurance.

Although insurance will remain Northwestern's core product, local offices are expanding their specialties in a variety of planning and other financial services. Part of the strategy includes alliances with companies that share Northwestern's "customer first" value. For example, Northwestern has launched a trust services pilot, sharing expertise with Northern Trust Corp. of Chicago, a leading deliverer of trust, investment and banking services.

What Northwestern calls "the Agency of the Future" will be built as much on intangibles, such as information and service, as on product reputation. Says CEO James D. Ericson, "People who are going to survive and thrive are those who can take this vast amount of information and present it in a way that is comprehensible for the customer."

Northwestern's managing director in Minneapolis, Gene Storms, thinks of the change in what he must provide the customer in terms of a pyramid. He visualizes a base called *raw data* at the bottom of the pyramid. At the next level there is *information*. From there, the higher but still narrower levels of the pyramid are called, first, *knowledge* and then, at the highest level, *wisdom*. Now, the data and information "that I used to provide people as a real service are available free on the Web," Storms says. "You don't even have to purchase a newspaper." To stay aligned with its market, Northwestern Mutual must move more of its service in the direction of providing knowledge and wisdom.

That, of course, means upgrading technology. Executive Vice President William H. Beckley says the company is investing more than $125 million in information technology to connect its agents to clients, to one another and to the head office. One aim of the effort is to have information available to policyowners 24–7.

VALUES THAT ENERGIZE: To anticipate—or even stay aligned with—market change, look to the value of service, which can energize all components, particularly market and technology (products and services). Every company can profitably elevate this value. Even the language of values in the marketplace suggests a hierarchy—from customer service, to customer satisfaction, to customer delight, to customer for life. Companies everywhere are struggling to climb one more step up that ladder. The rewards are worth the effort. As was noted in Chapter Five, nothing in business is a greater guarantor of sustained success than elevating values that promote customer loyalty.

QUESTIONS TO ASK:
- **Who are our customers? Today? Tomorrow?**
- **How well do we understand what our customers want today? Will probably want tomorrow?**
- **What societal trends will most likely affect our customers?**
- **How responsive are we to customers' requests? How could we respond faster? More comprehensively?**

Priority #2: Accelerate Response Time

We live in fast times that are getting faster. The question is not whether we will increase our time of response, but whether we will use human or systemic energy to do so. Rushing from task to task uses—and depletes—human energy. Systemic energy speeds transactions with far less expenditure of human energy.

Take the most basic system imaginable—a supermarket shopping list. Watch two people in the supermarket—one with a detailed and organized list and one relying solely on memory. Both push the same kind of shopping carts, both buy the same items. They both may actually complete the task in approximately the same time. But look closer. To achieve the same time, the person without the list will probably have to rush, cutting back and forth between shopping aisles to collect initially forgotten items. And, guess which one is more likely to forget a key item, spending still more energy on a return trip to the market?

> **The question is not whether we will increase our time of response, but whether we will use human or systemic energy to do so.**

Carry the same principle into a business transaction involving a half-dozen people, and the potential for saving energy and speeding results starts multiplying. Compare setting a meeting agenda with six people through one e-mail message with the effort it takes to call each one individually on the phone.

To be sure, the personal touch is often preferable to a mechanical system. Who has not hung on a phone, hoping for the sound of a live human voice when connected to a corporate voice mail message? Yet, even this hope can be a matter of expectation. Who has not listened to the sound of an endlessly ringing phone and thought, "Why don't they have voice mail?" The issue is not a choice between personal or systemic energy. In business today, the systemic is increasingly more appropriate for routine transactions, saving valuable human energy for the exceptional opportunity or crisis requiring a higher level of knowledge.

Most companies today are near the end of their employees' physical capacity to rush faster. However, every company still has vast untapped potential to accelerate systemic response time by improving processes and upgrading technology and training. The work that companies have already done to speed such activities as product development and delivery shows the potential. Integrated technological systems linking customers and suppliers are spreading rapidly, for example.

Companies today think of speeding response time as a technology challenge, but structure and skills are often as big a barrier to faster response as a lack of the latest technology. The evolving revolution in business-to-business e-auctions represents as much a structural as a technological innovation. And, an order taker's language skills or the computer skills of a data entry clerk sometimes have more to do with response time than the actual capacity of the technology system the employees are using.

VALUES THAT ENERGIZE: Speed, an all-purpose value, energizes whole companies or specific components. With speed as a value, companies focus on every component: answering customers faster, developing products in record time, organizing with fewer layers, training people to work in cross-functional project teams and publishing same-day financial information. Companies can also uncover opportunities by adopting the related value of simplicity, which can be particularly useful to companies with well-developed or obsolete systems and structures.

QUESTIONS TO ASK:
- **What were the last 5 to 10 transactions that were late?**
- **In each case, what were the reasons?** Inadequate systems? A lack of skills? Structural impediments? Obsolete technology? An attitude of complacency?
- **How can we overcome these impediments?** If you face complacency, take heart: Years of working with companies trying to speed their work convinces me that even the most basic review and corrective action can yield significant results, because the root causes of lack of punctuality run in similar patterns in different places throughout any company.

Priority #3: Develop All Your People All the Time

In scanning the environment, we regularly encounter the power of knowledge to change the destiny of nations, companies and individuals. Because knowledge increasingly determines competitive advantage, every company to stay competitive must invest in upgrading the knowledge base of its people.

The history of Motorola University (MU), which serves the $38-billion manufacturer of wireless communications technologies, semiconductors and advanced electronic systems, conveys a strong sense of the evolution of corporate education and training.

- **1981:** Motorola opens training center with a mission to build a culture of quality through skill-based training and problem solving.
- **1985–95:** Emphasis shifts to training plus education, with a greater focus on understanding the world in which the company operates and where it is headed.
- **1995–present:** Greater focus on building and managing knowledge and on developing skills to gather and distribute what is known within the organization.

Motorola requires all of its 130,000 associates to to engage in 40 hours a year of job-relevant training and education. MU's flagship Gavin Center in Schaumburg, Ill., is open 15 hours a day, 6 days a week.

MU operates seven state-of-the-art learning facilities around the world. In addition, some of its courses are available either in person or through technology at some 90 sites in 23 countries. In China alone, MU has trained 10,000 Motorola employees and partners.

All young people hired today by Motorola or a midsize company want answers to three basic questions: Is the work interesting? How will you develop your employees? How will you pay and reward them?

MU's Colleges of Technology, Leadership and Transcultural Studies, and Emerging Markets serve five geographic regions (the U.S.; North Asia; South Asia; Europe, the Middle East and Africa; and Latin America) with courseware, consulting and partnerships. In addition to serving employees, MU designs and develops courses for Motorola suppliers and strategic partners. Its consulting arm uses experienced Motorola executives to transfer critical skills to Motorola suppliers and customers. MU has established partnerships with educational institutions around the globe. Its Just-in-Time Lecture series is packaged on a CD, a film version of talks by experts, plus presentation slides and a running list of frequently asked questions. The CDs are sent overnight to members of project teams who may be in locations as scattered as Brazil, Scotland and China.

MU's president, William Wiggenhorn, says that large companies must now provide up-to-date education "on a global basis, in local languages, and all the time." MU used to design courses in one-to-four-hour blocks of time. Now modules are down to 15 minutes. "We have to figure out what people need to know, when they need to know it," he says. What Motorola requires are a technology that works, a faculty that speaks the local language, an understanding of local context and a support system to help people share knowledge.

Where does that situation leave the small to midsize company without Motorola's resources? With the same challenge but different solutions, says Wiggenhorn. With the exception of young people who are joining start-ups, all young people hired today by Motorola or a midsize company want answers to three basic questions: Is the work interesting? How will you develop your employees? How will you pay and reward them? Any company, any size must have good answers to attract people with high potential.

Wiggenhorn is a strong advocate of community colleges, which he calls "one of the beauties of operating in the U.S." Also, as was discussed in the previous chapter, more and more training software is available at low cost and online. When expensive training is needed, Wiggenhorn recommends that smaller firms form an alliance or consortium to share licensing expenses or the cost of having a community college design and deliver the training.

VALUES THAT ENERGIZE: Focusing on your people leads you to such values as respect for the individual, which can add power to corporate efforts to expand diversity. Development of people is another major energizer because it focuses attention on elevating everyone's knowledge and skills. Taken at its most expansive, as with Motorola, the value leads to efforts to extend training and development opportunities to other members of your supply chain.

QUESTIONS TO ASK:
- **What major knowledge and skills will we need to add,** given our assessment of our business environment?
- **How well do we communicate our values to new employees? Reinforce them with longer-serving employees?** (Motorola, for example, has a home-grown learning package, "Motorola: Yesterday, Today and Tomorrow"—a 52-unit review of the company's culture, history and values. All new employees are given access to the program as part of their orientation. Each unit takes 10 minutes to complete and contains a quiz, with answers.)
- **To what extent does our personnel turnover reflect a lack of development opportunities for everyone?** For women and minorities specifically?
- **How long has it been since we upgraded our employee orientation program?** Our other standard training programs?

■ What percentage of our revenues do we believe that we must invest in training and development in order to stay competitive?

Priority #4: Organize for Tomorrow

Our longest-enduring concept of organization was based on the principle that repetition of systems, rules, policies and procedures could be effective as long as one strong fixed center of authority directed the parts.

A corollary principle was that structure follows strategy. The fixed center of authority manufactured the master form of those systems, rules, policies and procedures consistent with what it wanted to accomplish and then relayed them for duplication to its subcenters. If the fixed center was powerful enough and consistent enough, it could duplicate itself across the earth.

This design, efficient and well-understood in the past, once worked well and it still works. We shouldn't dismiss the model out of hand, because over generations it has facilitated order, efficiency and prosperity. However, the design loses strength every day, with every newly educated person, with every new Internet subscriber, with every institution shifting from dependence on physical assets to dependence on knowledge, with every nation or organization that edges toward greater freedom.

The draining away of strength from the traditional model is irreversible, and it is picking up speed. Huge mergers of uncompetitive companies attempt to reclaim the productivity that once lay at the heart of centralized authority, but their limited success demonstrates only the declining power of the principle. Rigid enforcement of lockstep routines that would have been praised for their humanistic efficiency only 50 years ago now set off a disastrous exodus of an organization's prime intellectual assets.

RISK MEASUREMENT. Jumping too quickly from command and control toward more "uncentralized" models entails risk. The newer models depend on widely dispersed pools of knowledge, effective communication and the authority of mutually agreed upon values and standards. Lacking these, individuality prospers but productivity does not necessarily do the same. To see this principle work in miniature, talk privately with any CEO who jumped too quickly into a dressing-down policy without previously agreed upon standards.

Clinging to the past is equally foolhardy. Start-ups with a blank organization chart and an intuitive sense of the future can afford to be bold. Older companies are wiser to chance purposeful, sustained evolution rather than revolution.

Organizing for tomorrow must be conscious, swift and consistent, always exploiting or, better yet, creating new opportunities to shift authority from the center toward the periphery.

VALUES THAT ENERGIZE: For businesses seeking the most expansive strategy, freedom is the ultimate value. Communication and coordination help widen channels to disperse authority. Speed helps clear away structural and systemic barriers. Strengthening the value of teamwork is a powerful motivator, encouraging the creation of useful standards and the elimination of obsolete ones. Any of these values lifts performance in all components, especially in organization and people.

QUESTIONS TO ASK:
- **To what extent do we handle our routine operations, projects and paperwork on time?**
- **To what extent do we make and execute decisions promptly?**
- **How can we get more decisions made at the lowest level of authority possible?**
- **How effective are our systems to stay in touch with customers?** How current are the systems? How smoothly do we introduce feedback from customers into our operations? How can we update our systems for communicating with customers?
- **What inhibits a higher level of teamwork here?**
- **How clear are the responsibilities and accountabilities in our company?**

Priority #5: Elevate Operational Excellence
The values in any company are revealed in how it handles its routine operations. Successful companies express their highest

values in the smallest physical acts. For example, in an era when talent is scarce, Northwestern Mutual has strengthened rather than relaxed its recruitment procedures.

In Minneapolis, Northwestern Mutual's managing director, Gene Storms, has the daunting task of hiring new agents for commission-only jobs in a climate "where a sharp student will have jobs offers with a signing bonus six months before graduation." The natural temptation would be to fill your quota by settling for the best hires you can manage and hope that a certain percentage would manage to succeed. That would certainly be the strategy of other, more numbers-driven companies.

As knowledge becomes the primary asset for business success, human beings at last fully emerge as the ultimate and, in a real sense, the one limitless resource.

To the contrary, in 2000, Storms and his recruiters talked with 1,200 people before meeting their goal of hiring 24 salespeople. They tested applicants for their entrepreneurial bent and for their ability to finance the early stage of a commission-based career. The company analyzed the applicants' handwriting, and applicants participated in a trial run, completing market surveys in person with 15 prospective customers. Storms spoke with each candidate's parents or spouse to make sure that each could provide support at home for a career that will probably take a few years to produce sustained financial success.

Northwestern Mutual displays the same kind of care in hiring at its Milwaukee headquarters. It emphasizes assessment of its candidates' ability to work in teams, as well as their technical competence. The orientation program for new hires devotes considerable time to the company's values, says Susan Lueger, vice president for human resources.

All this attention to hiring practices pays off in ways that affect both the culture and the cost structure of Northwestern Mutual. Of the 65 agents Gene Storms has hired over the past five years, during one of the most volatile job markets in history, 31 are still in place. And, at headquarters in 1999, the turnover rate of employees, excluding retirement, was only 3.7%!

VALUES THAT ENERGIZE: Any routine operational task can be energized through values. Values such as systematic functioning, quality, or optimum use of resources are especially potent in identifying and overcoming issues that inhibit a company's development in the capital and organization components.

QUESTIONS TO ASK:
- **Which of our costs run the most—or the most frequently—over budget, and why?**
- **What would it take to lift our quality to Six Sigma level?** (See the discussion of this quality strategy in Chapter Six.)
- **How accurately and fully do we measure the productivity of our capital and our people?**
- **What activities could we outsource, thus freeing resources that we could apply profitably elsewhere?**
- **How well do we maintain the machinery, equipment and space critical to our operations?**

Summary and Conclusions

The development of business organizations always coincides with the development of society. Because the progress of business mirrors the evolution of society, this progress can be traced through a series of more complex and productive relationships with counterparts in other aspects of life.

In resources, business is moving from an emphasis on concrete materials to a reliance on technology and information. From an economic society based on land, the U.S. evolved into one based on money and other human-created assets. Americans are only now beginning to understand that knowledge has become our most valuable economic asset.

For most of human history, a leadership elite used force to motivate humans to produce. All the great wonders of the ancient world were built by sentient beings who labored as little more than human animals. An industrial society required a higher and more generalized intelligence for achievement. Rudimentary education was required. Pay rather than force became the principal motivator. Authority still flowed from the top, from the leader's capacity to extend or withhold compensation.

As knowledge becomes the primary asset for business success, human beings at last fully emerge as the ultimate and, in a real sense, the one limitless resource. Systems of authority, always slow to adapt, are now beginning to adjust to the enormous size of this change. Increasingly, pay is no longer enough by itself. Leaders are learning how better to extend their authority in meaningful ways to others, to provide new development opportunities. The team or network is replacing the pyramid as the most effective design to transmit ideas and expand creativity.

Just as this awareness gains momentum, an apparently sudden shortage of talented, knowledgeable people has caught most of the business world by surprise. In less than a decade we have gone from "lean and mean downsizing" to a frantic search for talent. We search for explanations in our nation's demographics, education system, government policies and societal attitudes. All provide important but partial clues.

The underlying explanation is now apparent. A technological civilization can only run on the primary energy source known as human brainpower. For that civilization to keep growing and expanding opportunities at the rate we are now moving, it must have access to more and better human brainpower every year. The search for better ways to find and unleash that energy source will from here on be a constant preoccupation of business.

A Creative Field of Endeavor

Business is a highly creative field of endeavor. It successfully converts individual ambition into communal achievement at the least cost to society. It identifies generalized desires and turns them into specific products and services that make our lives more productive, comfortable and enjoyable. Perhaps most important of all, business is an arena for personal growth and development for millions of people. The issue now is how best to harness that capacity to serve society consciously.

Humanity is now more aware of its potential not just to advance from one level to the next, but to skip three or four levels at a time. That is the real opportunity in the convergence of globalization, information technology and mass education. Innovations that used to take decades or even centuries can circle the globe in a few years or even months.

The best single force to accelerate this progress is an aware and energized business community. No other resource can bring to bear so much human creativity within an organized and flexible structure. No other institution can shift resources to productive avenues as quickly. No other arm of society has the capacity to turn theory into practical intelligence with such speed or efficiency. No other arena of human activity offers so many opportunities for growth and development of individuals and groups.

How well business employs these tremendous capacities will be a major determinant of human progress in the decade ahead.

CHAPTER ONE: A Moment of Opportunity

1 Figures cited come from "Work in Progress, Special Report," *The Economist,* July 24, 1999, www.economist.com/editorial/justforyou/19990724/sa7348.html.

2 Figures cited come from "On the Yellow Brick Road," *The Economist,* September 11, 1999, www.economist.com/editorial/justforyou/19990911/su3796.html.

3 Park, quoted in Louis Kraar, "What Pacific Century?" *Fortune,* November 22, 1999, p. 198.

4 Figures cited come from *The American Marketplace: Demographics and Spending Patterns,* 4th Edition (New Strategist Publications, Inc., 1999), and from *Digest of Education Statistics.*

5 David S. Landes, *The Wealth and Poverty of Nations* (W. W. Norton & Co., Inc. 1998), pp. 282–85.

6 James Traub, "Online U., How Entrepreneurs and Academic Radicals Are Breaking Down the Walls of the University," *New York Times Magazine,* November 2000, p. 92.

7 Beth O'Leary, "More Firms to Set Up Own Universities," Kiplinger Business Forecasts, December 7, 1999, p. 1., http://www.kiplingerforecasts.com.

8 Ibid.

9 Peter F. Drucker, *Management Challenges for the 21st Century* (Harper Business, 1999), pp. 149–51.

CHAPTER TWO: 21st-Century Demographics

1 Quoted in Barbara Crossette, "Europe Stares at a Future Built by Immigrants," *New York Times,* January 2, 2000, Section 4, p. 1.

2 Unless otherwise cited, figures cited in this section are from Elizabeth Kelleher and Pamela M. Prah, "Changing

Labor Demographics Pose Challenges for Employers," Kiplinger Business Forecasts, December 10, 1999, http://www.kiplingerforecasts.com/special/weekly/1999/dec10/laborforce.html, and from "The Graying of the Baby Boom," Kiplinger Business Forecasts, http://www.kiplinger forecasts.com/special/population/age/babyboom.html, and "A Look at Population," *The Kiplinger Washington Letter,* December 23, 1998, including supplementary KBF reports of the same date.

3 William L. Hamilton, "You're Not Getting Older. Products Are Getting Better." *New York Times,* June 27, 1999, Section 4, p. 1.

4 Geoffrey Coffin, "The 50 Best Companies For Asians, Blacks and Hispanics: Companies That Pursue Diversity Outperform the S&P 500. Coincidence?" *Fortune,* July 19, 1999, p. 53.

5 Cited in Diane E. Lewis, "As Women Dominate College Campuses, Some Wonder Whether Workplace Is Next," *Boston Globe,* June 6, 1999, p. F1.

6 Cited in Ellen Joan Pollock, "In Today's Workplace, Women Feel Freer To Be, Well, Women," *Wall Street Journal,* February 7, 2000, p. 1.

7 Cited in Patrice Hill, "In Jobs, Mothers Count on Flexibility: Family-Friendly Schedules Give Employers a Competitive Edge," *Washington Times,* September 19, 1999, p. C1.

8 Ibid., p. C9.

9 Cited in Paulette Thomas, "Closing the Gender Gap," *Wall Street Journal,* May 24, 1999, p. R12.

10 Peter F. Drucker, *Management Challenges for the 21st Century* (Harper Business, 1999), p. 46.

CHAPTER THREE: The Global Frontier

1 "What Is Globalization?" Part 1 of a 4 part series on Assessing Globalization, published by The World Bank Economic Policy Group and Development Research Group, Spring 2000, available on the Web at http://www/html/extdr/pb/globalization/ or from The World Bank 1818 H St., NW, Washington DC 20433, p. 1

2 Ibid.

3 Jennifer Ordonez, "Olive Garden Bets on Cachet of Cooking School in Italy," *Wall Street Journal,* October 19, 1999, p. B2.

4 Calvin Sims, "Japan Beckons, and East Asia's Youth Fall in Love," *New York Times,* December 5, 1999.

5 Harlan Cleveland, Garry Jacobs, Robert Macfarlane, Robert van Harten, N. Asokan, "Human Choice: The Genetic Code for Social Development," working paper presented at the 1998 Vancouver Assembly of the World Academy of Art and Science, p. 33. Available from www.mirainternational.com.

6 *Wall Street Journal,* October 12, 1999, p. A26.

7 Brandon Mitchener, "Border Crossings—The Internet Makes It So Much Easier to Go Global. And So Much Easier to Violate Local Laws," *Wall Street Journal,* November 22, 1999, p. R-41.

8 Rob Norton, "The Luck of the Irish," *Fortune,* October 25, 1999, p. 195.

9 Information in section on economic growth and poverty reduction from "Does More International Trade Openness Increase World Poverty?" Part 2 of a 4-part series Assessing Globalization, pp. 1–3; see note 1 above.

10 Information in section on international trade and inequality from "Does More International Trade Openness Worsen Inequality?" Part 3 of a 4-part series Assessing Globalization, pp. 2–3; see note 1 above.

11 Information in section on globalization and the environment from "Is Globalization Causing a 'Race to the Bottom' in Environmental Standards?" Part 4 of a 4-part series Assessing Globalization, p. 3; see note 1 above.

12 "The World's View of Multinationals," *The Economist,* January 29, 2000, p. 21.

13 Arnaud De Borchgrave, "Warm Up for the Long Haul," *Washington Times,* December 6, 1999..

CHAPTER FOUR: Business Evolution

1 Steve Lohr, "Welcome to the Internet, the First Global Colony," *New York Times Week in Review,* January 9, 2000, p. 1.

2 Cited in Harold Livesay, *American Made: Men Who Shaped the*

American Economy (Little Brown & Co., 1979), p. 141.

3 "To Pause and Be Refreshed," *Fortune*, July 1931, p. 108.

4 "Old and New Economy Companies: A Perfect Fit," *Trend Letter*, October 30, 2000, p. 6.

5 Cited in James Gleick, *Faster: The Acceleration of Just About Everything* (Pantheon Books, 1999), p. 86.

CHAPTER FIVE: The Market Rules

1 Clay Chandler, "Starbucks Going for All the Coffee in China," *Washington Post*, May 24, 2000, p. E21.

2 Seller Beware, *The Economist*, March 4, 2000, p. 63..

3 Penelope Patsuris, "Coke, Kraft, P&G, Sara Lee Launch New Marketplace," *Forbes*, June 14, 2000, http://www.forbes.com/tool/html/00/jun/0614/MU7.htm.

4 David P. Hamilton, "Inflection Point—Intel Chairman Andrew Grove Talks About How E-Commerce Will Transform Just About Everything," *Wall Street Journal*, April 17, 2000, p. R50.

5 Quoted in Jonathan Kaufman, "The Omnipresent Persuaders: Marketing in the Future Will Be Everywhere—Including Your Head," *Wall Street Journal*, January 1, 2000, p. R26.

6 Ibid.

7 Ibid.

8 Robert B. Reich, "Brand-Name Knowledge," *Wall Street Journal*, October 13, 1997, op-ed p.

9 Quoted in Jim Billington, "Customer-Driven Innovation," *Harvard Business Review*, July 1998.

10 "Dot-coms: What Have We Learned?" *Fortune*, October 30, 2000, pp. 96–98.

11 Frederick F. Reichheld's ideas and quotes here and below are excerpted from his book *The Loyalty Effect: The Hidden Force Behind Growth, Profits and Lasting Value* (Harvard Business School Press, 1996), and a *New York Times* interview with Fred Andrews (December 29, 1999), "A Man of Words Remains Partial to One Loyalty and E-Loyalty: Your Secret Weapon on the Web," with Phil Schefter, *Harvard Business Review*, July-August 2000.

12 Keki R. Bhote, "Beyond Customer Satisfaction to Customer Loyalty," AMA Management Briefing, 1996, p. 31.

13 Ibid, p. 35.

14 Oren Harari, "The Power of Complaints," *Management Review*, American Management Assn., July-August, 1999.

15 Daniel Lyons, "Make the Little Guys Feel Big," *Forbes* cover story, April 17, 2000.

16 Daniel Lyons, "Michael Dell's Second Act," *Forbes* cover story, April 17, 2000.

17 Geoffrey Colvin, "America's Most Admired Companies: How Frequently and Creatively Do They Use the Internet?" *Fortune*, February 21, 2000, p. 110.

18 Quoted in Robert Slater, *The New GE: How Jack Welch Revived an American Institution* (Richard Irwin, 1993), p. 260.

19 "Cisco@speed, Survey Business and the Internet," *The Economist*, June 26, 1999, http://www.economist.com/editorial/justforyou/19990626/su7156.html.

20 Brian Dumaine, "How Managers Can Succeed Through Speed," *Fortune*, February 11, 1989, p. 54.

21 Scott Kirsner, "Faster Company," *Fast Company*, May 2000, p. 162.

22 Ibid.

23 Matthew Rose, "Mr. Ryder Rewrites the Musty Old Book at *Reader's Digest*," *Wall Street Journal*, April 18, 2000, p. 1.

24 Kevin Maney, "Does Internet Time March On or Has Its Clock Been Cleaned?" *USA Today*, November 29, 2000, p. 3B.

25 http://www.demc.com/html/sponsor.html.

26 Quoted in Thomas A. Stewart, "Three Rules for Managing in the Real-Time Economy," *Fortune*, May 1, 2000, p. 332.

27 Cited in Jennifer Oridonez, "An Efficiency Drive: Fast Food Lanes Are Getting Even Faster," *Wall Street Journal*, May 18, 2000, p. 1.

28 Cited in Thomas A. Stewart, "How Cisco and Alcoa Make Real Time Work," *Fortune*, May 29, 2000, p. 284.

29 Constance L. Hays, "A Role Model's New Clothes," *New York Times*, April 1, 2000.

30 Cora Daniels, "A Fund Group Redefines Emerging Markets," *Fortune*, June 7, 1999, p. 234.

31 Ibid.

32 Lowell L. Bryan and Jane N. Fraser, "Getting to Global," *The McKinsey Quarterly*, 1999, No. 4, p. 28.

33 Figures on U.S. international business from Murray Weidenbaum, "All the World's a Stage," *Management Review*, the American Management Assn., October 1999, pp. 42–48.

34 Figures on U.S. international business from the Center for the Study of American Business, American Management Assn., October, 1999, pp. 42–48.

35 Cited in Beth O'Leary, "More Small Firms Will Go Global," Kiplinger Business Forecasts, June 14, 2000, http://www.kiplingerforecasts.com.

CHAPTER SIX: The Vast Profit Potential of Expanding Knowledge

1 *The New American Boom: Exciting Changes in American Life and Business Between Now and the Year 2000*, by the staff of the *Kiplinger Washington Letter* (Washington, D.C.: Kiplinger Books, 1986), and Austin H. Kiplinger and Knight A. Kiplinger, with the staff of *The Kiplinger Washington Letter, America in the Global '90s: The Shape of the Future—How You Can Profit From It* (Washington, D.C: Kiplinger Books, 1989).

2 California and Seattle electricity figures from Paul Johnson, *A History of the American People* (HarperCollins, 1997), p. 689–690.

3 Figures cited are from Philip Evans and Thomas S. Wurster, *Blown to Bits: How the New Economics of Information Transforms Strategy* (Harvard Business School Press, 2000), p. 13.

4 "Forecasts of Emerging Technologies," interview with William E. Halal, *Future Times*, World Future Society, Summer 2000, p. 1.

5 Ann Grimes, "To Keep the Teachers in Town, Rich Communities Offer Housing Help," *Wall Street Journal*, June 7, 2000, p. B1.

6 Michael Dell, "Building a Competitive Advantage in an Internet Economy," speech before the Detroit Economic Club, November 1, 1999.

7 For details about Medtronic history, see Frederick G. Harmon, *Playing for Keeps* (John Wiley & Sons, 1996), pp.

124–25. For Bill George's views of the next evolutionary steps in health care and at Medtronic, see George's speeches "The Future of 21st Century Health: Getting the Right Care," Harvard Business School Consumer-Driven Health Care Conference, November 18, 1999, and "Medtronic Vision 2010," Medtronic Global Strategic Direction Employee Meeting, January 11, 2000. For Medtronic's venture with Microsoft and IBM, see Thomas M. Burton, "Medtronic to Join Microsoft, IBM in Patient-Monitoring Venture," *Wall Street Journal*, January 24, 2000, p. B12.

8 Stan Davis and Christopher Meyer, *Blur, the Speed of Change in the Connected Economy* (Warner Books, 1999), p. 11.

9 Ibid.

10 Figures reported in 1999 IBM Annual Report.

11 Reuters, "I.B.M. Signs Wireless Deal With Internet Consulting Companies." Article appeared in *New York Times*, June 2, 2000.

12 "You'll Never Walk Alone: Survey Business and the Internet," *The Economist*, June 26, 1999.

13 GE, 1999 Annual Report, Letter to Shareholders.

14 Quoted in Rona Kobell, "Maid Service Reaching for New Markets," *Baltimore Sun*, July 5, 2000, p. 9c.

15 Cited in Eric Berggren and Thomas Nacher, "Why Good Ideas Go Bust," *Management Review*, February, 2000, p. 35.

16 Jonathan Rosenoer, Douglas Armstrong, and J. Russell Gates, *The Clickable Corporation: Successful Strategies for Capturing the Internet Advantage*, Arthur Anderson LLP, 1999.

17 For more information see http://www.bn.com.

18 Martha M. Hamilton, "All Day, All Night, All Week: From Copy Shops to Car Service Centers, Retailers Extend Hours to Boost Sales," *Washington Post*, July 1, 2000, p. A1.

19 Elizabeth Kelleher, "Stores Turning Away from Enclosed Malls," Kiplinger Business Forecasts, May 18, 2000, http://www.kiplingerforecasts.com.

20 Martha M. Hamilton, "The Latest Malling of America: Mills Corp. Draws Crowds to Unusual Shopping Environments," *Washington Post*, July 22, 2000, p. E1.

21 Mikel Harry and Richard Schroeder, *Six Sigma: The*

Breakthrough Management Strategy Revolutionizing the World's Top Corporations (Doubleday, 2000), p. xi.

22 Ibid., pp. 13–14.

23 Claudia H. Deutsch, "GE's Management Methods Are Put to Work on the Web," *New York Times*, June 12, 2000, http://www.nytimes.com/library/tech/00/06/biztech/articles/12web.html.

24 Harry and Schroeder, *Six Sigma*, p. 43.

25 Quoted in Sri Ramakrishnan, "Six Sigma Energizes GE: Manufacturing Method Used to Improve Services," *Washington Post*, November 26, 1999, p. E4.

26 Harry and Schroeder, *Six Sigma*, p. 3.

27 Eryn Brown, "9 Ways to Win on the Web," *Fortune*, May 24, 1999, p. 112.

28 Elizabeth Corcoran, "The E-Gang," *Forbes*, http://www.forbes.com/forbes/00/0724/6517145a4.htm.

29 Ibid.

30 Eryn Brown, "9 Ways to Win on the Web," p. 121.

31 http://www.bearstearns.com/evolve, April 20, 2000.

32 Joseph P. Manzi, "PDAs Offer Many Choices: Will Continue to Evolve," Kiplinger Business Forecasts, October 8, 1999, http://www.kiplingerforecasts.com.

33 James Pelz, "After Shift, Maytag Cleans Up on Profits," *Boston Globe*, June 6, 1999.

34 International Federation of Robotics, www.ifr.org.

35 "Robots Come of Age," *The Trend Letter*, September 16, 1999, pp. 6–7.

36 Knight Kiplinger, *World Boom Ahead: Why Business and Consumers Will Prosper* (Washington, D.C.: Kiplinger Books, 1998).

CHAPTER SEVEN: Toward "Uncentralized" Organizations

1 Julia Angwin, "Anatomy of Net Bookseller's Rapid Rise and Fall," *Wall Street Journal*, March 2, 2000, p. B1.

2 Thomas A. Stewart, "How Teradyne Solved the Innovator's Dilemma," *Fortune*, January 10, 2000, p. 188.

3 Account of origin of radio advertising from Daniel Gross and the editors of *Forbes* magazine, *Forbes Greatest Business Stories of All Time* (John Wiley & sons, Inc., 1996), p. 112.

4 Hal Varian, "5 Habits of Highly Effective Revolution," *Forbes ASAP,* http://www.forbes.com/asap/00/0221/073.htm.

5 Ibid.

6 Peter F. Drucker, *Management Challenges for the 21st Century* (Harper Business, 1999), p. 9.

7 Peter F. Drucker, *The Frontiers of Management* (Truman Talley Books, E.P. Dutton, 1986), p. 206.

8 See Michelle Kessler, "Position of 'Privacy Officer' Coming Into the Public Eye," *USA Today,* November 30, 2000, p. 1B.

9 Bernard Wysocki Jr., "Self-Organization: The Next Big Thing?" *Wall Street Journal*, July 10, 2000, p. 1.

10 Harlan Cleveland, *The Future Executive* (Harper & Row, 1972), p. 13.

11 Ibid., Chapter 3, "The Future Is Horizontal," pp. 30–47.

12 Harlan Cleveland, "Coming Soon: The Nobody-in-Charge Society," *Perspectives on Business and Global Change,* World Business Academy, December 2000.

13 Ibid.

14 Rich Miller, "Greenspan Says Dealing Fairly in Business Pays Dividends," *USA Today,* August 16, 1999.

15 OECD figures and analysis as reported by David Wessel, "Cross-Border Mergers Soared Last Year," *Wall Street Journal*, July 19, 2000, p. A 18.

16 "KPMG Identifies Six Key Factors for Successful Mergers and Acquisition," http://www.kpmg.com/about/press.asp?cid=271.

17 "How Mergers Go Wrong," *The Economist*, January 22, 2000, p. 19.

18 Jerome Idaszak and Michael Doan, "Mergers and Acquisitions Keep Rolling," Kiplinger Business Forecasts, askkip@kiplinger.com, September 17, 1999.

19 Quoted in "Spotlight on Rosabeth Moss Kanter," *Strategy and Leadership*, October/November/December 1999, p. 59.

20 See "The Science of Alliance," *The Economist*, April 4, 1998, http://www.economist.com/tfs/aarchive_tframeset.html.

21 Lewis Uchitelle, "Business-to-Business: It's Just the Beginning," *New York Times*, June 7, 2000, http://www.nytimes.com/library/tech/00/06/biztech/technology/07unchi.html

22 Ibid.

23 Matthew Coffey's comments are from his speech at the

National Tooling & Machining Assn. General Membership Assembly, Orlando, Fla., February 20, 2000.

24 Panos Mourdoukoutas, *The Global Corporation: The Decolonization of International Business* (Quorum Books, 1999), p.4.

25 Ibid.

26 Ibid., p. 2.

27 Ibid.

CHAPTER EIGHT: Capital—An End to Limits

1 Examples of the elevation of physical resources by organization, adapted from Harlan Cleveland, Garry Jacobs, Robert Macfarlane, Robert van Harten and N. Asokan, "Human Choice: The Genetic Code for Social Development," paper presented at the Vancouver Assembly of the World Academy of Art and Science, 1998, p. 9.

2 "Radical Robot Design Launches a Revolution," *Trend Letter,* October 30, 2000, p. 1.

3 Cleveland, et al., "Human Choice," p. 47.

4 Todd L. Treadway and Peter L. Blank, "Treasury Department Supports Modernizing Depreciation Schedules," Kiplinger Business Forecasts, August 18, 2000, http://www.kiplingerforecasts.com.

5 Barnaby J. Feder, "Deal Maker Takes on Manufacturing and Technology," *New York Times*, August 21, 2000, http://www.nytimes.com/library/tech/00/08/biztech/articles/21neco.html.

6 Thomas Petzinger Jr., "So Long Supply and Demand," *Wall Street Journal*, January 1, 2000, p. R31.

7 Martyn Chase, "More on New Oil Technology," Kiplinger Business Forecasts, December 18, 1998, askkip@kiplinger.com.

8 James Brooke, "Feeding the 'Energy Eater,'" *New York Times*, September 7, 2000, p. C1.

9 Quoted in, Ibid.

10 Chase, "More on New Oil Technology."

11 "The Electric Revolution," *The Economist*, August 15, 2000, pp. 19–20.

12 John McCarthy, "Frequently Asked Questions About

Nuclear Energy," http://www-formal.stanford.edu/jmc/progress/nuclear-faq.html.

13 Christopher Flavin and Seth Dunn, "Rising Sun, Gathering Winds: Policies to Stabilize the Climate and Strengthen Economics," http://www.worldwatch.org, reported by Dan Johnson, "Alternative Energy Sources Gain Worldwide," *The Futurist,* August-September, 1998, p. 15.

14 See Michelle Malkin, "Generators of the Electricity Mess," *Washington Times,* December 14, 2000, p. A22.

15 Facts and figures about the business of water are based on five articles published by Kiplinger Business Forecasts (August 20, 1999), under the title "Higher Costs, New Concerns in the Business of Water." Authors are Alan Kovski, Elizabeth Kelleher, Vandana Mathur and Michael Doan. Material available at askkip@kiplinger.com.

16 Quote is from Harlan Cleveland, "The Millennium Lecture: The Informatization of Development," M.S. Swaminathan Research Foundation, Chennai India, September 28, 1999. For a fuller discussion of this theme, see Harlan Cleveland, *The Knowledge Executive, Leadership in an Information Society,* Truman Talley Books (E.P. Dutton, 1985), pp. 19–35.

17 Thomas Petzinger Jr., Ibid.

18 Jane Tanner, "New Life for Old Railroads: What Better Place to Lay Miles of Fiber Optic Cable," *New York Times,* May 6, 2000.

19 "Study: Net Bigger Than We Think," *New York Times,* July 26, 2000.

20 Peter F. Drucker, *Management Challenges for the 21st Century* (HarperCollins, 1999), pp. 111–13.

21 "The Numbers Game," *Fortune,* November 22, 1999, http://library.northernlight.com/PN19991109040000416.html?cb=13&sc=0.

22 Thomas a. Stewart, "Managing Risk in the 21st Century," *Fortune,* February 7, 2000, p. 206.

23 Eric D. Beinhocker, "Robust Adaptive Strategies," *Sloan Management Review,* Spring 1999, pp. 95–106.

24 "E-cash 2.0," *The Economist,* February 19, 2000, p. 67.

25 Ibid., p. 68.

26 Joan Pryde, "For Entrepreneurs: Plentiful Capital, Various Sources," Kiplinger Small Business Monitor, August 21, 2000, KiplingerForecasts.com.

27 Joan Pryce, "No Letup for Venture Capital Deals," Kiplinger Business Forecasts, August 9, 2000, http://www .kiplingerforecasts.com.

28 http://www.businessweek.com/smallbiz/0003/vc000308. htm?scriptFramed.

29 Beth O'Leary, "More Help for Low-Income Entrepreneurs," Kiplinger Business Forecasts, August 9, 2000, http://www .kiplingerforecasts.com.

30 "A Lending Hand," *Business Week*, March 15, 2000, http://www.businessweek.com/smallbiz/fi/0003/fi3670061 .htm?scriptFramed.

31 Figures from Trickle Up Program, 1999 Annual Report, www.trickleup.org.

32 "Uncommon Opportunities: An Agenda for Peace and Equitable Development," *The Report of the International Commission on Peace and Food* (Zed Books Ltd., 7 Cynthia St., London N1 9JF, UK and 165 First Avenue, Atlantic Highlands, NJ 07716), page 158.

CHAPTER NINE: People—No Truce in the War for Talent

1 Carlos Tejada, "U.S. Economic Boom Spurs Despair Over Scarcity of Qualified Workers," *Wall Street Journal*, January 28, 2000.

2 Louis Uchitelle, "As Labor Pool Shrinks, a New Supply Is Tapped," *New York Times*, December 20, 1999, http://www .nytimes.com/library/financial/122099outlook-demo.html.

3 Stephen Barr, "Retirement Wave Creates Vacuum," *Washington Post*, May 7, 2000, p. 1.

4 John Schwartz, "To Find and Keep Techies, a Corps of an Idea," *Washington Post*, May 10, 2000, p. A27.

5 Devin Leonard, "They're Coming to Take You Away," *Fortune*, May 29, 2000, p. 91.

6 Robert Barner, "Talent Wars in the Executive Suite, Six Trends Shaping Recruitment," *The Futurist*, May-June, 2000, p. 35.

7 Reed Able, "Recruiters Ask for Equity and Get It," *New York*

Times, August 3, 2000, http://www.nytimes.com/library/ financial/080300recruiters-mktplace.html.

8 Jim Harris and Joan Brannick, "Finding & Keeping Great Employees," (AMACOM, 1999), pp. 13–15.

9 Ibid. p. 15.

10 Gene Bylinsky, "Women Move Up in Manufacturing," *Fortune*, May 11, 2000, http://www.*fortune*.com/*fortune*/imt/ 2000/05/15/int.html.

11 Lee Romney, "Franchisers Pin Hopes on Minority Entrepreneurs," *Los Angeles Times*, February 23, 2000, http:// www.latimes.com/cgi-binprint.cgi.

12 Geoffrey Brewer, "Older Workers are Thriving in a Tight Job Market," *New York Times*, June 21, 2000, http://www. nytimes.com/library/financial/062/manage-seniors.html.

13 "Brain Drain: Older Executives Are Set to Leave the Workplace in Droves. Keeping These Senior Stars on the Job Will Require More Flexible Management," *Business Week*, September 20, 1999, p. 124.

14 "Work Week," *Wall Street Journal*, October 5, 1999, p. A1.

15 Mark Tatge, "With Unemployment Low, a New Group Is in Demand: Ex Cons," *Wall Street Journal*, April 24, 2000, p. A1.

16 Pamela M. Prah, "Tapping the Ex-Offender Labor Pool," Kiplinger Business Forecasts, May 17, 2000; http://www.kiplingerforecasts.com.

17 Barner, "Talent Wars in the Executive Suite," pp. 35–41.

18 "The Real Meaning of Empowerment," *The Economist*, March 5, 2000, pp. 75–76.

19 David Leonhardt, "Joy for Second-String M.B.A.s as Firms Recruit," *New York Times*, February 23, 2000, http://www .nytimes.com/library/financial/022300manage-recruit.html.

20 Jay Matthews, "Exam to Help Make Liberal Arts Students Employable," *The Washington Post*, September 15, 1999, p. B4.

21 "Employers Recruit Early—Very Early—in the Hunt for College Grads," *Wall Street Journal*, October 19, 1999, p. A1.

22 Dana Hedgpeth, "If You Can't Hire 'Em, Train 'Em," *Washington Post*, June 6, 1999, p. E.1.

23 Gerry Moore, "Recruiting at Private Career Colleges," Kiplinger Business Forecasts, August 20, 1999, http://www .kiplingerforecasts.com.

24 Abby Ellin, "A Generation of Freelancers," *New York Times*, August 15, 1999, p. BU 13.

25 "Career Evolution," *The Economist*, January 29, 2000, p. 90.

26 Marlene Piturro, "The Temporary Executive," *Journal of Accountancy*, October 1999, p. 22.

27 Ibid., p. 21.

28 See Geoffrey Colvin, "The Truth Can Hurt—Get Used to It," *Fortune*, February 7, 2000, p. 52.

29 Michael Doan, "More On Job Training as an Economic Development Tool," Kiplinger Business Forecasts, February 12, 1999, mailto:www.askkip@kiplinger.com.

30 Ibid.

31 Quoted in Claudia H. Deutsch, "Instead of Poaching, Dot-Coms Cooperate to Keep Talent in Town," *New York Times*, December 19, 1999, p. BU 4.

32 Alan B. Krueger, "Rethinking the Economics of Immigration," *New York Times*, May 25, 2000, http://www.nytimes.com/library/financial/columns/052500 econ-scene.html.

33 Pamela M. Prah, "More Employers Will Use Foreign Worker Visa Programs," Kiplinger Business Forecasts, February 18, 2000, http://www.kiplingerforecasts.com.

34 Jeremy Kahn, "The World's Most Admired Companies," *Fortune*, October 11, 1999, p. 275.

35 Shelly Branch, "You Hired 'Em. But Can You Keep 'Em?" *Fortune*, November 9, 1998, pp. 247–48.

36 "Career Evolution," Ibid., pp. 89–90.

37 Bob Tedeschi, "Prospective Dot-Com Employees Grow More Selective," *New York Times*, July 31, 2000, http://ww.nytimes.com/library/tech/00/07/cyber.commerce/31ecommerce.html.

38 Peter Cappelli, "A Market-Driven Approach to Retaining Talent," *Harvard Business Review*, January/ February 2000, p. 106.

39 Allan Weiss, "The Rainmaker, Part One," *Consultants News*, March, 1999.

40 David Leonhardt, "Order of Compensation Universe Reflects Pull of New Economy," *New York Times*, April 2, 2000, http://www.nytimes.com/library/financial/Sunday/

040200biz-execs-options.html.

41 Quoted in Allan S. Boress, "Stopping Brain Drain," *Journal of Accountancy*, September 1999, page 69.

42 Leonhardt, "Order of Compensation Universe Reflects Pull of New Economy."

43 Ibid.

44 Patrick Barta, "Rises in Many Salaries Barely Keep Pace With Inflation," *Wall Street Journal*, February 1, 2000, p. A2.

45 Sana Siwolop, "At More Companies, Benefits Without the Wait," *New York Times*, August 27, 2000, p. bu9.

46 See "A New Retention Tool," *Management Review*, September 1999, p. 8.

47 Sue Shellenbarger, "From Harley Factories to Desert Gold Mines, More Bosses Get It," *Wall Street Journal*, July 21, 1999, p. B1.

48 Fred Barbash, "Where Web Will Benefit Businesses," *Washington Post*, July 16, 2000, p. H1.

49 Cappelli, Ibid., p. 107.

50 "The Real Meaning of Empowerment," *The Economist*, March 25, 2000, p. 75.

51 John A. Challenger, "24 Trends Reshaping the Workplace," *The Futurist*, September-October 2000, pp. 37–38.

52 Michelle Conlin, "9 to 5 Isn't Working Anymore," *Business Week*, September 20, 1999, p. 94.

53 Ibid.

54 Challenger, "24 Trends."

55 Wendy Bonds, "Give Me a Break!," *Wall Street Journal*, May 5, 2000, p. W3.

56 "Training Drain," *Management Review*, January 2000, p. 7.

57 "Corporate Universities: The New Pioneers of Management Education: An Interview with Jeanne Meister," *Harvard Business Review*, October 1998.

58 James W. Michaels, "Drucker's Disciple," *Forbes*, May 15, 2000, http://www.forbes.com/forbes/00/0515/6511084sl.htm

59 Mary Beth Grover, "Preshrunk," *Forbes*, March 3, 2000, http://www.forbes.com/forbes/00/0306/6506082a.htm.

60 *The Kiplinger Letter*, April 28, 2000, p. 1.

61 "Nation's First Act Center opens for Business: Workforce Testing/Training Network to Follow," http://www.act.org/

news/release/2000/07-31-00.html.

62 "Driving Cisco Systems Express Train," Interview with John Chambers, *Wall Street Journal*, June 1, 2000, p. B4.

63 Amy Zipkin, "In a Tight Labor Market, Thoughtfulness Is Wisdom," *New York Times*, May 31, 2000.

CHAPTER TEN: Riding the River of Opportunity: Aligning Your Company With Accelerating Change

1 Robert O'Brien, *Marriott: The J. Willard Marriott Story* (Deseret Book Co., 1977), p. 166.

2 For a fuller discussion of the role of values in development of societies, see Garry Jacobs and Harlan Cleveland, "Social Development Theory," International Center on Peace and Development, http://www.ICPD.com.

3 Quoted in G. Pascal Zachary, "Doves Marching: Obscured by the Roar of the World's Battles, Peace is Advancing," *Wall Street Journal*, March 27, 2000, p. 1.

4 Will and Ariel Durant, *The Lessons of History* (MJF Books), p. 81.

5 See Zachary, "Doves Marching."

6 "Riding the Third Wave, A Conversation with Alvin Toffler," Tom Johnson, and Laurence Bennigson, *Strategy & Leadership*, July/August/September 1999, p. 4.

7 *The Kiplinger Letter*, September 15, 2000, p. 1.

8 Quoted in Helene Cooper, "Trade Deficit Widened in July, Moving into Record Territory," *Wall Street Journal*, September 21, 2000, p. 2.

9 For details of impact of foreign trade on US economy, see Martyn Chase, "Exports' Star Role in the U.S. Economy: Background Briefing," August 24, 2000, http://www.kiplingerforecasts.com.

10 David Fromkin, *The Way of the World, From the Dawn of Civilization to the Eve of the Twenty-first Century* (Alfred A. Knopf, 1999), pp. 146, 150.

11 Paul Johnson, *A History of the American People* (Harper Collins, 1997), p. 329.

12 Maureen Milford, "DuPont Divests, Wilmington Adjusts," *New York Times*, Real Estate section, September 24, 2000, p. NE 43.

13 Fromkin, *The Way of the World,* p. 200-01.

14 "Government and the Internet, The Next Revolution," *The Economist,* June 24, 2000, p. 63.

15 Ibid.

16 See Kara Swisher, "A Contract With America.Com: Ex-Speaker Gingrich Wants the Government to Act More Like a Tech Firm," *Wall Street Journal,* June 19, 2000, p. B1.

17 For more detailed information about emerging challenges for government, see Bob Davis and Gerald F. Seib, "Technology Will Test a Washington Culture Born in Industrial Age," *Wall Street Journal,* May 1, 2000, from which this discussion of issues is adapted.

18 Quoted in Virginia Postrel, "Rich May Get Richer, But Poor Are Also Doing Better," *New York Times,* August 10, 2000, http://www.nytimes.com/library/financial/columns/081000econ-scene.html.

19 "Ten Years On," *The Economist,* November 6, 1999, p 16.

A

small business buying groups,
174
university courses on, 18
value as nonmaterial resource,
186
wireless Internet, 84
Internet Tax Freedom Act, 280
Ireland
economic growth of, 49
multinational corporation role,
52–53
telemarketing operations, 234
ISO, 134, 165–166
IT. *See* Information technology

J

Jacobs, Garry, xvii, 59, 150–153
Japan
evolving economy, 60–61
as global market, 46
growth of acquisitions, 168–169
immigration and, 29, 38–39
increased use of robots, 141
"Kaisan" system for quality
control, 134
military expenditures, 261
opposition to foreign takeovers,
168–169
Jobs, Steve, 284
Jones International University, 17

K

"Kaisan" quality control system, 134
Kinko's, 132
Kiplinger, Knight, 142
Klingel, John, 98
Kodak, 131

KPMG, 169–170
Kroc, Ray, 65, 67, 184

L

Lands' End, 48
Lang Group, Chartered, 37
Lear Corp., 32
Levi's, 49
Life expectancy, 47, 122
Long-term care insurance, 241

M

Macfarlane, Robert, xvii, 59, 150–153
Macroeconomics Advisers, 71
Maid Brigade, Inc., 130–131
Maids International, 130
Manpower, 106
Manufacturing businesses
new jobs in, 120
productivity and, 120–121
MapInfo, 233–234
Market
advertising strategy, 86–89
analysis of customers by segment,
102–103
availability of information and, 81
balance of power between
producers and customers and,
83–86
business-to-business Internet
exchanges, 84–85
consumer resistance to
advertising, 87
customer loyalty, 90–93
definition, 82
demographics, 102–106

About the Author

FREDERICK G. HARMON DOESN'T NEED A CRYSTAL ball. Thirty years of working in and reporting about business, including a stint as a staff writer for the Wall Street Journal, have equipped Harmon to lead his readers and his clients in identifying and answering the critical questions that will help them accelerate their progress at work through strategic planning. Harmon has acquired a sense of how organizations respond to opportunities and challenges and the ability to present his perspective in a style that is lively and accessible to intelligent businesspeople.

Harmon's clients range from individuals to divisions of large companies, and are a mix of for-profit and nonprofit organizations. He has worked with senior management groups in such organizations as: Merrill Lynch Trust Co., Prudential Insurance, the National Tooling and Machining Association, Mid-South Industries, Lebenthal & Co., Fleet Private Clients Group, the Columbia University Graduate School of Journalism, the Alliance for Children and Families, the National Aquarium in Baltimore, the Denver Museum of Nature and Science, the International Center of Photography, and Audrey Cohen College.

Prior to going independent, Harmon served as president of AMA/International, the division of the American Management Association that manages its overseas subsidiaries, and president of the Presidents Association, AMA's chief executive officers' division. While heading the latter division, Harmon was also responsible for AMA's Center for Planning and Implementation, which helped more than 1,000 organizations—private, public and nonprofit—to prepare strategic plans.

Earlier in his career, Harmon served as a line officer in the U.S. Navy, a staff writer for the *Wall Street Journal*, business editor of *The San Juan Star* (Puerto Rico) and editor-in-chief of McGraw-Hill's *International Management* magazine, published in the United Kingdom.

Harmon is the author of three other books: *The Vital Difference: Unleashing the Power of Sustained corporate Success* (AMACOM, 1986), *The Executive Odyssey: Secrets for a Career Without Limits* (John Wiley & Sons, 1989), and *Playing for Keeps: How the World's Most Aggressive and Admired Companies Use Core Values to Manage, Energize, and Organize Their People, and Promote, Advance, and Achieve Their Corporate Missions* (John Wiley & Sons, 1996).

Harmon holds a B.A. in history from George Washington University and an M.S. in journalism from Columbia University.

FOR MORE INFORMATION. Readers who wish to contact Fred Harmon with questions or comments about this book or to learn more about his strategic-planning consulting services may reach him as follows:

- **Mail:** 7873 Heritage Drive, Suite 532, Annandale, VA 22003
- **Telephone:** 703-658-3513
- **Fax:** 703-658-4552
- **E-mail:** fredharmon@msn.com